*Transforming
School Cultures*

LIVES IN CONTEXT

Series Editor: Mihaly Csikszentmihalyi, *University of Chicago*

Perhaps the most important challenge for contemporary psychology is to apply its conceptual models and experimental findings to the explanation and understanding of individual lives lived in the complex world outside the laboratory. This task requires a more integrative, holistic, socially and historically informed approach to the study of individual behavior than is usually practiced by psychologists. The Lives in Context series offers scholars an opportunity to take up the challenge, to publish their best work— work that combines empirical and theoretical rigor with an understanding of the whole person in natural settings.

Transforming School Cultures

MARTIN L. MAEHR
University of Michigan

AND

CAROL MIDGLEY
University of Michigan

In collaboration with the Elementary
and Middle School Coalitions

■ WestviewPress
A Division of HarperCollinsPublishers

Lives in Context

Cover photo courtesy of Microsoft Corporation

Published in 1996 in the United States of America by Westview Press, 5500 Central Avenue, Boulder, Colorado 80301-2877, and in the United Kingdom by Westview Press, 12 Hid's Copse Road, Cum-nor Hill, Oxford OX2 9JJ

A CIP catalog record for this book is available from the Library of Congress.
ISBN 0-8133-2743-1; ISBN 0-8133-2744-X (pb)

The paper used in this publication meets the requirements of the American National Standard for Permanence of Paper for Printed Library Materials Z39.48-1984.

10   9   8   7   6   5   4   3   2   1

Contents

Part One Introduction

Part Two School Culture and Student Learning

Tables and Figures

Preface

At no point in history has the importance of education been greater. Yet, instead of rising to the challenge, schools are often mired in a morass of conflicting expectations and demands, overwhelmed by an array of new things to try and to do. In this context, what is often lost—and what is desperately needed—is a vision of school and schooling, an overall view of purpose and direction. In the ensuing pages, we speak to this need. A vision of school is presented that can—and we feel should—guide school improvement and reform.

At the heart of this vision is a particular kind of culture, a complex of beliefs and values about what is worth doing in school and why. Briefly, the culture that is needed focuses students' attention on learning, challenge, and effort. It stresses the inherent worth and value of learning and minimizes the stress on relative ability and comparative achievement. Most especially, the focus is on the growth and progress of each student, not the demonstration of ability relative to others. In a word, we promote a "task-focused" rather than an "ability-focused" context for instruction and personal development.

Although this concept of school is based on an increasingly large body of knowledge, it has not as yet been extensively applied. To their detriment, and certainly to the harm of their students, many educators view schooling as a competitive game in which some win and others lose. This view is expressed in the way students are recognized, evaluated, and grouped as well as in the quality of academic work they are given. We describe not only what can but what actually does happen when schools and classrooms adopt a task focus. Not only does the level of student engagement increase, the quality of what is done is decidedly different from when there is an ability focus. An emphasis on task goals encourages the use of adaptive learning strategies and a thoughtful approach to subject matter. Ability goals encourage behavior that may suffice in the short term but effectively undermines the development of, commitment to, and capacity for becoming a "life-long learner."

However, this volume goes beyond making a case against school as a venue for academic competition. It lays out what can be done to move schools toward a focus on learning and growth. Building directly on current work in organizational culture, motivation, and learning, the exposition that follows is also firmly grounded in the day to day world of schools. Numerous real, typical, and recognizable examples of school make the theory concrete and usable. A highlight here is the presentation of two extensive case studies of schools in the process of enhancing their emphasis on task-focused goals. We offer these case studies as a realistic portrayal of the challenge, the trials, the possibilities for, and the processes involved in enhancing a task-focused emphasis in schools.

So we begin with a theory of school, but it is the way that this conception is embodied in practice that should provide meaning, encouragement, and a course of action for those who believe that all students can be successful under the right circumstances and deserve the very best.

Martin L. Maehr
Carol Midgley

Acknowledgments

This book is the product of many. More so than most. The title page names the two who framed, compiled, and edited but alludes anonymously and collectively to the many who worked alongside: The Elementary and Middle School Coalitions. At the outset, we wish to acknowledge the absolutely critical role played by the teachers, administrators, students, and parents where we worked. We cannot name them. We hope that in our work we have given them something more lasting and important than a listing in a book. Then there are the graduate students, many of them now professionals in their own right. There are many. They helped in different ways and in different degrees. Sometimes, their penetrating questions forced us to rethink or restate. Sometimes, they lent a hand when we were short of help or simply expressed interest or gave encouragement. We cannot name them all. We will name several who were most intensively and extensively involved: Eric Anderman, Amy Arbreton, Barry Arbreton, Jamie Beck, Rachel Buck Collopy, Lynley Hicks, Yongjin Kang, Avi Kaplan, Rob Roeser, Heidi Schweingruber, Julie Turner, Tim Urdan, Stewart Wood, and Allison Young.

Funding to support our collaboration with the schools and the data analysis that ensued was provided by the U.S. Department of Education (grant numbers R215A00430 and R117C80003). Funding for this type of "action research" is very limited and is gratefully acknowledged.

We note with appreciation that we were able to carry out this work in the context of the Combined Program in Education and Psychology at the University of Michigan. Faculty, students, and staff affiliated with the program are and remain a primary source of inspiration, stimulation, insight, and expertise. Among this larger group, we single out Paul Pintrich, whom we regularly consult. And of course there are colleagues elsewhere, too numerous to mention. Perhaps our list of references will indicate who they are. We mention especially Carole Ames, Martin Covington, and Willy Lens. And in that regard, we note with some sadness that one of this number, John Nicholls, did not live to see this work come to fruition. His ideas live on in this book, hopefully in a way that he would approve.

Special thanks are also due to those who played important "supporting" roles. Our secretary, Jan Blomberg, brought all the pieces together, kept us on schedule, and reduced the number of errors that might otherwise have crept in through the course of a rather complicated compiling process. Michelle Baxter and the Westview Press staff were especially helpful in the final stages of this effort with their suggestions, critiques, and encouragement. It was Michelle and Mike Csikszentmihalyi who convinced us that we really had a book.

Finally, and most important of all, were our respective families, our ultimate source of encouragement.

M.L.M.
C.M.

Part One

Introduction

1 A Story of Crisis and Hope

All who have meditated on the art of governing mankind have been convinced
that the fate of empires depends on the education of youth.

—Aristotle

Listen closely and you can hear the future banging its spoon on the high chair.

—Stefan Kanfer, "Good Things, Small Packages." *Time*, July 29, 1991

The importance of schools and schooling has never been greater.
This is as true in Chicago as it is in Beijing—or in Staplehurst, once a thriv-
ing community, now something considerably less than that. The grain eleva-
tor there and various pieces of farm equipment scattered about are tangible
reminders of the sources of livelihood; the deteriorating homes and buildings suggest that the national and world economy that conditions their
livelihood has been none too kind. Near what used to be a town square, a
school stands as a visible sign of hope in spite of it all. It is doubtful whether
that little village can continue for long in its present form. Probably the
school will not last either. But what it is doing now is perceived as having
much to do with the future of those who call it their own.

And so it is there and increasingly everywhere: Schools are at the center
of aspiration and hope. Much is expected, because much is needed. Those
needs are all too evident as societies and cultures and economies visibly
clash on our TV screens. Even in the most remote village of Hunan
province, the Chinese peasant knows that life is changing, that the old ways
will not last, that new competencies will be demanded and rewarded. No

3

society, no group, no locale, and finally, no person can escape the changes that new knowledge and technology are bringing. The African farmer herds his cattle while holding a transistor radio in his hand. Television is received in remote villages of India, making other worlds visible and new options possible. And no one needs to be reminded of the ubiquitous role of computers in changing the nature of work and the qualifications needed by workers. Worldwide, people engaged in diverse occupations question whether the job and roles they hold now will necessarily change in the future. Certainly, the future roles of sons and daughters are no longer assured. Children cannot count on following their parents into "the trades" or onto "the line," if indeed they want to. As a result, schools and schooling stand there, not just as an option but increasingly as a necessity to prepare children for the complexities of an uncertain future.

These concerns are part of the daily dialogue in the United States. Policy makers, educators, and the general citizenry continue to engage in a seemingly unending and agonizing appraisal of what schools can and should be, what they can and cannot do. Economists daily bombard us with numbers that reveal our vulnerability within a global economy (for example, Thurow, 1992). Many adults over fifty feel totally overwhelmed and inadequate when it comes to the new technologies. We are threatened by computers, even frustrated by our VCRs. When dealing with either we turn to someone under thirty, sometimes a ten-year-old, for help. We cannot even imagine what new technological challenges our children will face or what new complex problems will be theirs to solve, but we know that change will escalate. We want the next generation to be able to negotiate these changes, master the information systems that perplex us, and rise to the challenge of global problems. We can't even imagine the nature of work that will be theirs. And so as citizens, parents, and educators we worry about their preparation for an uncertain future. With these concerns, we turn to the institution of schooling for solutions. Today, as much as at any point in history, schools are viewed as critical to our children's intellectual, social, and personal well-being. Today, perhaps to a greater degree than ever, schools are a major factor in human development. Children spend thousands of hours there. It is there—perhaps more than any other single place—that talent is developed, identity defined, and aspirations framed (Csikszentmihalyi, Rathunde, & Whalen, 1993).

To compound the problem, schools today serve increasingly diverse populations of children and are asked not only to be surrogate parents but to address a wide range of society's ills. Schools face these problems often without the support of stable and strong family and community structures. Schools have, in short, become the last resort for the full range of children's needs, as well as the primary means for providing an "educated work force."

This is a story of schools and how they must change to meet these challenges. It is a story of crisis and hope.

The Crisis That Is School

Our narrative concerns the real world of schools, the school we know and maybe love. That school is in trouble. The school we teach in, the school our children attend, the school in our neighborhood—collectively and not uncommonly, individually, they are all under attack. The inadequacy, the failure of schools is common fodder for the media. Hardly a day goes by without a report of falling achievement scores and school violence. All too often there is direct and specific criticism of school staff and leadership. As one member of our collaborative team put it, "It is almost impossible for teachers [and school leaders, we would add] to feel good about themselves these days." Indeed, by many if not most accounts, the school is barely keeping its head above water—if that—in meeting this array of demands and expectations.

Newspapers regularly decry the level of literacy, the lack of numeracy, and the general level of achievement. Frequent cross-national comparisons tend to reinforce the criticism of public schooling in the United States. Harold Stevenson, for example, has been especially effective in arguing this case. In cross-cultural studies of American, Chinese, and Japanese students, Stevenson and his collaborators (Stevenson & Stigler, 1992) found that the American children scored highest on tests of cognitive skills in kindergarten and 1st grade. However, by the time they reached 5th grade, the Americans lagged far behind both the Japanese and Chinese students in mathematics. In fact, students in the Japanese classroom with the lowest average mathematics score still scored above the highest-scoring American classroom. There are ways to counter specific findings and handy explanations for why we are not doing better. The fact remains, however, that there is indeed a sense of crisis in the United States regarding the status of our schools and the quality of education our children are receiving.

But in an informal and more poignant way this story is reflected in the anecdotes told by our school collaborators. We listened to teachers talk about parent conferences and learned a great deal about what it meant to teach in their school. One mother reported her sense of doom after finding out she was HIV-positive, after having attempted to sell plasma to support the family's needs. There was the grandmother who struggled to raise the children of her daughters, mothers too soon and unable or unwilling to fulfill the role. Another mother haltingly wondered how her husband's severe bouts with alcohol or drugs might affect a child. A divorced father showed up at a conference to demand equal time and maybe seek "evidence" relative to child custody litigation. There were the stories told by children. A five-year-old discussed the shooting death of his cousin near his home. Another explained that his friend would not be in school for a while; his family had barely escaped a fire that destroyed all their possessions, forcing them to move to another school district and disrupting the school lives of seven children who could ill afford it. This too is the real world of school. It may be hard to convince parents living under these circumstances to collaborate with the teacher in fostering learning skills, motives, and values. It may be difficult to maintain a sustained course of progress when children live in chaotic contexts over which they or their parents have little control. It is perhaps not altogether surprising, under these circumstances, that achievement scores are so low and students drop out of school so often.

The crisis of schools is real. Change is needed to meet changing circumstances and new demands.

The Enduring Hope for Reform

Without question, today's schools are in crisis. But the ensuing chapters of this book are not just about crisis. They are, above all, about hope.

The Will and the Ways of Current School Reform

Perhaps because the crisis is so real, the problems so enormous, the implications so far-reaching, the past decade or so has witnessed many and varied attempts to reform schools. Not that school reform has ever really been off the agenda. On the contrary, we tend to reform again and again (Cuban, 1990). But there is at least as much fervor focused on reform now as at any point in our nation's history. Perhaps the crisis is greater, the stakes higher. Whatever the reason, the demand for school reform, even for a thorough renovation, is incessant. There are few schools that have not attempted serious change and fewer still who would admit it if they hadn't. Reform is a reality in the real world of schools. But that reform takes different shapes and forms.

Enforce and Enhance Standards

A common feature of many approaches to reform has been a focus on enforcing and raising standards. In this case, the problem is seen as one of not expecting enough or perhaps not expecting the right things. Certainly, this approach has often been followed in the current wave of reform. We have seen state legislatures and local school boards increase requirements for graduation, restrict extracurricular activities to students with certain grade point averages, deny driver's licenses to dropouts, and develop tests that had to be passed before students could graduate. As well meaning as this may be, there is little evidence that this concern for standards has resulted in better teaching, more favorable learning opportunities, or increased skills in problem solving and higher order thinking skills. Indeed, one of the results seems to be simply a renewed emphasis on tests and testing and subsequently on evaluating and recognizing students, teachers, schools, and districts on an all too limited and limiting set of criteria. It seems obvious that testing in and of itself does not assure excellence. As a matter of fact, an overemphasis on assessment can actually undermine the pursuit of excellence. When teachers break off essential instruction two weeks before a statewide test to drill students on questions that are likely to appear on the test, one wonders whether the true purpose of schools and learning has been polluted or lost. Even worse, when principals and teachers essentially cheat to ensure favorable scores for their students, their schools, and themselves, a concept of excellence, let alone its pursuit, has clearly passed from the scene. But as we shall discuss, the uses of tests and testing, necessary in some form and to a degree, always carry the potential for undermining motivation and learning (Covington, 1992; Hill, 1977, 1980, 1984; Hill & Wigfield, 1984; Howe, 1994).

Upgrade School Staff

Another solution that is periodically suggested is to improve the training and selection of teachers and administrators. Certainly, it is not a simple matter to reconstitute the current teaching force—and it is only somewhat less difficult to appoint a whole new cohort of principals and superintendents. And, in any event, focusing on personnel changes may be a bit like barking at the moon. What evidence is there that a massive retraining or replacement of school staff will address the problems, if there are not also some basic organizational as well as philosophical changes? As a matter of fact, schools often follow the pattern of hiring staff who "fit." As organizational and philosophical changes occur, different kinds of staffing will be sought. After we had been working in an elementary school for a year or so, the principal sought and hired staff who "agreed with the new philosophy."

But in many ways, the most disturbing aspect about making the school problem a personnel problem is what it says to incumbent teachers and administrators. Blaming school staff may not only fail to solve anything, it may and probably already has compounded the problem. How can an attack, general, indirect, or implicit though it be, encourage the best efforts of those we've asked to serve in the schools? In fact, we know that such an approach disheartens teachers. A news report prompted a teacher to tell us, "But they don't know what it's like here, how difficult it is, how hard we work."

Besides, is it really true that today's teachers are on the whole poorly trained and incompetent? They certainly do not appear to be inexperienced or lacking in professional training (U.S. Department of Education, National Center for Education Statistics, 1993). Our experience has taught us that lack of talent is not really the problem.

Reorganize and Restructure

Reorganizing, restructuring, even "reinventing" schools have been suggested recently (Murphy, 1991; Newmann, 1993). There are many proposals, including restructuring the school day, redesigning learning sites, changing governance and management, building partnerships and networks, increasing the participation of parents and the community, and, of course, changing the curricula (for example, Lieberman & Miller, 1990). But even these well-meaning changes may not lead to enhanced student competence and commitment.

Consider one example. Inspired by a multitude of changes in the methods of corporate America (Hackman, 1986), many school systems have considered transferring more authority to the building site, sometimes with the expressed hope of empowering teachers and parents. The thought is that the best decisions are made at the level the service is given. Possibly, but not necessarily! Additionally, it is argued that the transfer of authority will also elicit commitment. But to do what? As Newmann (1993) points out, structural changes in and of themselves hold small promise of effecting competence or commitment. They may provide the *occasions* for change, but they do not ensure it. Particularly troubling to us is the fact that the linkage between organizational change and *students'* motivation and learning is tenuous at best. Perhaps that is one reason why the rumblings of discontent with "site-based management" appeared soon after it was promoted as a desirable structural reform and continue to this day (for example, Timar, 1989; Midgley & Wood, 1993).

Enhance the "Working Conditions" of Teachers

Closely tied to issues of school reorganization and reform is another proposed solution: Improve the work environment. Certainly teachers are critical to school reform. But what does improving the work environment mean and how will it influence what happens to children?

Sometimes this proposal has been limited to salaries and perks. Increasingly, it has been tied to how schools should be governed. In this regard, several emphases are noteworthy. It is evident to most observers that school change must involve teachers and the school staff as a whole (for example, Newmann, 1993). Moreover, there is little argument against enhancing the professionalization and working environment of school staff. In addition to empowering teachers, school boards ought to increase teachers' salaries. These and other solutions stemming from an examination of teachers' working conditions (Smylie, 1994) are not to be ignored. Indeed, they will have to figure in any fuller solution. But in and of themselves they are distinctly limited. As desirable as it would be to provide teachers with more money and benefits, it is not an easy solution in an uncertain economy. Besides, the evidence is not overwhelming that more dollars directed to such ends would translate into better education. The work environment solution is no "sure bet" either. What may be good work environments for teachers do not necessarily translate directly into better learning.

Change and Enhance the Curriculum

In the post-sputnik reform era, there was a tendency to see the problem of the schools as largely attributable to the fact that they were not teaching the right things. Physicists were disturbed by the quality of physics that was presented. Historians decried what passed as history and so on. Although there are some who want scholars and scientists to determine what should be taught in the public schools, their numbers are not large. Yet there are serious reform issues within the broad domain of what children are to be taught. With that, there are new emphases in mathematics, reading and literacy, science, and social studies. Perhaps it is fair to say that the discussion relates also to how the content is approached, but content certainly is seen as critical (Westbury, 1992). Focusing on what should be taught without focusing on what and how students will learn is problematic. The test of worth of curriculum must in the final analysis reside in its effects on children. What the expert thinks is good course content is at least a step away from eliciting an investment of students in learning that content—and growing in the process.

Offer Choice

Still other proposals for change focus on developing a system responsive to consumer demand and choice. Several arguments are associated with this proposal, none of them well tested in practice. Competition is presumably good for business; shouldn't it be good for schools as well? And if you don't accept that argument, what about one based on psychological principles? Presumably, choice leads to greater personal investment on the part of the clientele; in the case of schools this means parents for the most part. The problem, however, is one of giving equal opportunity for choice to all. If choice depends on the availability of transportation, then some families will "choose" to send their children to the neighborhood school. Further, the existence of choice presumably fosters a market economy in which schools and school staff are working to survive. One may grant that market forces have been shown to have value, but only if there is a "level playing field." And clearly, that is often not the case. Indeed, observable differences in the buildings and the resources available to teachers and students are common. Moreover, market forces are likely to stress short-term efficiencies that may run counter to long-term striving for excellence. Increasing the opportunity for students to make choices regarding the school they will attend is still untested as a means of achieving school reform.

Increase Funding

Finally, there is the matter of money. Anyone who spends time in schools has heard it said repeatedly, "If only we had the money." Without question, we have not done all that we can and should regarding the funding of schools. Aside from the fact that taxpayers seem reluctant to come up with more dollars, how much more would it take? If we invested more, would things really change? One can always find ways in which additional funds could be used. For example, professional development is a necessity to retain one's expertise, but we confess to our dismay at learning about some of the programs that exist under this label. Is it worth the price of the dollars and the interruption of classroom studies?

Similarly, the press to bring computers to the classroom seems logical enough but only if teachers are made computer literate, good software is available, and there is a coherent plan for integrating computers into the regular or normal flow of instruction. We, as many others, have walked into classrooms where two or three computers were prominently on display but noted that they were not being used. In fact, in one case there wasn't even appropriate software available. Then there were the numerous instances where computers, new and with available software, were being used but only for skill and drill adapted from a paper and pencil drill sheet format. The bottom line is that one cannot presently assure anyone that investment of more dollars in most schools—without evidence of drastic change in business as usual—would really make a difference. Additional funding might serve to attract and retain a better cadre of staff, underwrite technology, and increase the "time on task," but all these may simply represent a case of pouring new wine into old bottles.

The Continuing Crisis

So the crisis continues—not because there is a lack of school reform efforts and ideas. Each of the ideas briefly reviewed arguably could contribute to a solution. Increasingly, however, it is evident that all of these attempts at reform are simply dancing around the edges of the problem. The schools certainly could use more money, but financial bankruptcy is not their primary problem. They could and should be more responsive to exploring, evaluating, learning, and growing in the process. But intellectual bankruptcy is not the fundamental problem either. At least, there is no paucity of ideas in the educational marketplace and no lack of readily available new and novel techniques and programs for doing just about anything the school might wish to do. There is, however, a growing awareness of a deeper underlying problem: philosophical or theoretical bankruptcy. Schools and school staff have lost a sense of what they are about. They have lost the "tie that binds." The "why" questions have been pushed aside by the "how" questions. Theory and philosophy play a small role in the minds of school staff or school leaders—or even in the minds of those who train them. As a result, there is confusion about what a school is or should be, about ideals or values, purposes and goals. Thus, adopting a new technique or program typically doesn't change anything of significance. Apparently, different things are done—if indeed what is done is really significantly different—for the same old reasons. And the same old reasons are the problem. This criticism of the underlying belief system of schools and school staff is increasingly made not by irredeemable agnostics but by those truly committed to the faith: Schools have lost sight of or perhaps are seriously confused about their purpose, their values, their role, and why they exist. They have a "culture crisis." That crisis must be dealt with first before other changes will have any value. In our view, the most promising action directed toward school reform has in fact called for the kind of modification of goals, values, and perspective that cultural transformation implies (for example, Covington, 1992; Hopfenberg, Levin & Associates, 1993; Perkins, 1992; Sizer, 1992).

Rethinking the Problem

Seymour Sarason (1982; 1990) was among the first to conceptualize school reform in terms of cultural change. Over a long career of commitment to schools and schooling, he has emphasized the need to rethink the nature of schools and the way schooling is done. According to Sarason, the "culture of school" needs to be changed. The norms of doing and believing, the values and beliefs—the very assumptions that underlie the existence of schools and schooling—must be examined, tested, modified, restructured, and perhaps even disposed of. Sarason's argument for culture reform is a point of departure for this book. It is the heuristic that prompts and guides our quest.

The Objective:"School Effectiveness"

It is a given that in the many and varied criticisms of schools, there is a convergence of opinion that the schools must be "effective" in what they do. Certainly in what we have said thus far about crisis and hope for schools it is clear that we share this basic notion. However, the nature of "effectiveness" is not an open and shut issue. It deserves definition and discussion. What do we mean by school effectiveness?

Effectiveness is generally thought of in terms of certain outcomes. The issue is effectiveness for what. As a result, discussions of school effectiveness often eventuate in irresolvable disagreements regarding differing assumptions concerning school objectives. While there is general agreement that the school, as any organization, must produce something that is valued by its supporting constituency, the constituencies of a school are not always in agreement. Although this is not an insignificant issue, the heart of effectiveness lies in how efficiently the organization accomplishes objectives. Effectiveness is the ratio of output to input. Some schools do a lot with a little; other schools do a little with a lot.

The problem comes in assessing inputs and outputs. Historically, this has been done in a number of different ways, none of them perfect. One recognized approach involves attempting to equate schools in terms of available resources and then compare their overall achievement scores. To a large degree, however, studies of school effectiveness have simply compared schools thought to be effective or ineffective, an appropriate practice in some cases (Linn, 1983; Dyer, Linn, & Patton, 1969), and then focused on the processes that differentiated these schools (for example, Lightfoot, 1983).

Effectiveness as a Motivational Issue

It is a small stretch to see school effectiveness as a motivational issue. Motivation is concerned precisely with how one invests resources and the quality of that investment. In applying motivational concepts to organizations and groups, one is asking the same kinds of questions one asks about individuals: Why do organizations or groups that possess seemingly equal resources exhibit different levels of achievement? Apparently, groups and organizations, as well as individuals, use their resources differently. They choose to invest in courses of action focused on learning or on other outcomes. They may focus on courses of action that seem to be learning-related but that are in effect bad choices. They may invest in anything in a qualitatively different fashion: persistently or spasmodically, mindfully or haphazardly, creatively or imitatively, systematically or only in moments of crisis. In short, current research on student motivation and learning can be directly applied to others in the school (for example, teachers) and to the overall functioning of the school as an organization.

School "Culture" as the Focus

Our theme is that a severe culture crisis is at the root of the educational malaise exhibited by many schools. The meaning and implications of that assertion must, however, be broached at the outset.

A focus on the organization.

Proposing culture as the cause of inefficient and nonproductive investment in schools draws attention to how individuals function within a group and to how groups draw on the resources and focus the efforts of individuals. The application of organizational principles to education is hardly new. In fact, it is a stock-in-trade of educational administrators (for example, Hoy & Miskel, 1995). However, with notable exceptions (for example, Sergiovanni & Corbally, 1984; Deal & Peterson, 1990), the focus has been on the selection and management of the professionals who make up that organization. As one administrator told us, "I just try to choose good staff and help them do whatever they think best." Focusing on school culture means looking at the relevant constituencies and groups and taking a view of how they relate and interact. It involves seeing the school as a functioning system.

Beliefs, values, and the construction of purpose.

The use of the term culture in talking about group life puts a particular cast on how one views the organization and motivation within the organization. As we will discuss, the use of the term culture emphasizes shared living and being that is derived from or related to beliefs and values but most especially purposes. Briefly, the type, focus, clarity, coherence, and shared nature of predominant beliefs about what school is and should be are at the heart of whatever effectiveness crises the schools might be experiencing.

The role of leadership.

Understanding that school effectiveness is a cultural problem has implications for leadership. Leadership is built into the very nature of organizations. In the schools, it is usually formally designated, but schools benefit as well as suffer from the quality of those who play formal as well as informal leadership roles. It is through managing the culture of the organization that leaders enhance and direct the investment that results in school effectiveness. In many ways, organizational culture has evolved as a concept related to how those in leadership roles can lead (Kaplan & Maehr, in press; Maehr & Buck, 1993; Maehr, Midgley, & Urdan, 1992). That topic is discussed throughout this book but especially emphasized in Chapter 8.

Toward Transforming School Cultures

In summary, this book is directed to those concerned with enhancing the effectiveness of schools. The argument will unfold that schools will be all they can be only if and as a culture is created that enhances student motivation and learning.

But the argument is not presented in terms of unreachable ideals. It is situated in the real world of teachers, students, administrators, parents, and citizens. This is a story of the real world of schools, not "model schools"—ideal or romanticized versions of school—but schools we know well. These are schools we both love and hate, take pride in and criticize. This is about the school our child attends, the school in which we work. But most of all it is the school we care about—warts and all; the school whose faults we know but which we hope to improve. That school is in trouble. It is beset by financial difficulties, overwhelming demands, and repeated and severe criticism. Maybe the school that you the reader have in mind is not experiencing this malaise. Wonderful! But the problems of schools and schooling in the United States, and to a degree throughout the world, generally are real and persistent—as even a casual reading of the popular press would indicate. They demand renewed attention.

Our perspective comes from years of living, working, and learning in schools. Our contribution to solutions emerges from collaborating with teachers, principals, parents, and others to experiment, intervene, fix, repair, reform, and sometimes restructure. Our efforts focused on changing two specific schools. Those two schools give meaning and form to our message. But the picture we describe of the struggles that school change demands is generalized. And most certainly, the theory of school that emerged from this collective effort applies to more than just two schools. Our experiences have emboldened us to propose that it is a readily applicable approach to school reform. It is applicable to schools as they now exist; we do not assume that schools have to be reinvented. But the approach requires a significant change in thinking—a cultural transformation. The nature of that transformation and how it can be initiated in individual schools is what this book is about.

A Theory of School

Although our work is situated in the everyday life of schools, it is framed by and in terms of generalizable theory. There are several implications of this.

Practicality

As Lewin (1952) said, "There is nothing so practical as a good theory" (p. 169). Theory represents the coherent and focused summation of the work and understanding of those who have thought about, worked in, and learned in schools. We build on the work of many who have asked similar questions and proposed answers. Theory has been useful to us and our school collaborators and will be helpful to any who wish to emulate and extend our efforts. At the least, it should provide a common language for talking about the experiences of school and suggest a hypothesis to be tested and an idea to pursue. As theory, it can and should be susceptible to and subjected to change and development through the efforts of practitioners and researchers who follow us.

Generalizability

The theoretical nature of our efforts relates to issues of generalizability and applicability. This book is based on our work in certain schools. That work is portrayed in a concrete and specific manner for the reader to interpret.

However, we are not merely interested in these schools; the reader likely would not be interested in what we had to say if we were. We have notions about the general implications for schools and schooling, and we express these as explicitly and directly as we can. They are there to be examined and criticized and thereby improved.

Applicability

From our work, we deduce specific principles that can and should guide school reform. We do not presume that our ideas are now and forever true. Only by applying these principles will we learn how and to what degree they are valid. This is only the first stage of what we hope will be a continuing dialogue. Subsequent stages will have to engage more practitioners, theorists, and researchers in a collective search if what we say here is to be more than just a story of a few schools, a few practitioners, and a few researchers.

Universality

Certainly, this is first a story about American schools for American policy makers, leaders, educators, and parents. Our objective was to address some of the problems thought to be critical in schooling in the United States in the late twentieth century. The basic theory is hardly as parochial, being a product of researchers and practitioners in many countries and places and cultures. Moreover, as the story evolves, we will make special reference to cross-national, cross-cultural research conducted by ourselves and others.

A Look Ahead

The book is organized into three sections. Following this introduction and overview, we outline a "vision for schools and schooling." At the heart of the cultural crisis is a misguided vision of what schools and schooling can and should be. Imagination is important, but a school's vision also should be tied to the experience and knowledge available. And just as important, that vision must work in the everyday world of schools. We outline our vision of school in Chapter 2, which provides the conceptual framework for the rest of the book.

In Part Two we specifically examine the nature and origins of school cultures. We use the plural, *cultures,* for a reason. On the one hand, it is convenient to think of the school as a culture. But within the school there are various subcultures associated with the different worlds of staff and students.

We consider cultural variation across classrooms, subject matter areas, and groups of students. We also look especially at the culture of school experienced by teachers and how this relates to the school experienced by students. The culminating argument in this section is that culture makes a difference; ultimately, culture affects the investment of students in learning. This argument is based on studies found elsewhere as well as data we report for the first time in this book.

Part Three presents a question that naturally follows: School culture in its varied forms makes a difference in the motivation and learning of students; what can be done about it? We present an analytic, descriptive, and prescriptive portrayal of our attempts to change school culture. The accompanying analyses and interpretations result in specific suggestions regarding how school leadership and staff can enhance the cultures of schools they know and experience and perhaps transform the culture of school as a whole.

Our work showed us that school change, certainly cultural transformation, will not occur without extensive participation from all concerned. But the sine qua non necessary to launch and sustain any such effort is the effective investment of those in leadership roles: certainly the principal but also those who are informal leaders. The social power that exists in many different quarters in an organization cannot be ignored. So we inevitably spoke especially to school leaders who were in a position to shift resources and attention. Cultural transformation will have a short life if it is initiated and sustained only by the individual teacher working behind the closed door of the classroom.

Our work of nearly a decade is not finished, but it is time to present our findings to teachers, administrators, researchers, and others interested in schools and schooling. We hope we will be able to solicit their participation, their attempts to test our conclusions, their insights, and yes, their criticism of the theory that emerges. And now to the vision and its grounding in schools we studied and continue to study.

2   A Vision for Schools

The letter (see Figure 2.1) from a rather typical middle school student is real; although it will draw a smile from most, at heart it is a reflection of a state of affairs all too often true. It is a situation that should be disturbing to parents and to those who are devoted to the practice of education. The reaction to school and teaching contained in this letter from a twelve-year-old to her aunt and uncle captures an aspect of school, a problem that should challenge educators. This situation inspired our book. Our goal is to reflect as well as illustrate the utility of a vision of school that capitalizes on the child's inherent interest in learning and enhances rather than diminishes it. This vision leads the Elizas of the world to experience schools as something that captures their interest, contributes to the best of aspirations, inspires their efforts, expands their world, and creates an enduring love of learning.

Envisioning what schools can or should be, of course, is not a new enterprise. The history of educational philosophy and practice has yielded many such visions. Indeed, as educators, politicians, and parents express their hopes, fears, and expectations, they inevitably reflect a more or less organized set of beliefs about what a school should be. Moreover, as we build schools and organize what should and must go on in them, we likewise reflect implicit assumptions, perhaps visions, that define teaching and learning.

The comparison is not new, but we have been struck by how much secondary schools continue to resemble factories. Not a current manufacturing unit, mind you, but more an earlier twentieth-century assembly line or even a nineteenth-century sweatshop. A generation or so ago, school designers began experimenting with open spaces, breaking down walls, creating movable learning zones, and generally providing an opportunity for the fluid and flexible movement of children and teachers. Too quickly, for us at least, the walls reappeared, first as bookshelves and later in stud and plaster. The framing of space as well as time has typically reflected a view of process and purpose—no less in school than in other life arenas. Not that we always

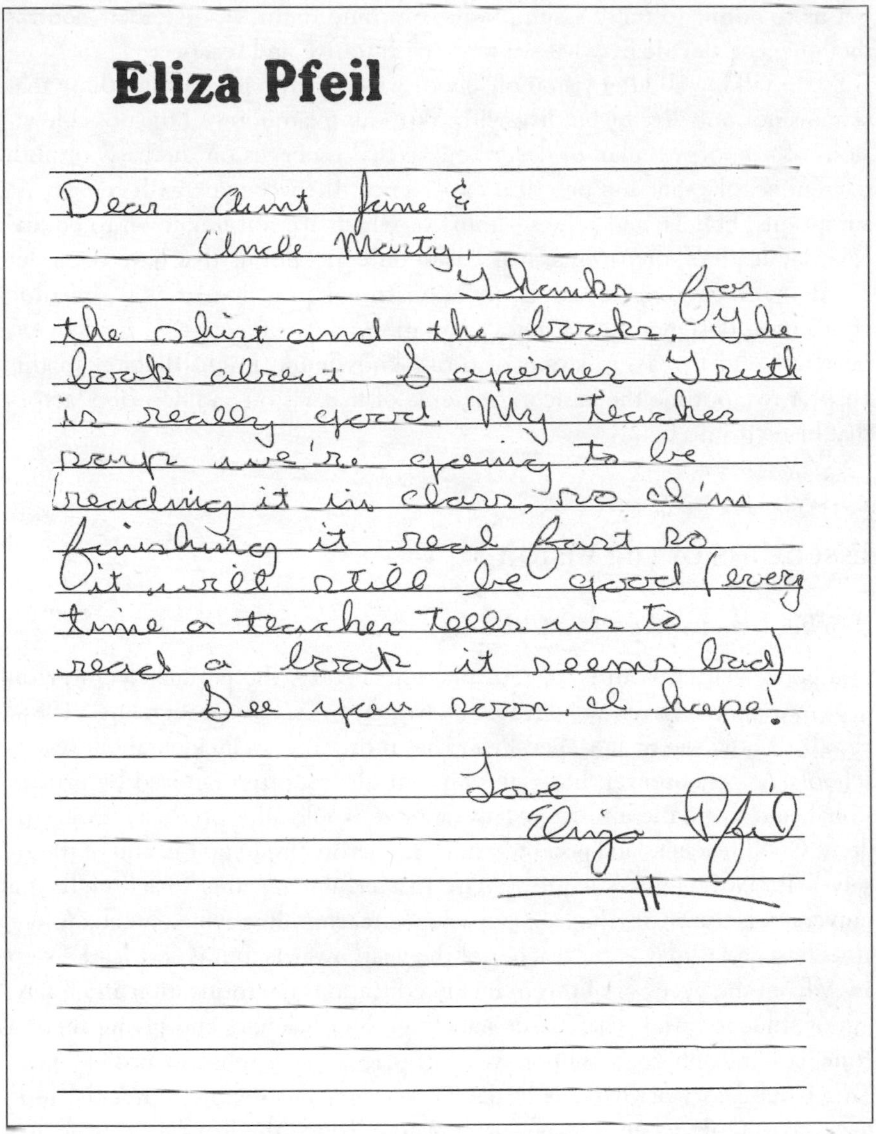

Eliza Pfeil

Dear Aunt Jane &
    Uncle Marty,
            Thanks for
the list and the books. The
book about Superior Truth
is really good. My teacher
says we're going to be
reading it in class, so I'm
finishing it real fast so
it will still be good (every
time a teacher tells us to
read a book it seems bad)
        See you soon, I hope!

                    Love
                    Eliza Pfeil

Figure 2.1   Letter from a student

examine our assumptions or core beliefs carefully and closely. Aside from whether we are conscious of a vision, we doubtless adhere to some set of beliefs regarding what schooling is about and what a school should be. It sometimes takes a good course in educational philosophy or more often, perhaps, a fellow staff member who has acquired a different perspective to get us to admit to these assumptions, examine them, resolve their contradictions, and decide by what we truly wish to live and teach.

So, in talking about a vision of school we are referring to something that schools not only live by but live with. Without examining all the possible visions of school, we plan to describe one that emerges on the basis of both current scholarship and practical experience. It too begins with certain assumptions, beliefs, and values—most of which are not unknown to educators, lay leaders, or parents. It is based on conceptions that have been derived from current research on educational practice. It is a dynamic conception designed for change, adaptation, and correction as further experience and the assimilation of more knowledge might dictate. In this chapter, we outline the basic ingredients of that vision and describe factors that bring it into being.

Essentials of the Vision

A School Focused on the Child

In a book written with Nancy Austin, Tom Peters, the popular lecturer on organization effectiveness, devotes a chapter to "school leadership" (1985, ch. 20). As the son of a teacher, Peters has more than an incidental interest in schools. As an observer, he argues a point all too often ignored by professional educators: the ultimate client (and we would add, product) is the student. Good teachers and good teaching are hardly important in and of themselves. It may be interesting to watch a masterful performer in action, be it a university lecturer or a high school science teacher. It may be entertainment at its best and it may earn "teacher of the year" awards, but it is at least a step away from the necessary bottom line in education: the motivation and learning of students. And what about selecting good teachers and giving them a collegial atmosphere, a supportive workplace, and a sense of professionalism? Doubtless worthy goals in their own right but definitely not the ultimate goal. Only when they enable staff to enhance the learning of students do these goals count. And why inaugurate site-based management or staff empowerment? Certainly, not just to make the staff feel good. Presumably, the only real justification for such restructuring or any other reform is that somehow it positively effects the life and learning of students.

The point is simple: The student is the ultimate client and product in the educational process. Priorities must be set and judgments made in terms of how the children will be influenced. As "ultimate clients," students must have the highest priority. Children must be well served. As the "ultimate products," they must be enabled and empowered in the present and for the future.

There are at least two major implications of this central point, both of which may be subject to argument. First, the school must be designed in terms of understanding the child's needs, developmental stage, sociocultural experience, emotional disposition, personal style, and potential. Second, the school's first commitment is to the student, not family or society. To be sure, the interests of parents and society cannot be ignored, but the school must direct itself first and foremost to the child. Generally, the needs of family and society converge, but when a choice must be made between child welfare and the welfare of parent or society, the school is the child's "friend in court." These assumptions are replete with implications and carry the potential for extended discussion and not a little argument. We will forego this for now and press on to the implications of taking this tack.

A child-centered approach to education, in one form or another, has been around for some time. While Rousseau himself hardly embodied the principle in his own dealings (for example, Johnson, 1988), much of his writing about education could be construed as a brief for such an approach. Certainly, one can see a fairly advanced form of child-created education embodied in the work of Herbart and Froebel. But most current educators received their dose of child-centered philosophy from Carl Rogers or his latter-day heirs and such popular authors as Jonathan Kozal, Robert Coles, and others. Perhaps some have delved into Dewey and might see there the origins of the vision of school we sketch out later in this chapter.

Although the notion of child-centeredness is so common that it is almost taken for granted, there are serious instances of divergence from it in the way we approach school. Many critics of schools talk more about the needs of business than of how the student is served. Parallel to that, curriculum concerns often revolve more around societal than student needs. There is room to focus on both, of course. Arguably, what is good for the child is likely good for the community. The conflict is often most visible in the priorities schools exhibit. Thus, one can readily observe that as grade level increases commitment to children decreases and commitment to content increases. Subject matter is primary in college, high school, and increasingly in the middle grades. Elementary and preschool teachers more readily accept and practice the child-centered assumption.

So not all teachers and others concerned with the profession of education are likely to accept our assumption of the primacy of the student without a quarrel. We are disturbed by what appears to be an accidental and incidental shift away from a child-centered focus in the training of teachers. Current emphasis on studying teacher behavior and teaching processes, in terms of the discipline that is taught, may have its merits. But it may also serve to turn attention away from the child. Recent emphases on teacher professionalism and concern with the work environment vis-à-vis staff, if not tied directly to the ultimate client and product, may be questioned. A good work environment for teachers does not necessarily translate into a good learning environment for students.

Most disturbing perhaps is the suggestion that teacher preparation programs can profitably ignore the study of child psychology and development and concentrate on abstract content or teaching processes. A child-centered approach demands that teachers have easy entree to current understanding of how the child develops, learns, experiences events, and acts. In short, in some fashion teachers need ready and easy access to the current theory and research on motivation, learning, and human development. Knowing your discipline is not sufficient for the task of teaching. Studying about and practicing teaching are not enough if they are not combined with knowledge about the children who are to be taught.

In sum, schools must be centered on the student. Educators must have an understanding of who the child-student is: the life that challenges them, their strengths, their developmental needs, their hopes and ambitions. The school must focus on the child as well as on learning.

A School Focused on Learning

Schools are viewed as a positive influence in a society; it is not surprising that they are asked to parent, counsel, and heal. But how are students best served by schools?

In one of the schools in which we worked, the teachers stated emphatically that their primary purpose was to provide a safe haven for students, a place where children could be protected from a harsh environment. Issues of subject matter and curriculum content were hardly at the fore of their thinking—and understandably so! Developing a love for learning was not either. Teachers saw their mission as providing affection, support, and comfort. One cannot deny that this represented a child-centered approach of value (for example Chira, 1991). Defensible in some instances, it cannot represent the ideal or the norm. A school may exist for healing, but ultimately it must stand for learning. Not that the two are incompatible. Indeed, the conditions that facilitate student learning are also more than likely to eventuate in general student well-being. However, the unique function of school is learning.

The school serves best and children are best served when the school is not only child-student centered but also learning-focused.

The issue, of course, is not really *whether* students learn. They do all the time in spite of or because of teachers, parents, peer experiences, resources, and opportunities. The question is *what* is to be learned or acquired in the course of schooling. There are many and varied answers. Too often, schools find themselves in the position of stressing what is of immediate importance. When the car became widely available to teenagers, it was driver education. Currently, it is sex education with an emphasis on birth control and AIDS prevention. Or as former U.S. Surgeon General Joycelyn Elders put it: "Now that we've taught them what to do in the front seat, we have to teach them what to do in the back seat." In perhaps the worst case scenario, preparation for the statewide achievement test has become an informal but regularly evident part of the curriculum. Most schools, in principle at least, are committed to conveying generalizable knowledge and skills, attitudes and values. The debate over what should be learned continues. What is not at issue is that children must not only learn to learn but must become lifelong learners. We live in a changing world. It is difficult to predict whether this or that piece of information will be useful in the future. Those of us who can remember when computers became part of the research scene will recall that it was almost a necessity to develop program writing skills. Many of us who learned Fortran have not only forgotten it but wonder why we learned it in the first place. But few can afford to stop acquiring new skills and updating or enhancing old knowledge if they want to remain fully functioning members of society. It is critical that in the course of schooling everyone can and must develop a personal, life-long investment in learning.

We do not wish to gainsay the continuing dialogue on curriculum. Designating areas of study and topics within these areas must be viewed as one of the most serious of concerns for society as well as educators. In this book, however, we concentrate on an equally serious question. *How* does one engage children in acquiring the knowledge and the skills deemed necessary by parents, educators, policy makers, and community leaders? This book is not about curriculum theory and practice; we will not pretend to present a thorough discussion of subject matter options. We will not argue the case for vocational education, for traditional subject matter content, for basic skills, or for aesthetic experiences. Rather, we concern ourselves with the issue of motivation, surely among the most critical issues for teachers, principals, parents, and ultimately society as a whole (for example Cross, 1990). Whatever the curriculum, children must be engaged in the learning process in such a way that they don't reject the process—a disturbing and very real possibility!

It is no secret that not all children like school. This is sometimes treated lightly, as a humorous part of child development as when an adult asks a child whether he or she likes school, fully expecting an automatic "no" and evaluations of school as "boring," not "cool," or worse. Consider that when children are interviewed on TV, they seem obliged to say that they "hate school." Of course, such comments are said in what seems to be jest. But the fact that they are so often stated does not reflect well on the ability of school to attract the investment of children in learning. Even commercials reinforce the assumption that school is likely to be dull and boring. Generally unattractive. Something to be avoided if only it were possible. One recent commercial portrayed a father skipping and cheering as he goes down the aisle of a store buying supplies for the new school year. Simultaneously, his children look despondent and dejected. It is hard to miss the point. The underlying assumption about school is painfully obvious. What a society accepts as humorous is often most revealing, as are the portrayals of life that are chosen to capture our attention and shape our buying habits. These are but a sample of instances where schooling and the idea of continuing investment in acquiring the knowledge and skills that schools represent is not universally promoted. The value of school is sometimes at best grudgingly accepted—even by parents.

As we have worked with teachers and administrators in rethinking schooling, we have regularly endeavored to incorporate parents in the process. Early on, we learned an important and disturbing lesson. To many parents, what schools stand for is by no means attractive. In attempting to involve parents of "at-risk children" in the educational process, we quickly learned that these parents too were once judged at risk. How often we have heard a parent, when told that his child is having problems in school respond, "Yeah, I'm not surprised. I had trouble too." Their experience in school was decidedly bad. They hated it. Even as adults they worry about meeting with teachers and school officals—not just because it often means bad news but also because they themselves feel uncomfortable in any place called school. It was and is a place that seems to summon up all their worries of lack of competence, efficacy, and worth. Many of these parents desperately want their children to succeed in school but they are handicapped by their own experiences. The parents are unsure of what they can do. They are even hesitant to ask for help.

Even more disturbing is that one finds an occasional educator who herself does not accept or grasp the value of creating a love for learning or has resigned herself to the fact that for most kids school and learning is "work" and there is "no gain without pain." A primary objective of the schools—

teachers, administrators, parents, and community leaders—must be that all children become invested in learning.

A School That Creates Life-Long Learners

There is an array of knowledge, skill, values, and attitudes thought to be critical to education. So wide and varied is the range that educators have found it necessary to lean on sophisticated, detailed, and extended taxonomies (for example, Bloom, Engelhart, Furst, Hill, & Krathwohl, 1956; Bloom, Krathwohl, & Masia, 1964). Yet, one can reasonably reduce this complexity to two primary questions regarding what should be taught. First, what is durable? Second, what is propaedeutic or instrumental? Answers to these questions can, must, and should guide school learning.

What is the most durable knowledge? What really lasts? What has a continuing and enduring quality to it and will empower the student throughout a lifetime? Dealing with that question seriously will, of course, rule out a lot of nonsense. It will possibly lead to a new perspective on curriculum and teaching. The primary objective of schools must be to develop life-long learners. The question that educators and policy makers must continually place in the forefront is: How will teaching this or that enable and encourage the student to keep on learning?

Engaging children in learning has immediate importance for attaining other valuable school outcomes. Most broadly, it equips students to deal with a future that teachers, parents, policy makers, and soothsayers can hardly divine. Knowing about the food chain is important for passing a test, but being able to apply that knowledge enables one to fish, grow crops, and tour a new environment. But preparation for, personal investment in, and a love for learning are not only desirable but necessary. These are no longer—if they ever were—the prerogative of scholars and scientists. All need them to survive and to realize a full and complete life. If one ever could, one cannot now afford to stop learning. But it is not just individual self-interest that forces learning; the survival of communities and societies demands it. Now as never before, it is unacceptable and self-defeating to permit talent to die on the vine. The nature of contemporary society is no less interdependent than a tribal group confronting a threatening environment. We live, die, stand, and fall together. Stressing the development of life-long learners is not elitist; it is and must be broadly inclusive.

Thus, our answer to the question of *what* should be learned stresses the primacy of an acquirable, enduring orientation, or trait of character. The essential argument here is that school is about creating learners. It is impossible to inculcate all the knowledge that can and will be useful. Skill development has a durable ring to it, but really, how useful is penmanship to most of us? Moreover, many of us did not appreciate the durability of typing skills until the personal computer era arrived. And this too is probably a passing phenomenon. Certainly, there are skills and types of knowledge that seem to exist as a *sine qua non*. For example, the ability to communicate, especially receiving and transmitting ideas through written symbols, seems durable as does modeling and solving problems of the world and daily life through numeracy. Important also is certain social knowledge: how democracy works; an awareness of the wider world of work; an appreciation of a diversity of peoples, customs, values, interests, and opportunities. But can one imagine acquiring, retaining, and continually updating this knowledge without becoming personally invested?

In this book, we shall concentrate on enhancing the personal investment of students in learning for several reasons. There is perhaps no orientation more important than the predilection to continue learning. Especially in today's world, one has to learn new skills and acquire additional knowledge regularly. Throughout their lives, most adults find that demands of work and living inevitably lead them back to "school" in some form or fashion. Besides, learning is and can be a redeeming and invigorating force for enhancing the quality and enjoyment of life—as senior citizens are increasingly finding as they participate in "elder hostels." In short, developing a love for learning is decidedly instrumental in meeting major life objectives. As a broadly useful and widely generalizable educational outcome it merits attention (Maehr, 1976). But seldom is attention paid to this outcome. Although most agree that creating life-long learners is important, this agreement is largely of the lip-service variety. Moreover, there is strong reason to believe that schools can and do affect whether children become life-long learners.

But of course, whether or not one can accept the importance of personal investment within the school curriculum, this seemingly elusive concept must be discussed in more detail.

The Nature of Student Investment in Learning

The words "personal investment" roll easily off the tongue. We have found that educators feel comfortable with them as well. But clearly, the serious issues at stake here demand that we be specific about what we are proposing when we argue that a personal investment in learning is critical. What is the nature of this desideratum? More precisely, what is it and how do we get it? It is time to be specific, to speak in terms that every educator can grasp.

Personal Investment

We use the term *personal investment* as an alternative for the common term "motivation." We do so not to make the topic seem easy or esoteric, but because we want to reflect a specific perspective on the nature of motivation. Investment suggests a metaphor regarding what motivation really is like. Referring to motivation as investment suggests an image in which all students have certain resources they may use in different ways. All students have time, energy, and abilities; they bring a history of experience, information, and knowledge to any situation—be it school, a social group, work, or whatever. The primary issue of motivation, then, is not whether students have it. They do. It is a matter of how they choose to invest it. Motivation is like money—it can be used in a variety of ways. The issue is how these resources are invested and with what results.

Direction

The term personal investment reflects that we are talking about the kinds of choices individuals make, the direction of behavior they pursue. Each time one visits a classroom or a learning group, one sees children pursuing different options. Either by design or happenstance, they are doing different things. Seldom are they all doing the same thing and they often shift from one thing to the next. One day, one of us happened to drop in on a 5th grade class. It was a tightly ordered class, desks all lined up in a five-by-five square. Free movement was not the expectation; directed action to closed specific ends was clearly the intent of the teacher. Yet, when the teacher talked, only some students appeared to be attending more to the teacher than the person in the next seat. When seat work was in progress, here and there a student focused on circling this or inserting that. Another student could be seen drawing a stick figure, another apparently daydreaming. A student in the back of the room was communicating to a friend with facial gestures. Another seemed to be more interested in what the outside "guest" was doing than in the task at hand. This is not a surprising or unusual observation when one drops in on any 5th grade class—even a highly structured one. These are examples of the kinds of choices and the variation in the direction of behavior that every teacher, most principals, and an occasional researcher see regularly in the school behavior of children. These kinds of choices suggest the nature, degree, and quality of investment in a task at hand. These choices may or may not sum up to a pattern and may or may not eventuate in major effects on the course of learning and development. Other choices may loom larger in the developmental history of the child-person, such as dropping out of school and taking a job. The choices may also be more dramatic, such as returning to school at middle age and in mid-career. And small choices may cumulate into big effects: Not setting aside time to do one's homework may eventually rule out any hope of getting into medical school. The point, of course, is that we are all regularly confronted with multiple options, and we do in fact go in some directions and avoid others. This directionality of our behavior over the short and long terms is specifically embraced in the term personal investment. We participate, engage, invest in some activities and acts and not in others. Personal investment infers that an individual does one thing when other possibilities are presumably open to him.

Intensity

It is not only that individuals make different choices to engage or not to engage in academic learning tasks. The nature of the investment in any given task may vary. Choices such as we have described can also be characterized in terms of intensity or degree of engagement. The actual energy directed toward a particular course of action may vary. The desultory way in which a teacher sometimes grades papers is at variance with the level of energy and engagement exhibited when that same teacher teaches a class or gives a speech. We all have low energy periods during the course of the day and through the life span. Sometimes these relate to internal and physiological causes: fatigue, medication, illness, age; sometimes, however, they seem to reflect our interest in and our enthusiasm about a given course of action. It may be that a teacher's desultory grading is attributable to the fact that it is done at a time of the day when the energy level is low—late in the day or in the evening in front of the TV. Intensity often is situational. But the fact that we regularly relegate it to a time of day when we are typically tired or have something else to do may indicate an enduring level of (lack of) investment in that particular activity.

Persistence

Choices can also be characterized by their persistence, the continuation of a course of action once taken. Thus, when a child spends the better half of the evening on a science project and only ten minutes during the breakfast period doing a math assignment, a variation of a degree of investment is shown. More interesting, perhaps, is the child who spends half of the evening on the science project and returns to the same project the next night—without anyone telling her to do so! Indeed, at the heart of the development of a long term investment in learning is the "continuing motivation" to invest in a particular task across varying circumstances for one's own reasons (Maehr, 1976; Hoffman, 1992; Hughes, Sullivan, & Mosley, 1985; Pascarella, Walberg, Junker, & Haertel, 1981). It is this example of an investment in learning over the long term that is especially of interest to educators. And, we would suggest, is and should be a major objective of schools.

Quality

Of course, it is not just the direction or intensity of an activity that interests us. Those concerned with developing the minds of children care about the quality of investment. Most of us choose to spend some time reading a newspaper, perhaps each day. However, that investment of time and effort is played out in different ways. On some days, we may simply check headlines, focusing on getting an overall summary of what's happening in the world we inhabit. At other times, we go beyond headlines, maybe giving special attention to a continuing story or a series of articles. The media regularly reports the problems besetting inner city America. Perhaps the *New York Times* has a special feature on how schools are becoming full-service social agencies. This may attract more than a skim of the headlines, especially if one is interested in public education. A different reading strategy will ensue and the reading may be accompanied by some reflection; perhaps the section will be clipped, filed, duplicated, and shared with a colleague or friend. The thoughts contained will be processed in quite a different way than simply noting NFL scores and standings. In a not dissimilar fashion students approach school reading materials. Ten students may all "read" the same passage or document, but *how* they read it will vary, sometimes dramatically. Thus, we cannot limit ourselves to the choices—investments—people make; it is necessary to consider how they invest when they invest. So we refer both to the intensity as well as the *quality* of investment. When we refer to the quality of investment, there are a number of issues to consider, including the following.

Academic venturesomeness.

Researchers concerned with school achievement have recently devoted considerable attention to the quality of investment, viewing it as a critical factor in learning and achievement. An early concern was with what might be called "academic venturesomeness" (Clifford, 1988; Maehr, 1983). Academic choices always involve a degree of risk. One may wish to work on this or that task, take this or that course—but might we "get in over our heads"? Translated, this means one may be open to failing in some sense, or appearing stupid, or engaging in a task that is frustrating and leaves one with negative feelings. Yet, choosing the "safe path" may have its disadvantages. In our discussions with teachers, we often ask them to think back on their own schooling experiences, particularly in regard to a class they would have liked to take but which they avoided for fear of perhaps reducing their grade point average. Such questions usually generate an interesting and active telling of tales. It is no surprise that most express regret over having avoided an interesting and perhaps important learning experience because of a fear of the risk involved. Of course, growth often demands taking the uncertain and risky path. Simply repeating what one does well or feels secure doing reduces the opportunities for optimal expansion of one's talent. Those who have taught know all this quite well as they observe it in students who are too fearful to try something, unwilling to think themselves capable of understanding calculus or chemistry or learning how to play a violin. One of the true joys for teachers is to learn that they have helped someone to accept a learning challenge. Some students remember fondly the help teachers have given them in enhancing self-understanding. We can cite our own favorite anecdotes in this regard. The large number of such anecdotes indicates the importance of academic venturesomeness as well as the teacher's and school's role in encouraging it.

Strategic learning.

Other facets of the quality of investment have been the subject of particular interest in the past decade or so. These involve the use of different strategies and thinking processes as one learns and include how students go about the task of learning (for example, Pintrich & DeGroot, 1990a, 1990b; Pintrich & Garcia, 1991). Every teacher has witnessed students approaching learning in maladaptive and adaptive ways; take the reading of a textbook assignment, for example. Even relatively sophisticated college freshmen sometimes exhibit maladaptive strategies in carrying out their reading assignments. Instead of beginning with a kind of survey of what the assignment is about, setting some sort of expectation for what they should look for, and then proceeding to read, they often get lost in the fine print, ignoring the boldfaced titles and subtitles. They simply read from beginning to end or for a certain period of time without engaging in behaviors that embed the information in their memories. Recent work on reading and study practices has given rise to the concept of "self-regulated learning," a core set of strategies for approaching a task thoughtfully and with a workable and useful strategy (Pintrich & Garcia, 1994). What is interesting is that although individuals can be taught about these procedures and encouraged to use them, often they will not. And in other cases, they will use these strategies spontaneously without the benefit of advice or wise counsel. Emotional factors such as anxiety and instructional conditions that affect motivation generally seem to play an important role in this regard (see for example, Covington, 1992).

Thoughtful learning.

Most educators would also agree that students not only need to adopt effective learning strategies, but they also need to approach the tasks critically (for example, Pintrich, Cross, Kozma & McKeachie, 1986; Pintrich & Schrauben, 1992) and creatively (for example, Amabile & Hennesey, 1992). Students need to consider what they are reading, raise questions about it, and discover alternatives to the solutions that an author proposes. In particular, we hope students will exhibit a degree of creativity in coming up with novel, socially useful responses to questions and approaching problems in new and different ways. Certainly, the activities of teachers and schools do not all suggest that thoughtful learning is a major objective of instruction and schooling. However, as one thinks ahead to the needs of children and the society in which we hope they will be full contributors, it can hardly be denied that this facet of investment cannot be ignored. Indeed, innovation deserves special and increasing attention. Originality is not only needed by society, it is needed by individuals as they make their way in society. It will become increasingly clear that such outcomes figure prominently in the vision of school we present.

Table 2.1 presents examples that sum up to a picture of what we have in mind when we use the term personal investment. By no means is the concept of personal investment merely a metaphor. It is a metaphor, of course, in that every student is portrayed as having resources of time and talent that can and will be used in some way. But this metaphor translates readily into behaviors that can be specified, observed, and assessed. Students invest in different ways and begin to project that the direction, degree, and quality of their investments will affect the course of their lives and the community in which they live. Different investments will yield different outcomes.

Table 2.1   Dimensions of Personal Investment

Dimension	Variables	Examples
Direction	Choice/preference	Mary, a 3rd-grader, comes home from school and "chooses" to watch TV rather than do homework, practice the piano, or play with a friend.
	Persistence	Frank, age 10, spends five minutes on an English assignment at 7:00 p.m., after which he goes to the basement and works on a model car he is building. He has to be "dragged" to bed at 10:00 p.m.
	Continuing motivation	Mike, a 4th-grader, picks out a book during his class's biweekly library session. He brings it back to his classroom, begins reading it, puts it aside upon his teacher's request to work on math but brings it home and, as his mother puts it, "couldn't put it down."
Intensity	Number of items attempted/problems solved	Peter was introduced to magic markers during the morning kindergarten session. Within twenty minutes he managed to turn out ten separate pictures.
	Activity level observed	Angie was sent upstairs to do her homework. She lay on the bed with her book for twenty minutes, mostly gazing up at the ceiling, finally falling asleep.
Quality	Strategic learning	A class of 10th grade students was told that they would have to write an essay on a "famous scientist." Within a day, Bill asked the teacher for possible references and took advantage of a library period to quickly survey a few references. Later he checked out several books, began reading, and started writing his paper a week before it was due. On the day before the assignment, Joe called the library for help, got multiple references and books, reading each through from cover to cover. But by 7:00 p.m. the night before the assignment was due he had not come across sufficient information to write the essay. Desperately, he called his brother at college and asked if he had any old essays he could "use for a guide."

Thoughtful learning

Mr. Jones's class of 5th grade science students is expected to do individual projects each year. Liz checks with her older sister who had the same assignment two years earlier and basically gathers the same types of seeds, mounts them on poster board, and labels them, much as her sister had.

After the teacher introduced a unit on electricity, Jane was intrigued with how water could generate electrical power. She began building a water wheel and got help from her father in crafting a generator. The whole project turned out to be too cumbersome to bring to school. But Jane did manage to build a water wheel that generated electricity.

Academic venturesomeness

Walt was a junior in engineering when he realized he had taken mostly math and physics courses. The world of the humanities was a strange world. One semester, he decided he would enroll in the course Persian Language and Literature to see what it was like—to heck with his GPA!

Different Investments; Different Outcomes

The choices people make and the nature and quality of the activity that ensues are critical facets of human nature and life. The term investment appropriately suggests the essence of what is involved in making choices. Basically, all people have resources of time and energy to be used and some discretion as to how they will be used. As people use time and energy, they *invest*, applying these resources with some specifiable results. In line with another meaning of the word invest, they also confer some meaning, value, even power to the endeavor or course of action. What is done at one point affects subsequent choices and courses of action. The direction, intensity, and quality of investment is likely to eventuate in different outcomes. As children invest so they build the frame of the persons they become. As such, investment patterns in school are characteristically related to achievement: the ability to move to the next level of schooling, to pursue this or that career, to excel as a musician, a scientist, or an athlete (Csikszentmihalyi, Rathunde, & Whalen, 1993).

Questions relating to the quality of life necessarily arise as we consider personal investment. How investments culminate in the framing of the person are crucial and necessarily a part of the continuing dialogue among educators. However, we accept the proposition that a crucial, if not *the* crucial, investment of students must to some significant degree culminate in their being continuing learners. An investment in continual learning pays dividends in life generally.

The Development of Continual Learners

In our vision for schools students increasingly exhibit a certain investment pattern. Specifically, that they develop a continuing involvement with and a love and appreciation for learning. Continual learning is more than just having fun in school. It involves experiencing success and self-fulfillment and perceiving the day-to-day relevance of acquiring new knowledge and skills. The persistence of this orientation, however, depends significantly not only on immediate emotional reactions but also on the adaptive value and long-term efficacy and the knowledge, skill, and personal orientations that endure from the experience.

But how does one get this to happen in a school? That is what this book as a whole is about. In the remainder of this chapter we review some basic principles that lay the groundwork for the fuller story of how schools can assist children in becoming life-long learners.

Personal Investment: Causes and Processes

The past two decades have given birth to an impressive body of knowledge on how, why, and when individuals invest in any endeavor, especially learning.[1] The way many of us think about learning and teaching processes has been transformed. The guiding principle that has emerged is that action is mediated by beliefs and perceptions. Individuals invest as their beliefs and perceptions dictate. Out of this work has emerged a body of thought, data, and dialogue that is especially useful in understanding teaching-learning processes and schools and how they affect the development and learning of children. Essentially, any individual's investment is formed by three essential and interrelated concepts: purpose, self, and options. Briefly, individuals invest in an activity only if it is a perceived option. Sociocultural experiences outside of school play a major role in forming options. Family, peers, and to some degree the media frame what is available as well as what is worth investing in. One's view of oneself can foreclose options or open the person up to new possibilities. The school contributes significantly to how individuals construct personal options, in part simply by conveying knowledge and skill, but also by expanding the view that one has of oneself. Whether and how the school does this depends on how the school defines schooling for the individual.

The Primacy of Purpose

Purpose is basic to the understanding of human behavior. Recent research has underscored this central fact. In particular, research on the role of goals in shaping behavior has emerged as a major force in exploring why and how individuals engage in any course of action. Theoretically, one can imagine an array of purposes that might guide learning—or teaching. In fact, it is possible to construct a meaningful and rather complete picture of learning processes by concentrating especially on two: task and ability.

Task and Ability Goals

These represent contrasting purposes in pursuing a course of action (see Table 2.2). Ability-focused goals relate especially to social competition, demonstrating one's ability to outdo or outperform others. In a learning situation this takes the form of demonstrating that one is "smart"—actually, "smarter"—than others. In sports, it takes the form of winning at all costs (Duda & Nicholls, 1992). In parenting it can take the form of making sure that one's children are trained earlier and are better behaved than the

Table 2.2   Definitions of Task and Ability Goals

	Task	Ability
Success defined as	Improvement, progress mastery, innovation, creativity	High grades, high performance compared to others, relative achievement on standardized measures, winning at all costs
Value placed on	Effort, attempting difficult tasks	Avoiding failure
Basis for satisfaction	Progress, mastery	Being the best, success relative to effort
Work/performance context	Growth of individual potential, learning	Establishing performance hierarchies
Reasons for effort	Intrinsic and personal meaning of activity	Demonstrating one's worth
Evaluation criteria	Absolute criteria, evidence of progress	Norms, social comparisons
Errors viewed as	Part of the growth process, informational	Failure, evidence of lack of ability or worth
Competence viewed as	Developing through effort	Inherited and fixed

Source: This table builds on earlier analyses by Ames and Archer, 1988.

neighbors' children. Task goals relate especially to progress and mastery; the intrinsic and personal meaning of performing a task is central. Schools, parents, peers, and students represent this goal as they refer to the "excitement" in acquiring a new skill; emphasizing that all can learn; stressing the importance of effort, improvement, progress, growth.

Generally, in schools as in most achievement situations, individuals will be more or less inclined toward one or the other of these two goals. Ask a 7th grader a series of questions about why he studies and when he studies, and he is likely to give a series of reasons that reflect definitions of purpose that are task- or ability-oriented. Through questionnaires or interviews he will indicate that school is not so much about learning as about performing well, coming up with the right answers, completing work on time, and being at the top of the class. School is all too often viewed as a competitive game in which some win and others, unfortunately, lose.

In contrast to emphasis on *demonstrating* ability, some students believe that schooling and learning are about *developing* ability. In more concrete terms, one child leaves for school saying, "I want to win the spelling bee today. I hope I do better than Susie on the math test." Another child says as she leaves, "I hope I can figure out what I'm doing wrong on these long division problems today. I can't wait to read the next chapter in our Greek mythology book." The latter child believes that learning in and of itself is worthwhile and her goal is to improve ability rather than to prove ability. Many students hold both these seemingly contradictory conceptions of school simultaneously with one or the other conception predominant in any given situation.

A substantial literature exists that allows for several conclusions about the nature of goals. The existence and salience of the achievement purposes in learning situations have been widely recognized (Ames & Ames, 1989; Maehr & Pintrich, 1991). The labels applied to task and ability goals vary somewhat among different research groups.[2] But in the main, there is convergence on the importance of these two purposes. And in the social sciences there has been a surprising degree of agreement on conception and measurement. Clearly, goals are cognitions; thoughts that individuals hold about situations. The construction of task and ability goals are set within the broad domain of cognitive theory. In some ways, they parallel earlier conceptions of needs and motives. In particular, they derive in part from work on achievement motives and needs (McClelland, 1961). But in several important respects they represent a clear break from this tradition. As cognitions, thoughts in the first instance, they are reportable. If properly asked, people can probably tell you what their purposes are in performing in a situation. The practical implication is that one can use direct questioning and surveys in determining purposes; there is no need to employ projective techniques or indirect methods to unveil affective undercurrents of one's psyche (McClelland, Koestner, & Weinberger, 1989). Individuals are reasonably forthright in defining a situation—or at least, what they say about their purposes in achievement situations is typically related to what they will do. Children at an early age (Nicholls & Hazzard, 1993) as well as college students (Pintrich & Garcia, 1991) and adults (Maehr & Braskamp, 1986) have been shown to hold thoughts of purpose that frame their actions.

Of course, many questions remain. Goal theory is not static but remains a dynamic venue for inquiry. Among questions that are currently under scrutiny are the enduring nature of these thoughts, their status as a personal characteristic over time, and their subjection to change along with situations and circumstances. Another question relates to the degree to which these are partially framed by or incorporate basic emotional reactions that are part of what used to be thought of as the "unconscious." Moreover, it is especially clear that task and ability goals do not embrace the full range of purposive life. Individuals operate with multiple goals. Social goals (for example, Urdan & Maehr, 1995) have been recognized as playing an especially important role in schools and classrooms as well as in other domains of life and work. The unfinished nature of goal theory and the degree of complexity of purposive life does not detract from a central principle that forms the basis for the thrust of this book. Two goals, task and ability, are especially crucial for how we go about understanding the emergence of a predilection for life-long learning. And so it is that we will build our narrative around task and ability goals: what they "do" and how they "emerge."

Goals and Personal Investment

The central point of holding task and ability goals, of course, is that these conceptions of school purposes play an important role in whether or how students will invest in school activities. In this regard, it may be helpful to review well-established findings in the literature. How does holding a task or ability goal relate to the indicators of personal investment we outlined earlier? Figure 2.2 suggests a possible causal flow of events.

Choice, direction, and intensity.

Holding task or ability goals is related to how one is oriented toward learning and to one's engagement in any course of action. This shows up in the attitudes that students express toward school—or what they are doing at any given time in a classroom (Dweck, 1991; Garcia & Pintrich, 1994; Maehr, 1983; Nicholls, 1984). It shows up in adults in expressions of job satisfaction and organizational commitment (Maehr & Braskamp, 1986). People simply seem to be more positively disposed toward a task when they hold task goals. The reasons for this are not obscure. The social competition associated with ability goals has a definite downside (cf. Nicholls, 1989). There are winners and losers and in such situations most indeed will be losers. Many will be losers most of the time. So, it is not surprising that ability goals are less likely to be associated with positive feelings than task goals.

Task and ability goals are differentially associated with the intensity with which a person engages in a task. When an individual holds a task goal she is not only more likely to be fully engaged in the task but also engaged for a longer period. A task orientation probably also breeds what is called "continuing motivation" (Maehr, 1976). It is not just that task and ability goals are differentially associated with attitudes and feelings, they clearly relate to patterns of motivation that will be exhibited by students.

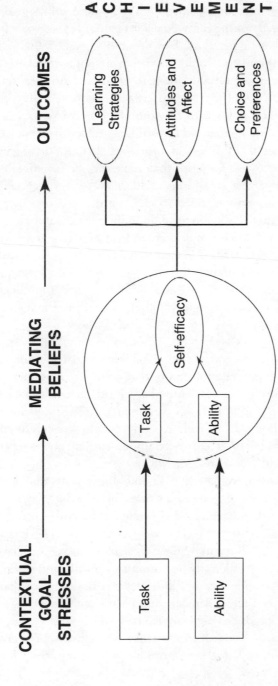

Figure 2.2 Schematic representation of goal theory model. *Source:* Adapted from Maehr, Pintrich, & Zimmerman, 1993

Quality of investment.

Of equal if not greater importance is that task and ability goals are associated with the *quality* of the individual's investment. Task goals frame different types of behavior patterns than do ability goals. When an individual adopts a task (rather than an ability) goal vis-à-vis a particular activity, she is more likely to exhibit a willingness to try hard and take on challenges (Ames, 1984; Dweck, 1991; Maehr, 1989; Nicholls, 1984). She dares to risk failure in reaching forth to try something new. We have seen the role goals play in how elementary school students select their projects for a science fair. Believing that this task is some sort of competitive game, it is natural for students to risk no more than necessary. In practice, we observed that under ability stress conditions children were less inclined to do what they wanted to do, more inclined to seek out their parents' help, and often prone to replicate what a sibling had done the year before. This is not "academic venturesomeness." It is not likely to lead to personal growth and actualization of one's potential. It is definitely *not* what most educators have in mind as a desirable orientation toward learning. Seeking learning challenges and academic venturesomeness is a desirable feature of intellectual life and growth. It can hardly be thought of otherwise within the context of teaching and learning in schools.

So the fact that task and ability goals are differentially associated with variation in this type of academic risk-taking is hardly unimportant. But there is also a raft of data indicating that ability goals undercut basic and necessary learning processes. Thus, Paul Pintrich and others (Pintrich & Garcia, 1991, 1994; Pintrich & Schrauben, 1992) have shown repeatedly that holding ability goals is likely to undercut the use of effective learning strategies that eventuate in enhanced understanding and retention (Anderson, 1980; Entwistle & Ramsden, 1983).

Finally, it is worth noting that task and ability goals may figure into the demonstration of creativity in one's work. This possibility was anticipated in the early work of John Nicholls (1972) and has recently emerged as worthy of special attention within the context of goal theory. There is a large body of literature that has illustrated how extrinsic rewards often have a negative effect on motivation, especially on continuing motivation (Elliot & Harackiewicz, 1994; Harackiewicz & Elliot, 1993). Building on that literature, Amabile (1983) and Teresa Amabile and Beth Hennesey (1992) have shown how extrinsic rewards can undermine creativity as well. It is not difficult to extrapolate from these results on intrinsic and extrinsic reward conditions to hypothesize that task goals are more likely to foster creativity than ability goals. Indeed, the very fact that task and ability goals have been associated with venturesomeness, deep processing, and generally adaptive patterns of problem solving and learning almost inevitably leads in this direction. And Jennifer Archer (1990), in an early test of this prediction, did in fact find a relationship between holding task goals and creativity in writing poetry by high school students. Although this seems to be a reasonable extrapolation from present knowledge, clearly more work needs to be done to see how task and ability goals might be related to this elusive but desirable outcome of an educational experience.

Learning with and from others.

Learning in schools is inevitably a social act. Indeed, much recent research would indicate that the nature and quality of learning as well as the investment in learning are affected as students share insights, construct understandings together, and in effect teach each other (Brown & Palincsar, 1989; Palincsar & Klenk, 1992). What should also be clear is that ability goals are not designed to facilitate the sharing of knowledge, cooperative learning, learning in groups, helping or seeking help from others, and so forth (for example Arbreton, 1993; Gutierrez & Slavin, 1992). When individuals view the classroom and educational settings as places to demonstrate that they are better than others—when comparative performance is the goal and classroom activities a competitive game at best, a dog-eat-dog scramble at worst—then one cannot expect to find good social and interpersonal relationships among participants. The notion of the classroom as a place where students construct understandings together, gain from each others' insights, and learn to share and help certainly is not fostered by an ability-goal emphasis.

A preference for task goals.

We have portrayed two learning or achievement goals as being at the center of learning and task goals as having a preferred place in designing the nature of schooling. Achievement and learning, of course, are not all there is to life in or out of school. Multiple goals frame behavior (Maehr & Braskamp, 1986; Urdan & Maehr, 1995; Wentzel, 1991). In studying adolescents one cannot help but be impressed with the degree to which making friends, getting along with others, and being accepted are important. But so are goals such as serving, helping, enabling, and giving to others (Farmer, Vispoel, & Maehr, 1991; Kohn, 1990). Establishing and maintaining social solidarity, a sense of community and belonging, are important in the life of students and also affect their investment in learning. But presently, the evidence is overwhelming that these two goals are most directly important in framing the course of learning and schooling. A large body of literature portrays a coherent picture of learning and schooling when one or the other of these two goals is primary. When expressing what a school should be, that literature yields an inescapable conclusion: School should emphasize task goals. And so our vision of schooling will revolve especially on how task goals emerge in educational settings and what happens when they do.

The summary point is simple. Task and ability goals are not incidental in the lives of students and are significant in creating an investment in learning. Task goals are at the root of the development and maintenance of a positive and productive commitment to life-long learning.

Goals and Thoughts About Self

Task and ability goals have differential effects in part because of the way they define the learning situation and focus the learner. On the one hand, task goals make the process of learning primary with individual improvement and progress the ultimate purposes of the effort. It is the person vis-à-vis the task that is at issue. In contrast, ability goals make learning a socially competitive endeavor. The objective is to define who is "competent" (and who is less so) relative to others. One's place in a hierarchy of ability is at stake. Thus, one's self-image is likely to be a more important part of the motivation equation in the ability than the task goal situation. And that is an important point!

Concept of self and investment of time and effort.

Certainly, one of the more commonly held views of student motivation is that the student's sense of self is at the root of her motivation to learn. Countless books and articles have been written on the topic and it seems to be a hypothesis about which teachers feel strongly—and with some merit. Students avoid taking more math than they have to because they *believe* that they *aren't good at math*. If a person believes he lacks the ability to do something, he is more likely to be wary of trying. The relationship between such judgments of self and motivation has not only been noted by teachers, parents, and people in general but is well established in the research literature (for example, Bandura, 1993; Harter, 1992).

This engendered avoidance, of course, can be most serious for the life course of individuals. What happens when a 7th grader feels that she isn't good at math? In most instances she can't elect to avoid it completely even though confronting math not only elicits disinterest but also anxiety. One option is to enroll in a less demanding section of math. That may spell temporary relief temporary because it could create further problems. A young friend tells of taking that route, even though all the "objective data" indicated that she was indeed quite good in math. This choice to avoid proved problematic when she became interested in policy studies, entered a graduate program, and confronted formulas defining economic trends and statistics. Fortunately, she had not avoided math to the point that she took no math at all. She had taken enough to keep on the "college and prospective graduate student path." But returning to algebra upon one's entrance into graduate school without a basis in high school or college can be and often is fraught with problems: anxiety at the least and failure at the worst. Although not the case with our young friend, many avoid math too much, and in the 7th grade their life choices are set in a way they do not fully realize at the time.

Concept of self and quality of investment.

Even when judgments of competence don't appear to affect the direction of behavior, they can and do impact the quality of the investment that will be exhibited. The fear of being shown to be incompetent is likely to eventuate in poor learning and study techniques, as the large body of research on "evaluation anxiety" has pointed out (for example, Hill, 1980; Hill & Wigfield, 1984). When something so serious as their self-esteem is at stake, students do not respond thoughtfully or even rationally. They use poor study techniques and are creative primarily about avoiding the kind of engagement that is necessary to learn. Martin Covington (1992) has summarized how this focus on the self, particularly when there is the sense that one may be inadequate, eventuates in the most inappropriate of learning strategies. In particular, he points out how individuals engage in complex maneuvers to provide reasons for their possible failure, reasons that don't touch their sense of competence and self-esteem, such as not studying until the night before a test. These so-called "self-handicapping strategies" are good at temporarily shifting the blame for failure on something besides one's ability. They are, however, decidedly self-defeating so far as gaining knowledge and understanding is concerned (Midgley, Arunkumar, & Urdan, in press; Midgley & Urdan, 1995).

Goal stresses, self-concepts, and children at risk.

It is the focus on the self and one's ability relative to others that is likely at the root of the maladaptive approach to learning taken by students who come to school "insufficiently prepared." These may be children who have not had the advantages of early tutoring in preschool or extraschool programs. They may come to school with little sense of the order, style, and expectations of the classroom. It may be that they simply know from the color of their skin, the cut of their clothes, or the words they use, that they are not only different but possibly disadvantaged for this seemingly alien experience. Their lack of experience in the expectations of teachers and schools jeopardizes these children, particularly if all this is tied in with their sense of competence (as it often is) and if relative ability figures strongly in the value system of the school.

In short, it is difficult if not impossible for children of certain backgrounds to think of themselves as competent at many things the school demands. How can these students not notice that many are ahead of them in school knowledge and skills? It would seem that the inevitable choice when one is confronted with one's inability is to avoid those situations. And that's what they—and most of us—tend to do. Or perhaps we try to devalue schooling, make a joke of it or rebel against it.

Most educators have recognized this dilemma for a long time, although they have not really dealt with it very effectively. One line of attack has been to initiate special "self-esteem programs" of varied quality and type (cf. Kohn, 1994). For the most part, these programs assume that the source of negative self-concepts lies in the lives that children live out of school: the quality of their family life, the racist attitudes that they experience, the stigma of being poor. Undeniably, these factors are at work to the detriment of many children and few would argue with the school's interest in ameliorating these situations. The action taken, however, is often misguided. For example, it is a practice in school to have individuals begin the day by shouting something like, "I am somebody," "I can do it," or "I'm beautiful." Many teachers make a point of honoring all students for something: gold stars for having the "nicest smile," being the "best rester," or a "good helper." These techniques may not hurt, but it is doubtful whether they will have enduring effects on one's self-regard. Certainly, there is little evidence that this enhances children's sense of competence for learning. Besides, it misses a fundamental point: Maybe it is not just what happens outside of school that is the problem; maybe the school itself is the problem. If so, it is doubtful whether verbal or physical hugs by teachers can counter what school cultures create.

Indeed, we would argue specifically that a school emphasis on ability goals makes it virtually inevitable that a large group of children will develop all too many misgivings regarding their competence to learn. In particular, children who come to school with little preparation and with no continuing support will begin to view themselves not only as different, but also dumb and, worse, of lesser value. The rewards in the ability-oriented school lie in doing better than others regardless of the opportunities or resources you have been granted. It is a race with the participants starting at different points on the track and with those behind having little or no chance to catch up. So it does little good to hug or praise when the whole environment is sending a message that winners—not learners—count.

We will revisit this point later in the book. It has broad implications for dealing with diversity of background and heterogeneity of entering competencies and orientations that are typically represented in school. For now, we will sketch the theoretical model that frames our vision of school.

The Experienced Environment Affects Goal Orientation

Interwoven with our discussion thus far are two different, but ultimately compatible, notions about goals. On the one hand, goals are beliefs that guide an individual's actions, thoughts, and emotions. Students—perhaps even in kindergarten—enter a classroom with certain beliefs about the purpose of schooling. The child certainly is not a blank tablet at the beginning of her formal schooling experience and the nature of the new situation can also have strong effects on changing these thoughts. Indeed, the very way in which much of goal research and theory building has been carried out forces attention on how the situation, factors in the social context, eventuate in the goals that become primary in shaping a person's thoughts about self, actions, and emotions. Specifically, schools and classrooms have been shown to vary in how they lead individuals to construe the purpose, meaning, and the *goals* of a situation. Recently, research in achievement settings has increasingly underscored this basic point. It has been regularly observed that students in different classrooms tend to view the purpose of learning and schooling differently (Meece, 1991; Nicholls, Patashnick & Nolen, 1985). This has been shown to be related to student perceptions of the teacher and of what goes on in the classroom, including summary judgments of emphasis on task or ability goals and reports of specific instructional and management practices employed by teachers, such as how they group, evaluate, and recognize children and how they organize the learning tasks (Ames & Archer, 1988; Meece, Blumenfeld, & Hoyle, 1988; Meece, 1991).

There is a wealth of evidence that classrooms—how they are organized and managed, who the teacher is and what he does—play a significant role in determining the purposes children adopt in learning. It is not only that children construct meaning in a situation; construction of meaning is lawful, predictable, and controllable. Certain acts lead to certain perceptions which in turn affect the level and quality of personal investment.

But clearly, the classroom is only one learning site in the school. An important one, to be sure, but by no means the only one. What happens in the gym, at band rehearsals, and on the playground is also important, albeit too often ignored in studies of school learning. Moreover, each classroom exists within a wider organizational context whose influence is doubtless of significance. Educators often give the impression that school reform is simply a matter of obtaining good teachers, treating them as professionals, and then empowering them to practice their craft. How can one be against good teachers and teaching? But the issue is decidedly more complicated than that. Putting good teachers into bad schools is not unlike putting new wine into old bottles. Certainly, given the high rate of school staff turnover, it is not reasonable to expect that school reform will burst forth from the creation of a new and strikingly distinguished teaching force. And maybe it's not that we don't have "good teachers," but that we have school organizations that cripple their efforts.

Sarah,[3] a teacher with whom we've worked, tells of how during a district reorganization she moved from teaching 6th grade in an elementary school to a "junior high" transformed into a "middle school," where she taught the same age students. The significant change was the "organizational context." Sarah confessed that at first she was very distressed by the different emphases and vowed adamantly that she would remain true to her former ways of teaching and dealing with children and subject matter. She would not forsake her basic philosophy about education and the ideals to which she dedicated herself, even though the middle school was a decidedly different place. The staffing was obviously different; the norms for teachers and students were different. Less child-centered and more content focused, certainly. The atmosphere was more organizationally complex, involving more constraints on what could be done and how one might experiment. She observed somewhat uncomfortably that after a year or so in the new environment she had changed as well, becoming more like the rest of the middle school staff and less like the elementary teacher she had been. This insightful observation gave her pause to reflect as she participated in meetings of a school improvement team that was examining programs and considering possibilities for change.

Sarah, of course, is not alone in this experience and that is one reason why in recent years increasing attention has been given to the nature and structure of the school as a whole: its culture, its values, the beliefs it promotes, and its operation. And in that regard it is interesting to note that parallel to research at the classroom level, research on school climate and culture indicates that *schools as a whole* reflect different goal stresses (Krug, 1989, 1992; Maehr, 1991; Maehr & Buck, 1993; Maehr & Fyans, 1989; Maehr & Midgley, 1991). Just as the smaller unit of the classroom has been found to define learning, it now appears that the larger unit of the school may likewise define learning and with that have a pervasive influence on student beliefs and behaviors.

Although the specific types of learning sites consciously sponsored within schools are important and thus the primary focus of our interest, other contexts cannot be ignored. We point out two of these for special attention and analysis: family and peers. Although the significance of family and peers in optimum development and learning of school-age children is widely acknowledged, the role that these groups play in how children respond to schooling and generally manage their world is of interest and importance. In this regard, current research has just begun to scratch the surface of this area for understanding (for example, Ames & Archer, 1987; Epstein, 1983; Urdan & Maehr, 1995; Buck & Schweingruber, 1992). Enough has been discovered to indicate that these contexts cannot be ignored. Moreover, there is an indication that these contexts, like those of school and classroom, can be described as more or less likely to lead to the adoption of task or ability goals. As a result, they too are factors in the equation leading to the student's construction of purpose and goals in schooling and learning.

Toward Realizing a Vision of School

The bottom line to the nature of student investment in learning is that schools not only affect it, they cause it. This issue scares or angers practicing educators: "You mean it's our fault that SAT scores are low, that kids drop out of school too soon, that too many kids say they hate school and think learning is stupid?"

In a word, yes! Or, on a more positive note, it is our responsibility to do something about the "continuing crisis" in education. Blaming parents, social disintegration, poverty, lack of funding, or meddling legislators simply will not do. The crisis is everyone's problem, but schools should lead in taking action. The schools are not only the problem but the potential solution. The good news is that schools and school staffs can do something to make a difference. In the ensuing chapters we describe how the school, while often the problem, can be the solution.

Evidence is accumulating that critical social contexts affect goal adoption. The evidence suggests that goal-adoption is to a significant degree a function of experienced contexts and that the psychological character of these contexts can be changed to affect goal adoption patterns. Childrens' spheres of experience are not inevitably destined to stress relative competence and thereby eventuate in a perception of schooling as a competitive game in which there are always winners and losers. In this regard, preliminary work suggests that classrooms (for example, Ames, 1990, 1992; Ames & Ames, 1993) and schools (for example, Maehr & Midgley, 1991; Maehr, Midgley, & Urdan, 1992; Maehr & Buck, 1993; Kaplan & Maehr, in press) can be altered so that ability goals will be minimized and task goals enhanced. Indeed, we intend to portray how learning environments of schools can be constructed to stress task rather than ability goals.

Conclusion: School Is Not a Home . . . or a Factory or . . .

School is about *learning*. It must also care about social, personal, and moral development. But its uniqueness lies in other domains. The enhancement of intellectual growth, understanding, and continuing investment in learning has to be the salient feature of the place called school.

Experiencing the life and worlds of many children who come to school inevitably draws some teachers to "parenting" and encourages serious consideration of creating "full-service schools" designed to meet the social needs of students (and families): medical, nutritional, judicial, vocational, personal, social, and psychological. While schools often are expected to provide or coordinate the meeting of all needs exhibited by children, essentially taking the place of home, schools play this role only to a degree. The school is not a home. It's primary task is not the same. It should not pretend that it is.

The school is not simply a tool of the economic system. Certainly, society correctly expects that what happens in schools will enable students to make their way in the world and to contribute to the community, society, and human good. Too sharp a focus on the economic ends of school, however, may serve to foreshorten consideration of the intrinsic worth of pursuing schooling and learning for their own inherent worth to the individual as well as for a multiplicity of desired outcomes for society. School must be considered an institution designed to meet basic human needs: to learn, to grow, and to master within a context in which relatedness as well as individuality are stressed. Schools are and must be concerned with self within community. A school is not really a "job" for young people, and schools should not be designed as factories turning out parts for some larger enterprise. School should not be "work" in the sense that it is done for extrinsic reasons and simply by and for the command and demand of others. In fact, it should be closer to "play" in the sense that it is natural, developmentally appropriate, self-sustaining, and as much as possible "fun."

In sum, school is and has to be a very special place revolving around two key concepts: learning and community. In fact, schooling is learning *in* community. That, in a few simple phrases, is our vision for schools.

Notes

1. A sampling of this work can be found in a series of research annuals (Ames and Ames, 1984; Maehr, Pintrich, et al., 1984) and a recent text (Pintrich & Schunk, 1995).

2. Multiple terms are employed in the literature to designate what we here term "task" and "ability" goals. For this volume, we adopted terminology that made most sense to the school staff with whom we worked.

3. References to school personnel are not fictitious but the names used are pseudonyms.

Part Two

School Culture and Student Learning

3   The Cultures of School

Schools are both the problem and the solution to the continuing crisis in American education. They will continue to be both until we change what goes on there. Many would agree to that. Many would agree also that more than a minor adjustment here or there is necessary. The introduction of a new reading program, self-esteem days, the addition or replacement of staff, the upgrading of technology, or one of a number of similar additions, without basic organizational change, will not do it. Externally imposed standards cannot save education and may have done as much harm as good. Site-based management doesn't help a school that is handicapped by a lack of intellectual and economic resources, a clear sense of purpose, and a will to act. The jury is still out on the worth of managed competition among schools. These and other highly publicized "quick fixes" are marginal to the solution as we see it. The problem of schools is not one of bad teachers, poor administrators, unsupportive parents, or inadequate curriculum. Although more resources would be welcome, lack of resources is not the problem either.

The problem is rooted in the core beliefs held by staff, leaders, and teachers; it lies in the perceived purposes, goals, and personal incentives that are associated with schooling. In short, with Seymour Sarason (1982, 1990), we accept the assumption that it is the *culture* of the nation's schools that must be transformed. And a careful reading of our portrayal of a "vision for schools" makes it clear that we are asking for a review, a revision, and a transformation of core values, beliefs, and practices in many schools. Our vision demands an examination and transformation of school culture. How can this be done? we asked ourselves. The answer that evolved was composed of several parts: What is this thing called "culture"? What form does it take in schools? How does it influence what goes on in school? And can it indeed be changed?

We begin answering that set of questions in this chapter. Our answers reflect a concern for theory which gave us perspective in asking questions. We sought answers in the experiences of practitioners and in focused research conducted by ourselves and others in a variety of school settings. We searched for generalizable principles that could generate hypotheses and be tested. This is not just a report of our own experiences or the story of the community of researchers and practitioners that contributed to the effort. It is a composition of facts, generalizations, principles, issues, ideas, and questions that might contribute to a theory of schooling. We will cast our answers especially in terms of four schools and a school district in which we worked intensively for a period of almost three years. We may have begun our quest in a university setting, but the effort could not and did not end there. In effect, involving ourselves closely in the lives of several schools for a considerable period of time gave us new insights into what we were about. It caused us to ask different questions as well as reframe the nature of our quest. Initial answers had to be discarded, rethought, or reformulated. This chapter and those that follow represent constructions and reconstructions that could not have been made without our school-based collaborators. The theory that initially shaped our efforts became something more—something better—as the result of living and working alongside teachers, principals, students, parents, and others in intensive school change efforts.

Early in our research, the concept of school culture figured in our thinking as a metaphor or perhaps a heuristic. Increasingly, it became a construct that could be defined, assessed, and measured. School culture became a set of *variables* that effectively described a school as different from other schools. It was associated with how the school functioned but also with what it produced. It seemed to make a significant difference not only in the work life of teachers but also in how they felt and what they did. Most importantly, it seemed to relate to the investment patterns of students: how they felt and what they did. As a variable, school culture could change and be changed. And increasingly, we came to see that it could be changed by leaders working with staff and concerned others.

Of course, the concept of school culture was not our creation. Indeed, it is a rather popular notion though an idea more often employed than analyzed. The term derives largely from the literature on organizations (for example, Denison, 1984, 1985) where it has been found to have considerable utility. At times, it has been thought of as a framework, even a constraint, within which leaders must work and as a mechanism through which leaders can effect change. The story we tell has some of the former, but it is directed ultimately to making a case for the latter.

So what is this thing called "culture"? What difference does it make in the life of schools? Can it be transformed? In this chapter we focus on the first question.

What *Is* School Culture?

It is commonly held that schools have a culture (for example, Deal & Peterson, 1990; Sergiovanni & Corbally, 1984). Many educators have found this characterization to be rich in meaning. At the least, it is a provocative metaphor for thinking and talking about schools and is particularly apt for those in positions of leadership, both as they operate in terms of a social system and as they attempt to change that system. Although discussions of school culture depend heavily on organizational theory generally, the impetus for thinking about schools this way can be traced to widely shared experiences, observations, and facts about school operations, processes, and outcomes. The concept probably derives most immediately and directly from a repeated observation: Schools differ one from the other in the way they work as well as on the "effects" they have on the lives of children. It builds on a line of investigation that has shown that schools differ in their effectiveness (for example, Good & Weinstein, 1986). Although many if not most schools are designed to be comprehensive—to provide a little of everything for diverse groups—schools can and do differ in their claims to excellence. And certain schools seem to have more to boast about than others. Some schools turn out scientists and scholars. Others boast excellence in music and the arts. Some are noted for their athletics programs. Others serve the community through health care curricula, vocational guidance, job internships, and partnerships with business and industry. These schools can identify areas of effectiveness and convince students they are indeed on the right path.

Social class, ethnicity, parenting skills, early experiences, peers, and extraschool experiences notwithstanding, schools do make a difference. Moreover, some schools make more of a difference than other schools. There is considerable evidence in support of this assertion (Bock & Wiley, 1967; Maehr, 1991; Maehr & Fyans, 1989). Indeed, such findings of differential school effects have been a driving force in the school effectiveness literature (Brookover, Beady, Flood, Schweitzer, & Wisenbaker, 1979; Brookover, Beamer, Efthim, Hathaway, Lezotte, Miller, Passalacque, & Tornatzky, 1982; Rutter & associates, 1979; Purkey & Smith, 1982; Edmonds & Frederiksen, 1979). There seems to be something that differentially characterizes schools associated with how students perform, how they relate, and how they invest. Some schools do a lot with a little; others appear to do a little with a lot.

School Differences and School Culture

Often, the term culture is used to express this difference in the character of schools. Indeed, parallel with research on organizations in general, a large body of literature has emerged related to the culture of schools (for example, Sashkin & Walberg, 1993). This literature is, to say the least, broad and diffuse, but it has yielded several intriguing ideas. There is the possibility that ways of describing human groups generally may prove helpful to those who must participate in or play leadership roles in these groups. Each school has a kind of social psychological life of its own that can be described by employing standard social science procedures. Thus, like societies or subsocieties generally, one school can be thought of as holding shared answers to certain basic questions that are somewhat different from those held by other schools. School culture implies a perspective and a definition of variables that have evolved out of study of the properties and processes of more or less interdependent groups of individuals living and working in a given locale over a period of time—time enough for individuals to think of themselves as part of a given group, to recognize the existence of this group, to attribute some identity to it, and for each member to accept a role. The primary observation is that such interdependent groups of individuals confront problems and characteristically come up with a set of shared answers.

Culture as Shared Answers

By defining culture as answers to questions, we are stressing that *culture is a matter of the mind.* Culture is a thought, perception, or belief; it is primarily part of one's cognitive life but also associated with behavior, objects, forms, and functions. But it is what people have in their heads that counts. Culture embraces not random thoughts but thoughts individuals hold vis-à-vis a group or organization. And, as we will discuss later, some of these thoughts are more—some less—important as far as the functioning and effectiveness of the organization are concerned. We stress that the use of the term culture implies a set of answers that are *shared* by a designated group of persons. The answers are thoughts that coordinate living and working together, simplify decision making, focus effort, reduce conflict, and generally make group life livable. They have a function, are maintained, and are defended and transmitted as they serve these ends. Some degree of acceptance of these answers is required for membership in the group. They are normative because conformity is expected and demanded.

Answers That Cultures Give

So to what questions are the shared answers of schools directed? What is the range of answers that are given? Generally, the answers are directed at how the group and its members should comport themselves if they are to remain full participants in the group and if the group is to survive let alone thrive. The answers are of five distinguishable types, though in substance and influence they not only interact but overlap. They are in fact complementary and interdependent. But for purposes of portraying the whole of what we take to be culture, it may be helpful to focus on somewhat different categories of questions that are asked and answered.

(1) There are questions that stem from and relate to how *basic human needs* are to be handled: what to eat, how to dress, and where and how to live. We refer to this set of questions as matters of style and preference. (2) Another set of questions relates to the definitions of the *tasks* to be done by the group: *jobs* to be done and the *technology* available for doing them. (3) A third set of questions relates especially to *how the group is organized,* how interactions are facilitated and controlled, power distributed and shared. (4) A fourth question concerns the *symbolic life* of the group, the rituals and rites, the myths and artifacts that symbolize a shared purpose and raison d'être. (5) Finally, there are questions regarding the *meaning of existence,* issues of value, and what is worth doing and why.

What are the answers to these questions and how do they define the system of interacting persons called a "school"?

Style and Preference

As one moves from Katmandu to Dallas, it is these kinds of differences that are evident. Such differences exist not only among societies but also among schools within the same society, though perhaps more subtly. They may not be the most important of differences that distinguish societies or organizations, yet they are noteworthy and may reflect broader beliefs and attitudes of the organization as a whole. Thus, they are on occasion taken quite seriously as when teachers or students are directly or indirectly encouraged or required to dress a certain way. All schools have some norms for dress. They may be specific and explicit such as when dress codes are drawn up by school staff or school boards. They may be implicit and seldom noted, products of "youth culture" and the media, sometimes subject to informal negotiation with parents and teachers.

When one arrives in a foreign country, it is style and preference that make an initial impression. When one visits schools in Beijing one is likewise aware of style differences compared to schools in the United States. It may appear there is little difference in the way students in Los Angeles and Detroit dress, since they all participate in the same media world. But the differences are probably just more subtle.

Aside from preferences and style exhibited by various participants in the organization, as, for example, the way in which they dress, there are differing ways in which various functions are carried out. Most schools have bulletin boards and place signs of one type or another here or there in the building. At a very general level, bulletin boards and signs serve similar functions across different schools. But their *nature, placement, and use* differ in interesting and significant ways from school to school. For example, in some schools virtually all messages are confined to a locked bulletin board under the obvious control of the school administration. In other schools pictures, slogans, and posters are pasted to walls and doors throughout the building, a product of a variety of authors and a range of style and purpose.

It is interesting to observe how schools seek funding outside of normal budgetary categories. Some schools sell candy, hold raffles, cook chili suppers, or make contacts with business groups. How this is done is different from school to school and community to community. What especially captures our attention about fund-raising is the variety of purposes for which extra money is sought. Here the community's theories of education and schooling often combine in interesting ways to create a program that may or may not be compatible with the vision school leadership and staff are endeavoring to realize. For example, fund-raising ventures may exacerbate the sense of difference among students and families, or worse. Asking children to sell or buy candy to support some worthy school cause may make it all too clear that some children are different in their access to financial resources. When the selling is framed as a competition among students or classrooms, a new set of unwanted learnings may also ensue. But of course, the culture of a school may also be reflected in the objectives that are selected. It may be computers, a trip for a special group such as the choir, or a dinner for an athletic team. It could be to support scholarships or to underwrite school parties (to make school fun under the assumption that learning itself cannot be?). Whatever the reasons, the choices made in selecting and administering these endeavors are not only interesting, they may be of some importance in understanding the nature of school culture and its purposes.

Knowledge, Technology, and the Tasks to Be Done

In common parlance, the term culture is often equated with knowledge, expertise, and a level of sophistication, particularly with regard to the aesthetic. But it is also widely used to describe the general level of knowledge and technology that is available and in common use. Certainly, in applying the term to organizations, one cannot imagine avoiding a description of the tasks to be done and the sources and nature of the knowledge that are employed in getting these tasks done. A typical report on any culture usually involves describing the patterns that the citizens follow in obtaining food and sustenance, providing shelter, propagating and caring for the young, taking care of those in need, and organizing and ordering social relationships. What is the knowledge source in doing this? What technology is used? When visiting a strange and exotic place, one wants to know these things. Most organizations, including schools, also can be characterized by the knowledge base out of which they operate, the technology they have available and use, and most particularly, how they define tasks to be done—by students, teachers, administrators, and parents. One of the more obvious differences between schools is available technology, ranging from paper and pencil through textbooks to computers and state-of-the-art audiovisual equipment and services. Relatively easy to index—if not define absolutely—is the knowledge base of teachers: years of schooling, certificates for this or that, specified workshops attended, and so forth. These are not unimportant to be sure. However, they often represent a striking but somewhat superficial difference among schools. Perhaps more intriguing and harder to come by are the definitions of tasks to be done: What are teachers and administrators asked to do? What are their jobs? And most important, what are the tasks given to students? How is the activity or process of learning defined? What are children asked to do? About this, we will have a great deal to say in this chapter as well as in subsequent chapters.

Social Organization

It is crucial for any organization that certain operating procedures and organizing principles be followed. These include a number of facets.

Groups and grouping.

This is common to all organizations. It is also true of schools. We group students according to grade levels and within grades according to ability levels and sometimes, unfortunately, according to social and ethnic backgrounds. We also organize instruction into subject matter areas and route children to groups to ensure a designated level of exposure to the "true, right, and beautiful" ideals the school believes it has been established to promote. Teachers may be isolated within their own classroom or they may be encouraged to "team teach." Group structure in classrooms may be fluid and regularly changing or set at the first of the year and not easily changed. The importance of groups and grouping in schools is reflected in the amount of ink that has been used in writing on the topic (for example, Cohen, 1994; Oakes, 1992).

Roles.

Roles are another often more subtle feature of group life in schools. By roles we refer specifically to the set of widely shared expectations held regarding individuals in certain social positions. Roles associated with being male and female are an obvious example. But important also are roles and attendant expectations associated with being a teacher, a principal—and a student. As individuals fit into these categories, the group expects them to act in certain ways. Sometimes these ways pose few if any problems. Sometimes, as in the case of gender roles, they have detrimental inhibiting effects (for example, Steinkamp & Maehr, 1984).

Status.

Status is also an important descriptor of how groups and organizations operate that figures in to what is meant by the term "culture." This involves several subcategories, such as how status is accorded, who has it, and how it is exercised. Who runs things in the school? What is the degree of input from different quarters? To what degree are there clear and stable hierarchies of student groups? These are the kinds of issues that the term status designates. Clearly, anyone who has experienced school at any point has an opinion about who has power, who doesn't, who is or was "in." Where power resides and how broadly it is distributed is an important variable in understanding the character and culture of a school.

Management mechanisms.

Management mechanisms comprise a readily evident feature in how groups in general and schools in particular are organized and operate. Thus, as schools have norms, roles, and status hierarchies, there are also ways to enforce the maintenance of these. Tasks and functions must be coordinated. A degree of commitment to the goals of the group must be promoted. With the term management mechanisms we call attention to procedures used in getting individuals to conform to the organizational structure. In particular, we have in mind action taken to elicit participation. How does the school generate investment in achieving certain goals? Obviously, this is critical, and we have singled this feature out for special attention (see particularly Chapter 4). For now, the point is that varied management mechanisms are employed by different schools, presumably to meet similar objectives. The decisions made here not only reflect the culture, they reinforce that culture. The management mechanisms are very likely one critical entry point for changing school culture.

Myths, artifacts, and symbols.

If one visits Peking, Bangkok, or Israel, one is impressed with their temples, statues, artifacts. These exotic locales have rites and rituals for approaching meals, celebrating events, mourning, and recognizing changes in status. The essence of culture may lie largely in normative structure associated with answering basic questions of living and the meaning of life. But it is through myths, rituals, and various symbols and artifacts that these expectations, meanings, and purposes are communicated, conveyed, and reinforced. Similarly, in the day-to-day life of schools, the stories that are told, the pictures that are displayed, and the content and phrasing of the signs and posters are noteworthy. They may reveal something about the dominant theories of education and the attitudes toward children. They may reveal what principals, teachers, and students really think schooling is about. Ethnographic and other qualitative approaches to the study of organizational culture in particular have emphasized that anecdotes, reminiscences about revered figures of the past or present, and stories about significant events provide an important entry point for understanding the nature of any organization (for example, Deal & Kennedy, 1982). They often reflect the mission of an organization. The degree to which these stories are widely shared can demonstrate the cohesiveness of an organization, especially its shared sense of mission and purpose (Peters & Waterman, 1982; Maehr & Braskamp, 1986).

Similarly, artifacts such as the slogans that appear on school walls or on bulletin boards (closed or enclosed) suggest something about how the school is run. The prominent listing of an "honor roll" in an elementary school or the posting of grades in high schools shows how learning is viewed as well as what is valued. In our own work, we have found it helpful, not just to observe what is happening in individual classrooms, but to attend schoolwide convocations—"fun nights," parent meetings, and faculty meetings. The outsider is given a general "feel" for what the school is dealing with beyond observations obtained in individual classrooms. It also provides more objective data on topics at issue and decisions made that are likely to project the life of the school as a whole as well as what goes on within the various instructional units. But it is also interesting to listen to the anecdotes and stories that are told and to be aware of the emphases placed on events and the conclusions drawn. As observers of organizational culture often point out (Deal & Kennedy, 1982), nestled within these stories is evidence of values held and basic beliefs about purpose and meaning of actions taken. The rites and rituals serve as a more visible symbol of the beliefs that hold the community together. The organizational literature provides many anecdotes on the role of rites and rituals in symbolizing the core values of a group (cf., for example, Bolman & Deal, 1991). We worked in a school where the principal took honor-roll students out to lunch. By this gesture the principal meant to emphasize that the school valued "excellence." Unfortunately, it might have reflected a stress on comparative achievement rather than learning; in the course of our work in that school, the practice was dropped.

Beliefs, values, and goals.

All of the general categories just reviewed can and often do prove useful in providing dimensions along which schools differ. But cutting through and across all these various aspects of culture in general and school culture in particular are beliefs, goals, and values. Schools differ in the core set of beliefs that give focus to the organization and guide how it operates and functions. Of course, there is a wide variety of beliefs that may be considered critical in this regard.

The renowned anthropologist Florence Kluckhohn (1961) made an insightful observation about the variables that give groups their character or culture. She suggested that all groups of individuals operating in some sort of shared relationship over a period time have to deal with certain issues that frame core values of shared existence. She of course was not referring specifically or directly to schools but to society in general. All of the issues she designates serve to suggest the range of beliefs that give rise to cultural differences. Some, maybe all, have relevance to understanding belief systems that may differentiate schools.

First, there are issues regarding the *essence of human nature:* Are humans basically good or bad, and if either, to what degree are they malleable? Of course, a complementary form of this question for schools relates to the nature of children and how we feel about their moral and their intellectual natures. The answers given here are likely to find their form in the way we discipline, control, or motivate. It also is related to how we approach instruction. In this regard, Stevenson and his colleagues (Stevenson & Stigler, 1992) have repeatedly emphasized that an important difference between the parents and teachers in certain Asian countries and the United States revolves around assumptions about the capacity to learn. Briefly, whereas U.S. parents and teachers are more likely to stress ability as a factor in achievement, Chinese and Japanese parents and teachers are more inclined to stress effort. This is perhaps especially true in such areas as mathematics, where parents, teachers, and students in the United States are inclined to believe either "you have it or you don't." These cross-national differences are interesting and important in their own right. However, they may also suggest the possibility that schools differ in the degree to which they hold or promote certain assumptions about the nature of a child as a person and learner.

Closely parallel to questions of the nature of human nature are questions of the *nature of human relationships*. Are people first and foremost a part of a collectivity, a family, tribe, group—or is the individual primary? Recent cross-cultural work has given enhanced meaning to this distinction (for example, Triandis, 1995). The distinction helps us understand the different orientations toward achievement brought to school by children of various sociocultural backgrounds. It may also be that the cultures of school vary in this way. Certainly, the opportunity for cooperative learning is more available in some schools than others. Likewise, schools differ in stressing the achievement of individuals in sports, academics, or the arts—as opposed to "team spirit." They also make a greater or lesser point regarding the importance of contributions made to one's family, to the community, and to society at large. In short, schools exhibit a complexity of variation in how they reflect social consciousness.

Questions regarding concepts of *time* are subtle but no less important. Some of the most difficult and embarrassing experiences in cross-cultural contexts relate to the way individuals understand and value time. One o'-clock, actually means 1:10 p.m. in the class schedule at the University of Michigan, something that new professors as well as students do not immediately realize. Time truly *walks* in some cultures but seems to *run* in others. On the surface, at least, schools in the United States seem to be controlled by bells, rigidly held class transition times, and forty- to fifty-minute instructional hours. This is particularly true at the secondary level, but we have observed precise schedules in many elementary classrooms as well. There is, however, some variability in how firmly teachers adhere to these schedules. For example, how willing are schools to interrupt established class schedules to arrange for special events? What kind of events are they most likely to insert into an established schedule? There are beliefs about how much time children need to learn a particular concept or skill. There are assumptions regarding how much time can be spent on "learning" during the course of a school day. After all, it is "work" and therefore must be relieved by regular intervals of play. We have heard more than one teacher argue that "serious instruction" (and student learning presumably) really only happens in the morning. You can't expect to accomplish much in the afternoon. Walk into most elementary schools and compare them with the last high school you've visited and you can't help but notice that time is viewed and treated quite differently. And by no means are we implying that all high schools or all elementary schools are essentially and necessarily similar in this regard. The point is that organizations in general and schools in particular hold certain beliefs about time, its use, its control, and the degree to which it is a resource or a variable.

These beliefs are appropriately considered within any comprehensive definition of school culture. Among these beliefs, none is more important and influential than the *purpose of school*. Indeed, we would argue that the larger questions of purpose frame much of the believing, and consequently the doing, that may be called culture. There are many things we can talk about when discussing school culture, but none are more important for the motivation and learning of children than how the purpose of learning is defined in the cultures of schools. Purpose cuts across all the issues we have discussed and provides an integrated perspective on culture and a manageable way to think about its change. To that essential argument—or hypothesis, if you prefer—we now turn.

A Theory of School Culture

A Focus on Purpose

Clearly, the concept of school culture has been and will remain a multifaceted construct. One cannot ignore the range of beliefs that are often incorporated under the label of school culture, and we have described them in the previous section. As fascinating as this complex phenomenon may be, much of it is of limited value in helping school leadership and staff understand themselves and project the changes they want. It is not totally useless, of course. One has to be sensitive to a broad array of norms, mores, roles, thoughts, beliefs, and values that operate in schools if one is to understand school. However, a concern with changing schools necessitates a greater focus. Among all these dimensions, characteristics, or variables, what does one concentrate on to effect school change, specifically change that encourages individuals to adopt task rather than ability goals for schooling?

In the preceding chapter we endeavored to show that student investment is significantly influenced by the adoption of two purposes for schooling: task and ability. Now we propose that among the multiple "answers" that can be associated with school culture, there is none more important than the answer to the question of why school exists. What is its purpose? Why should children be there? To what ends should teachers teach and administrators lead and manage? The existential question is basic. How it is answered will be reflected in all the other answers that we have associated with school culture. Moreover, participants can and will sense what this answer is. As they sense that their school puts a stress on performance and comparative ability, rather than growth and the inherent value of learning, it will affect not only how they feel about that school but likely also what kind of persons they will become. It will affect the goals they adopt for learning and in turn the quality of their personal investment in learning. Associated with the way a school is organized, with its policies and practices, is a differential stress on task and ability goals.

So when individuals refer to the culture of schools, they can and do refer to all of these many and multifaceted aspects of what happens when 500 or so children spend six or more hours a day with each other and with certain adults doing a variety of things: playing soccer, reading a book, drawing a picture, listening to a teacher, watching a video, talking to a friend, discussing how a conflict can be resolved, working on a project, solving an equation. We suggest, however, that the nature and effects of these activities—how they are carried out and how they influence the lives of children, especially their investment in learning—is determined by the purposes they hold in doing them. More specifically, we suggest that the differential stress on two types of purposes is the critical feature of the culture of school as it relates specifically to motivation and learning: task and ability definitions of schooling.

Of course, the notion that goals, objectives, and purpose are critical to the effectiveness of an organization is hardly novel. Most school improvement groups work long and hard on mission statements, goals, and objectives—as do teachers as they plan their activities for Monday morning. Whether it is a health care organization, a church, or Public School No. 95, a sense of what the group is about, why, for what, and for whom it exists is critical. And the more the mission is shared by and salient to all who are a part of the organization, the more likely it will be that those who are part of the organization will invest in it. After all, you are not likely to put your life and future on the line for something about which you know or care little. So the sense of purpose plays a primary role in determining not only the nature of an organization but also how it will work and the degree to which it will elicit the allegiance of all those it encompasses. Thus, the interminable writing of objectives, while it may seem a bit silly at times, does in fact reflect an important endeavor: Organizations cannot be effective unless they focus on their efforts and have and promote a sense of what they are and what they hope to do.

The first point here is that the purposiveness of an organization is at the heart of its culture, and it is that sense of purpose that is needed to elicit investment. The second point is that the task and ability purposes defined in the previous chapter are differentially stressed in schools. Their cultures reflect and are significantly organized around these two different goal emphases. The school's definition of the purpose of schooling as primarily task- or ability-oriented is exhibited in a variety of ways that can be and regularly are apprehended by students. Students perceive that the school tends to stand for learning (task goals) or for classification and sorting (ability goals) and act accordingly. Specifically, they will tend to adopt the school's definition of what the schooling enterprise is about. Certainly, students are influenced by other experiences in adopting task and ability goals. The point is that the school stands as a major causal agent to be considered in this regard.

The causal flow of events we have just described is portrayed in Figure 3.1. The critical variables to assess are student goals in doing school tasks, which lead to qualitatively different patterns of personal investment. As noted earlier, it is a well-established basic hypothesis in the literature. The point at issue in this chapter and this book as a whole is that school culture is likely to significantly shape the individual goals students come to hold. As the culture of the school serves this purpose, it frames the quality of motivation and learning that will be exhibited. This conceptualization of culture and its effects, if valid, could be useful to understanding motivation as well as designing school change. One must consider whether it makes any sense

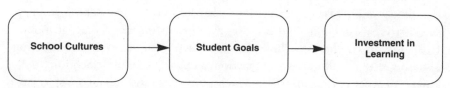

Figure 3.1   School cultures and student investment

to view school effects in this way: Do children really perceive schools as differentially stressing task and ability goals? Are these perceptions collectively different in subcultures of the school? Do they vary across classrooms and curricular areas or among student types? In later chapters, we will examine how these views of schools make a difference in the way children invest in schooling and learning.

How Do You Know a Culture When You See One?

Clearly, our work has led us to view culture in a particular way. We make no claim to study culture in its holistic richness. Our intention is to use culture as a variable, to think of it as a specifiable and ultimately manageable antecedent of motivation and learning. Thus, we have brought the work on organizational culture face-to-face with the study of motivation and learning. This leads us inevitably not only to narrow our focus but to adopt a certain set of procedures for specifying culture. For us, culture consists of perceptions that individuals hold and share to varying degrees with others. These perceptions can be assessed and can be used in predicting and explaining behavior. They are useful in particular in defining when and how school children will invest in learning.

Historically and presently, organizational culture has been examined, understood, and interpreted by employing so-called "qualitative procedures" (for example, Deal & Peterson, 1990). Such study more or less follows an ethnographic model used by anthropologists in assessing a native culture in South America or Africa. In the main, it involves living and working in the environment for an extended period of time to observe firsthand what is going on. In addition to systematic observation, interviews with a selected sample of role players are usually conducted. Organizational documents are secured, read, and interpreted. In the end, an attempt is made to portray the organization in such a way that the reader will have a sense of the general character of the organization, especially how it differs from other organizations. Occasionally, specific deductions are made and concrete advice on action to be taken is rendered. Often, the conclusion is left to the reader.

Such methods yield "thick descriptions" that can be rich in insight, provocative, and helpful. In reading a well-composed portrayal of a school that is based on such an approach, one seems to experience the life that is actually lived there. It is like reading a fascinating piece of good reporting in a newspaper. The school is more than numbers on a page. It comes alive as a dynamic, concrete entity. Above all, the school is not seen merely as a number of isolated parts but as a meaningful whole. It is of particular interest that such qualitative descriptions have often called attention to the symbolic aspects of the organization—rites, rituals, myths, and heroes—and stressed the formative role of these in shaping the direction and purpose of the organization. Indeed, it is perhaps too easy to overlook the symbolic significance of many activities if one does not live and work in an organization as an ethnographer typically does. Stories told by principals about the present, the past, and the future, about teachers or students, may not readily take on the proportion of myths but probably reflect meanings that are relevant to identifying what goals, purposes, and aspirations are thought to be of value. Stories told by teachers and students are perhaps of even greater significance. But the ethnographer can (and profitably) also pay attention to slogans, jingo, and jargon, all of which contribute to the "feel" of what is happening in the school in the present and might happen in the future.

Such qualitative methods have particular appeal for "getting inside" the organization. Much of our reporting of findings will be complemented by information gleaned through the use of such methods. Needless to say, ethnography and other qualitative methods of this nature are time-consuming and have their limitations. They do not lend themselves well to a quick analysis of the workings of any particular social group, corporation, workplace, or school. The insights obtained from these methods are heavily dependent upon the quality of the people gathering the data. All of this tends to limit the number of schools that can be studied and the number of people in the school whose stories can be recorded. Thus, the objective of achieving a richness of data, perhaps a depth of understanding, is achievable only in the case of a smaller sample. Moreover, they provide little to the typical school in the way of tools for their own self-examination. Given these and other limitations, there is point and purpose in complementing qualitative procedures with more standardized procedures designed to gather very specific bits of information from larger numbers of individuals. And most especially, in confronting the gargantuan task of showing that school cultures affect student motivation and learning, one desirably wants and needs data that yield testable relationships and hypotheses that can become part of an enlarging and enriching picture painted by multiple artists. Finally, it is significant that current theories of motivation, especially theories of learning and achievement, have moved to a social cognitive approach that not only specifies the role of perceptions in affecting motivation but provides guidelines for assessing these perceptions. So, we currently have much to build on in constructing a model of culture and motivation that is accessible through standard procedures of data gathering. We have much to build on in arguing for and testing a social cognitive theory of culture and motivation.

The concept of "subjective culture" (for example, Triandis et al., 1972; 1975) served as a heuristic in our efforts in several ways. First, it prompted us to think about culture as something that is in the minds of individuals who compose a group and not just something that is in the minds of individuals who define and study the group. Culture is a construct made up of the perceptions that individuals have about critical areas of life and living within a group. Thus, we talked earlier about culture being "answers" to certain "questions." Obviously, this concept of culture is conveniently compatible with social cognitive theories in general and a social cognitive approach to motivation in particular. A broadly shared view in this regard is that individuals behave in response to and in terms of their perceptions, thoughts, and beliefs. Second, the concept of subjective culture represented an attempt to treat culture psychometrically. That is, it provided a rationale for and tools to be used in objectively assessing culture as a variable or set of variables following standardized measurement procedures. The rationale and tools have served as guidelines in our own thinking, but so has work on organizational climates, learning, and work environments (for example, Fraser & Walberg, 1991). Thus, we based our work heavily (though not exclusively) on questionnaires and standardized interviews that had demonstrated reliability and replicability and that could yield indices of measures appropriate for applying sophisticated statistical analyses.

Finally in this regard, it should be noted that the concept of *subjective* culture makes culture an individual difference variable in the first instance. That is, in viewing school culture's effects one is interested in how the individual student's grasp of the culture affects her behavior. It is the child's view that the school defines learning in this or that way that should make a difference in the child's thought and behavior. Yet, the term *culture* puts stress on the shared nature of the perceptions: that a school, for example, tends to reflect a certain view of learning. And so, we will examine how individual perceptions make a difference in the lives of individual students, faculty, and others, but we will also consider these individual perceptions in the aggregate as an index that may distinguish schools, classrooms, teachers, subgroups of students, and other distinguishable groups defined by those who are more the actors in our studies as well as by those of us who are recording the stories or painting the picture of their schools and classrooms. Clearly, using the concept of school *culture* as an element upon which one can work in effecting comprehensive change makes it incumbent to view effects aggregately as well as individually. We need to know how broadly school policies and practices are associated with and reflected in the definitions of learning held by students and faculty.

Origins of a School Culture Survey

Operationally, our work on methods to assess school culture had its beginnings in a venue somewhat remote from schools and was, as a matter of fact, somewhat accidental in nature. A decade ago, Martin Maehr and Larry Braskamp (1986; Braskamp & Maehr, 1985) initiated a study on motivation in the world of work. The initial focus was on personal incentives that individuals held for work and how this affected their investment in the job. The interest in "environments" was initially confined to the nature of the job in which the person was engaged (Hackman & Oldham, 1980). We began our work by interviewing people—in this case, employees in a wide variety of occupations. We asked them about their aspirations and motives and what they liked about their job. We often asked them to describe experiences. We asked them about times when they felt good about themselves and to describe their feelings as well as why they thought they came to feel that way. While we focused on their personal incentives or goals and how these might be realized in the job they held, they often changed the focus to the organization. Indeed, they were sometimes more willing and able to talk about the organization in which they worked than about themselves or their particular job. They had something to say about what the company as a whole was promoting, the kinds of values that seemed to guide its action. They focused especially on what the company stood for, what it recognized and rewarded, how it defined the place of the worker, and how they felt about that. In brief, they seemed to be more than willing to talk about goal stresses in the organization and the effects of these on their level of engagement and investment. Sometimes their thoughts were primarily negative; sometimes they were positive; sometimes they were very analytical, reflective, and somewhat devoid of affect. But it became increasingly clear that the organization, its values and goals, was something of significance in determining how they thought about their work and how they invested in it. The hypothesis implied by others (for example, Schein, 1984; 1990) jumped out at us: Organizations stress goals and these emphases may have much to do with motivation. And so, somewhat as an afterthought, we constructed an organizational culture survey.

Four scales were developed that paralleled four personal incentives we found to be an important part of achievement motivation. They came to be called *accomplishment, power, social solidarity, and recognition.*[1] Additionally, we included a scale we called sense of mission. Our interviews as well as the organizational literature generally (for example, Deal & Kennedy, 1982; Peters & Waterman, 1982) indicated that organizations with a clear sense of mission and purpose were more likely to elicit the engagement of participants. Or, more importantly, organizations in which the mission was clear and salient to employees or participants were more likely to attract a firm allegiance.

In general, our work eventuated in reliably distinguishable dimensions of what we thought of as the heart of organizational culture so far as affecting motivation was concerned. Moreover, in the application of this work it became clear that different kinds of organizations could be distinguished by these scales. Different organizations exhibited different profiles on these dimensions. Some were high in both accomplishment and social solidarity, such as certain management consulting companies we studied. These companies stressed achievement and productivity but also a "team spirit," emphasizing good relations with others inside and outside the organization. Some companies were high in power and very low in social solidarity, such as a large real estate company where the sales representatives were highly competitive, individualistic operators essentially using the "home office" as a clerical backup but with little investment in anything other than having their paperwork done right and their phone calls transferred. Of course, some companies were rather like a club, high in social solidarity, low in power, and moderate in accomplishment. And of course there were other combinations or profiles as well. In the case of some, the lack of emphasis on accomplishment made one wonder about the ultimate future of the organization. Most for-profit organizations cannot exist for long as a club. The point is that preliminary research began to suggest that the profiles on the organizational culture scale scores might be a valid index and a potentially useful tool for analyzing organizations. But especially important in the present context is that adaptation of these scales was put to use in examining school contexts—the "subjective culture" of students.

Leslie Fyans (Maehr & Fyans, 1989) and Martin Maehr (1991) adapted the items for use with school children and incorporated them in a large statewide school assessment program with interesting results. The school culture items/scales reliably indexed perceptions that children had of their schools. These perceptions seemed to vary among children of different ages and socioeconomic groups. Perceptions of what the school stressed as separable from what was emphasized at home or by peers differed increasingly with age. And, as we shall discuss in Chapter 4, came to play an important role in school-related attitudes. Interesting also in this early data set was preliminary evidence of the existence of various possible "subcultures": students enrolled in different curricula (academic, vocational, and so forth) and of different socioeconomic background and ethnicity. And perhaps most importantly, evidence was provided that the subjective culture made a difference in the school behavior of children.

This work served as a preliminary confirmation of the idea that the way in which students perceived the school culture was related to their motivation. And of course, there was reason to believe also that these perceptions held by students emerged from what they saw happening in their schools regarding policies and practices in managing students and instruction. Later, this work was followed by more extensive scale development on the organizational facets of school life (Maehr, Ames, & Braskamp, 1988). More recently, these ideas have been incorporated in a comprehensive measure of school cultures, motivation, self-beliefs, and action that serves as the basis for our quantitative analyses of schools and students, the Patterns of Adaptive Learning Survey (PALS) (Midgley, Maehr, Hicks, Roeser, Urdan, Anderman, & Kaplan, 1996).

The Patterns of Adaptive Learning Survey

PALS is a multidimensional survey that includes scales that assess students' perceptions of the culture (task goal structure and ability goal structure) in the classroom and the school, their personal goal orientation (task, ability), their sense of academic efficacy, and their use of cognitive and motivational strategies (self-regulated learning, "deep" cognitive strategies, and self-handicapping strategies). In addition, PALS includes scales assessing teachers' perceptions of the school culture for students (task goal structure and ability goal structure) and for teachers (accomplishment goal structure and power goal structure), their personal teaching efficacy, and their instructional strategies (task-focused strategies and ability-focused strategies).

During a four-year period from fall 1990 to fall 1994, students in grades 3 through 8 and their teachers and parents filled out various versions of the survey at different times. As we analyzed the data, scales were revised and refined to improve reliability, validity, and utility. More recently, the survey has been administered to more than 850 students in 5th grade in elementary schools and the following year when they were in 6th grade in middle schools. During the same time frame, teachers in twenty-one elementary schools and ten middle schools filled out the teacher survey. The most recent version of the instrument is now available to other researchers, and a paper describing its validation is now being prepared for publication (Midgley, Urdan, Kaplan, Roeser, Hicks, & Maehr, 1996). In addition, a survey eliciting more "objective" data regarding the emphasis in school policies and practices on task and ability goals has been developed and given to a group of elementary and middle school principals. Preliminary analyses of the data gathered from elementary school principals indicates that these objective indices are related in predictable ways to teachers' subjective reports of the school culture for themselves as professionals and for students (Wood, Roeser, & Linnenbrink, 1996).

In the final analysis, the definition of culture is determined by the methods used in identifying, observing, or assessing it. In this case, the measures we developed and employed in this particular program of research contain and embody our definition of school culture and, therefore, need to be described. Selected scales from the most recent version of PALS, with items and alpha coefficients, can be found in the Appendix. But the point to be stressed at this juncture is that culture is defined by a differential stress on task and ability goals as perceived by major participants in the culture. These measures may be treated as characteristics of the individual or aggregated to consider broadly held beliefs in schools, classrooms, or among different types of students or teachers. By considering the variance between and across groups one can assess homogeneity or cohesiveness within the culture or a wide degree of divergence. That is, one can assess the degree to which the definition of a task or ability learning culture is widely shared—and by whom.

Several Cultures of School

There probably is little question about the utility of such measures—both for research purposes as well as for purposes of school self-study and evaluation. Of greater interest at the moment are questions of validity. Essentially, this book is concerned with the validity of the perspective on school culture we have described. In this chapter, we begin to validate our approach as we examine how it can yield data of interest in the understanding of schools and what they do. Basically, do these kinds of measures really distinguish cultures that are part and parcel of schools? We focus on several such cultures that are of interest to us and that form a major part of our story as a whole, primarily classroom and school cultures.

In many ways, all schools look quite similar in nature. Their reasons for being, the persons and groups of which they are composed, and the way they operate can be easily distinguished from airlines, supermarkets, hospitals, and churches. In broad outline at least, schools have much in common. Moreover, as one reads about different schools' objectives as written by school improvement teams, the objectives are remarkably similar, even in schools in different regions of the country. As we studied this issue in depth, however, it was clear that this acceptance of similarity of purpose was superficial. In fact, stated objectives characteristically mask over what we believe to be the most important distinctions in the way the school goes about its business. This becomes clear when one spends more than a passing moment in classrooms and in school corridors, observing and talking to teachers, students, and the custodian.

Walking into a school on any given afternoon, one can observe this, that, or the next thing that might distinguish it from the school you visited in the morning. There is the "official" school bulletin board—where it is placed, what it says, what it highlights. There is evidence of cleanliness, maintenance, control, concern with safety. There may or may not be posters on the wall, broken windows, hall monitors, crowded classrooms. These are all interesting observations and not without merit. However, what cannot be seen or sensed so readily is how a school frames learning, defines the purpose of schooling, and develops a rationale for all the activity, posters, bricks, and mortar. In the preceding chapter we only hinted at an important possibility: The school environment plays a major role in how students will define the purposes and goals of schooling. Students construct a meaning of schooling from certain things that go on in that environment. In this chapter we begin to examine that possibility by demonstrating that school cultures vary, especially to the degree they stress task and ability goals for schooling.

Different Classrooms, Different Cultures

The classroom is a meaningful and manageable place to test the role of learning environments since it is in many ways the primary instructional unit and to many the essence of what the school is. In fact, the school has been described as a collection of one-room school houses, each pursuing its own agenda, somewhat apart from and not fully in coordination with the next (cf. Maehr & Buck, 1993). There is a growing body of research that strongly suggests individual classrooms can be characterized as having different "cultures" in regard to the way they present learning.

While not necessarily applying the term school or classroom culture in their work, a number of researchers have anticipated our argument, particularly as it applies to the classroom level. Carole Ames and her colleagues (Ames, 1990; Ames & Archer, 1987, 1988), for example, have pointed out how learning environments might be framed in terms of varying emphasis on learning and task goals. As children sense this variation in stress, so they are likely to exhibit qualitatively different patterns of motivation for learning. Moreover, in an ongoing research program Ames and her colleagues have laid the basic groundwork for identifying practices and policies that likely give rise to a definition in primarily task- or ability-goal terms, indicating what "variables" in the classroom can be changed to affect not only the culture but also the quality of learning exhibited.

Parallel to that work, John Nicholls and his collaborators (for example, Nicholls & Hazzard, 1993; Nicholls, Patashnick & Nolen, 1985) made sense out of subject matter, conventions, expectations, concepts and experiences as they enmeshed themselves thoroughly in the subjective world of students. Using a variety of procedures they systematically revealed something about the "theories" of school and learning students construct, which in turn appear to shape how students engage in learning tasks. These theories incorporate definitions of purpose as well as related notions about the definition of subject matter and the nature of knowledge. Similar to our notion of a subjective culture, individuals presumably come to view the learning environment as taking this or that form and presenting certain possibilities that are grasped by the student and that relate to the ways he will (or will not) invest.

Building on this line of thought, members of our research group (Anderman & Young, 1994) specifically sought to determine whether classrooms as a whole reflected distinguishably different cultures so far as the emphases placed on task and ability goals. In this case, a large number of students within approximately thirty different classrooms in two different middle schools were surveyed using the PALS measure of classroom culture described earlier. Using current hierarchical linear modeling techniques (Bryk & Raudenbush, 1992), Eric Anderman and Allison Young (1994) found that students' perceptions of the purposes for learning varied significantly across science classrooms. This was not attributable to differences in background, in gender, or in level of achievement. All the evidence pointed to the existence of a certain environment, or culture, that had evolved or been created within the classroom. Again, as students perceived the classroom, so they defined the purpose of instruction and schooling and oriented themselves to it. In interpreting their results, Anderman and Young also made an interesting observation. A number of researchers have called attention to the decline of motivation that occurs between grades 6 and 7 (for example, Eccles & Midgley, 1989; Wigfield, Eccles, MacIver, Reuman, & Midgley, 1991). Anderman and Young point out that this varies with classroom experience and argue persuasively that such declines in motivation are probably not universal and inevitable. They are in fact attributable to the learning context or culture.

That classrooms reflect different task and ability cultures is an important observation. It may be that in many cases this difference is associated with subject matter areas so that math classes, for example, may differ from science or literature classes. But an exclusive focus on classroom cultures is too limited, especially as one moves beyond the elementary grades to middle school and high school where children experience a variety of classrooms in the course of the day—as well as a variety of cocurricular experiences—all of which are part of the mix called school. Do schools in some sort of holistic or pervasive sense also exhibit differential stresses on task and ability goals and in this sense yield quite different cultures so far as learning and motivation are concerned? Indeed, it might well be the case that the culture of the school shapes significantly the culture of the several classrooms that compose it. At the very least, one cannot limit oneself to observing what happens within classrooms if one wants to understand how schools affect goals.

Different Schools, Different Cultures

Early in our work we sensed that classrooms not only differed in goal stresses but that schools as a whole did. We also began to foresee the possibility that this differential schoolwide emphasis might play a major role in how instruction was carried out in classrooms. This possibility had its roots in two major lines of evidence.

Following the work of James Coleman et al. (1966) and Christopher Jencks (1972), which seemed to indicate that schools did not and possibly could not do much to change the patterns of motivation and achievement especially in the case of poor and disadvantaged minorities, a line of activity emerged that challenged that assumption. It was based in the first instance on systematic observations of differences between schools defined as "effective" and "ineffective" (for example, Brookover & associates, 1979, 1982). However, at some point it evolved into intervention programs designed to foster school change (see for example, Edmonds & Frederiksen, 1979) and virtually became a "movement" for a decade. We draw several conclusions from this line of activity that remain especially relevant to the present. We agree that a clear sense of mission within an organization is associated with effectiveness. To a degree, the movement also provided some point of emphasis on academics. But it fell far short of making a crucial distinction between purposes revolving around task and ability goals. In any event, much of the discourse that filled the literature began to stress the role of the school as a whole in fostering adaptive student behavior. The idea that schools could and did reflect a certain kind of learning environment, even a culture, began to emerge.

Perhaps, however, it was the work with organizations in general that gave rise to the concept of school culture we have adopted (Denison, 1984). Conducting studies in a broad array of organizations we learned several things that were important for this developing notion of school culture and motivation (see for example, Maehr & Braskamp, 1986). We quickly learned that people were not only willing to talk about themselves, they were also willing to talk about an organization to which they belonged. In work organizations, employees readily told us about the incentives, rewards, and opportunities that existed in their job. They also could and would tell us a great deal about the organization as a whole: what they thought it stood for and promoted—what it really "believed" in. In this early work on organizational culture, we also sampled a few schools and interviewed school staff members. The teachers conveyed their perceptions about schools in a manner not unlike those in other organizations. Such a willingness to talk about organizations and ability to sense direction and purpose—or sometimes the lack of it—intrigued us. It led us to begin constructing a survey of work-related attitudes that in particular asked about the belief systems stressed within the organization, especially the definition of purpose, goals, and objectives. Thus, if a critical feature of any organization was such purposiveness, it seemed quite possible that it could be rather easily assessed through the use of mass-administered, standardized survey procedures. This supposition was complemented by the fact that cognitive theory was beginning to show that perceptions and cognitions of this nature were primary data that could be used in predicting behavior in the organization: motivation and investment in the tasks to be done and a wide range of other outcomes.

This recognition of the possible utility of readily expressed perceptions of the organization led to the development of an organizational culture survey (Braskamp & Maehr, 1985) and to various studies of the cultures of organizations from the perspective of the participants. It also eventuated in the development of procedures for assessing school culture and a line of research in this regard. It is with the latter that we are especially concerned.

Four scales were formed that were designed to reflect four major purposive emphases in an organization. These were labeled accomplishment, power, affiliation, and recognition. In content, accomplishment and power essentially parallel task and ability personal goals. Additionally, a scale eliciting an overall perception of the school as holding a clear and salient mission was included. The scales were subsequently shown to have reasonable levels of reliability—but what about validity? What does it really mean to collect perceptions of the goal stresses of the organization? Can schools be significantly defined and distinguished in such terms? And even if they can be, what does it mean for how the school functions? The answers to that question represent a continuing, open-ended story, but a significant beginning on that story has been made.

Preliminary work showed that the profile of purposes differed for different types of organizations, suggesting that different goal stresses indeed existed in these organizations (Maehr & Braskamp, 1986). More recent work specifically on schools has shown similarly that schools can be distinguished in terms of such goal and purpose profiles. One example is especially instructive in this regard. Educators perhaps have long sensed that there is something qualitatively different in the way elementary and secondary schools "live, move, and have their being." Educators describe this sensed difference in a way that is very close to what we have called culture. The experienced world of the practitioner has more recently been confirmed by systematic observations (Anderman & Maehr, 1994; Anderman & Midgley, 1995; Midgley, 1993; Midgley, Anderman, & Hicks, 1995). More specifically, evidence is currently accumulating that the goal profile of middle grade and elementary schools is decidedly different. Carol Midgley, Revathy Arunkumar, and Timothy Urdan (1995) recently profiled the culture of elementary and secondary schools as differing in their emphases on task and ability goals. While that essential difference had been hinted at or speculated about before (Eccles & Midgley, 1989; Eccles et al., 1993), this study is the first to profile the difference in terms of the varying stress on task and ability goals, leading to a fuller understanding of why motivational problems increase during the middle grades (Anderman & Maehr, 1994). In short, the perceptions of purpose held by participants in an organization seem to reflect something that distinguishes the organization and the way it goes about its business. As a result, survey questions about such purposes are proving to be reliable and valid—perhaps a useful means for describing and analyzing a potentially important part of school culture. These are not *just* perceptions; they are perceptions that make a difference (see Chapter 4).

One School, Several Cultures

It is interesting to note that preliminary work has also indicated the existence of several cultures within schools. This is not altogether surprising to individuals who study organizations in general and schools in particular, but it is important nevertheless. Martin Maehr and Larry Braskamp (1986) found that different facets of an array of different manufacturing, educational, service, and health organizations (executive-administrative, clerical, and so forth) were likely to see the purposes of the organization quite differently. In making this observation, they suggested that a critical variable in any organization might be cultural "cohesiveness," that is, the degree to which all participants shared the same perceived purpose profile. Thus, wide divergence in perceived purpose among subcultures presumably organized around the same objectives may pose a problem. But in any case, one cannot consider the cultures of organizations without taking account of the possibility of subcultures. This is no less true of schools than other organizations.

Teacher and student cultures.

The issue of several cultures is particularly relevant to schools. The math department, special education faculty, music teachers, and the janitorial staff likely have different views of the school. Although all cultures are interesting, the two distinguishable between teacher and student are of greater significance. Curiously, work on school restructuring has focused more on changing the work culture for teachers than the learning culture for students. The assumption has been that somehow the right work culture would automatically translate into the right learning culture. Perhaps! There is reason to believe that a strong emphasis on accomplishment in the work environment combined with a sense of collegiality may be the sine qua non for a staff to feel committed and satisfied, and invested in their school. Indeed, in transforming school culture as we propose, this may well be an early and necessary step. However, it does not ensure that school staff will in fact invest in a way that is most facilitative of student learning. Simply put, a stress on accomplishment in the work environment for school staff does not necessarily eventuate in a task environment for students. To obtain the latter, specific attention must be given to the ultimate client in the educational process (Chapter 5).

Student cultures.

Of special interest is the possible existence of distinguishable differences in purpose profiles among differing groups of students. The history of schools in the case of students with different cultural backgrounds and ethnicity in the first instance makes this an interesting and important topic. Equally important are groups that seem to be alienated for one reason or another, often to be judged at risk for school failure. In any case, it is clearly important to be sensitive to the multiplicity of groups and cultures that may exist in a given school. The first issue concerns the degree to which there is a certain cohesiveness in the sense of what the school is about. The second is the degree to which the purpose is noted but not adopted as one's own.

In this regard, one is likely to be interested in how at-risk students, students from varying socioeconomic and ethnic backgrounds, may share the perception of school culture held by others. Early in our work on school cultures we recognized the importance of examining the effects of school culture on various subgroups. It should not surprise anyone that these subgroups from time to time do in fact have a different view of school. Thus, Anderman (1992) showed that students judged by the school to be at risk, special education students, and "regular" students differed in their perceptions of the purposes stressed in their schools. Essentially, they saw different schools. This finding probably can be generalized across many schools, but the point here is not the state of affairs in the nation's schools. Rather, we wish to make two other points. First, these results provide evidence of the validity of our measures and the conceptions on which they are based. This bodes well for the further use of PALS (and similar measures) in assessing the character of schools. Second, such findings suggest also that in examining school cultures, the variation among subgroups presents a possibly very important piece of information on the character of the school as a whole.

Subject matter areas.

A final point of interest is the possible existence of subcultures associated with subject matter areas. Are there in fact different definitions of learning extant within math departments compared to what exists within the social studies department? Allison Young, Amy Arbreton, and Carol Midgley (1992) examined middle school students' goal orientation in four subject domains: English, social studies, mathematics, and science. They found that students were significantly more oriented to task goals in math and in science than in English or social studies. They also found that students were more likely to hold an ability-focused orientation in social studies than in the other content areas. Although this is a preliminary study, it lays the groundwork for additional studies that consider differences in goal stresses across subject domains. There is doubtless variability among schools in this regard, and the point is to examine what the situation is in any given school and how it possibly detracts from the functioning of the school as a whole. Measures of school culture such as we have proposed provide tools for doing just that and have utility beyond simply conducting a piece of re-search on school culture. They also suggest ways in which one may examine the several interlocking subcultures, determining how cohesive or diverse the organization as a whole is, suggesting points at which organizational change can and must occur. So the concept of school culture we have pro-posed, the degree of discriminant validity it seems to exhibit, also has po-tential utility in diagnosing schools and pointing to change (see Chapter 7).

Conclusion

Clearly, the concept of school culture has been and will remain a multifac-eted construct. One cannot ignore the richness of data on a range of activi-ties and beliefs that can be and are often incorporated under the label of school culture. As fascinating as this complex phenomenon may be, it is of limited value in helping school leadership and staff understand themselves and change. It is not useless, of course. One has to understand a broad array of norms, mores, and roles that are operative in a school setting if one is to work effectively as an educator, especially if one wishes to effect change. However, our argument is that it is necessary to provide a focus for one's concern with school change. In particular, we suggest that one has to focus on beliefs about purpose and value, sense of direction and mission. As we have implied throughout—but will explicate in detail in the following chapters—it is perceived purpose that directs personal investment. As one defines purpose, so one acts.

And thus, in this chapter, we have moved from a broad, virtually all-encom-passing definition of "culture" to a rather narrow band of cultural variables: what the purpose of school is, why one is there, what the social interaction is essentially about. Theory, research, and common sense all press us to narrow our focus. It is difficult for anyone to get a grasp on something so complex as school. Recognizing that the culture of school is composed of a complex amalgamation of many more or less shared answers to what should and should not be done there helps little. What is needed is a narrowing focus that comes in the essential hypothesis of this book—that schools can be defined in terms of purposiveness. They can be essentially and effectively characterized in terms of a more or less shared sense of direction, really a definition of school-ing. And, most important, as they define purpose so they act.

In this chapter we have shown how that purpose can be readily accessed, not just through qualitative procedures (though they do prove very useful) but also through more economic and usable survey methods. It is hoped we have at least in part dispelled the notion that school culture is a mystery that must be sensed and tiptoed around to be managed effectively. This chapter is about the fact that school culture—or at least specifiable essential parts of it—can be assessed, analyzed, and just maybe, manipulated. In no sense do we wish to ignore the richness that is the school or denigrate the use of qualitative methods in studying schools. Indeed, as we proceed, it should become quite clear that we have benefited from a catholic view of culture and an ecumenical perspective on methods. But the bottom line is that school culture is a variable that can be assessed and perhaps ultimately influenced.

So now to the issue: If school culture is a variable, what does it do? What does school culture determine or cause?

Notes

1. We have used various terms in reference to these four dimensions of organizational culture. Throughout this book we will use the four terms accomplishment, power, social solidarity, and recognition. These organizational stresses on accomplishment and power have their parallels in the task and ability goals that are the primary focus of our discussions in this book. Social solidarity also has its parallels in work on personal social goals (Urdan & Maehr, 1995) and recognition relates to "extrinsic rewards," regularly at issue in the discussion of individual goals as well as group emphases (for example, Cameron & Pierce, 1994).

4   School Cultures
Make a Difference

Introduction

The portrayal of the cultural landscape of a school can charm, inspire, excite, and disturb as much as any work of art or product of science. It can also inform, provide insight, and possibly prompt action. If such portrayals do more than intrigue us, they do so usually because we assume that cultures make a difference. It isn't just that cultural differences are interesting. It is that these differences relate to something else we think is important. Typically, we are prone to single out certain distinguishing features of a group's life and relate these to something that has broader importance and societal value: "achievement motivation" (Maehr, 1974a; 1974b), the acquisition of scientific knowledge or mathematical ability (Stevenson & Stigler, 1992), the tendency toward violence (Nisbett, 1993), and so forth. The objective is to see how a variable characteristic of groups may lead to desirable or undesirable behavior. Often that way of thinking leads to issues of intervention and management.

Many of the ethnographic portrayals of organizational cultures, including school cultures, seem to have been written for those in leadership positions (for example, Deal & Peterson, 1990). Those who lead are assumed to somehow negotiate around the normal ways of doing, thinking, and believing within any organization (for example, Bolman & Deal, 1991). Everyone knows that each organization has a range of acceptability beyond which any person who wants to remain in the organization, especially work effectively as a leader, dare not go. Clearly, those who are practically interested in a school, who want to work effectively within it, must have some sort of notion of what the school is about. It is in this sense that school cultures make a difference. One has to take account of extant norms, styles, beliefs, and values in operating, managing, and *changing* an organization. Much of the writing to date has tended to stress this facet of the importance of organizational cultures.

However, there is increased interest that culture is important not just as something to negotiate around but as a factor that influences the decisions, planning, performance, and effectiveness of organizations. In particular, there is interest in how culture influences the investment of individuals (for example, Maehr & Braskamp, 1986). Culture is thought of as an organizational variable, something that can be influenced, manipulated, managed. Building on this essential idea, some have specifically argued that it is through managing culture that leaders lead (for example, Schein, 1985). With that, organizational culture becomes a primary tool through which the leadership of an organization can and should work, and ultimately this is the raison d'être for the study of organizational culture. There is point and purpose to obtaining an awareness of the workings of the organization so as not to operate in ways that may violate principles held sacred by those within the organization. Thus, new leaders are justifiably interested in the culture of an organization simply to avoid gaffes as well as to recognize possibilities for pursuing an agenda. Such concerns are justified and important, and we will take them up again later in this volume, especially as we consider how organizations can change. However, in this chapter we focus specifically on whether and how school culture affects the motivation and investment of students in learning. As we emphasize throughout, students are the true bottom line of school reform. When we consider transforming school cultures, the ultimate and primary question is this: How does school culture make a difference in the learning and motivation of students (Maehr, Midgley & Urdan, 1992)?

In summary, the point of examining culture is two-fold. First, culture makes a difference, not just in general, but ultimately and specifically in the motivation and learning of students. Second, but by no means of secondary importance in this book, is that culture is potentially manageable; it is a manipulable variable. It will be there whether managed or not. More importantly, it can be modified by the self-conscious action of those within the school.

In this chapter we begin the systematic examination of this basic set of assertions. First, we outline a theoretical model that guides our efforts. Second, we describe research results that support the model and suggest how school culture translates into student investment in learning.

A Theoretical Model of School Culture and Motivation and Student Learning

Fundamentally, culture is a concept that must help us understand schools: how they look, how they function, and what they do. Most important for us, however, is that culture makes a difference in the life and learning of students. How this happens is a complicated matter, but not so complicated that the process cannot be understood and ultimately controlled by those who manage and teach. An outline of that process is presented in Figure 4.1 and will serve as a guide to our theory of how school culture influences student investment.

Simply put, the hypothesis we propose is that culture determines personal investment. In its broadest and most general form that hypothesis is not particularly controversial. Most studies of school effectiveness assume, and to some degree demonstrate, that something within the broad range of what we have called school culture in fact shapes what happens in the lives of those who participate in that culture. In the case of students, it should affect their learning, their motivation to learn, and what they do in the course of a school day. Obviously, the selection of what is to be learned—the curriculum and the content of the material that composes the curriculum—narrows the range of options. In anything called school, there are clear definitions of what is worth learning. Indeed, that fact was and still is at the heart of curriculum debates: German and other immigrants to the United States in the nineteenth and early twentieth centuries wanted German customs and lore as well as language and literature to be available in schools their children attended. Those from Roman Catholic religious traditions wanted practices,

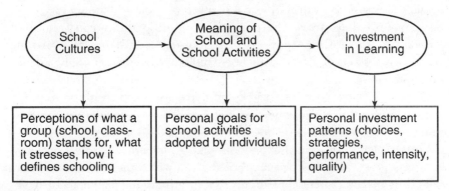

Figure 4.1 The relationship of school cultures to student motivation

rituals, and a curriculum that was not so blatantly Protestant. African-Americans today want schools to expand the range of options for literature, art, music, and history. Those from the Near or Far East may prefer that schools not delve into history and literature that denigrate their eastern heritage but concentrate instead on basic skills and knowledge widely generalizable across cultures. Certainly, a broad definition of school culture embraces the fact that schools vary in how they provide options in what is to be learned, what is a fitting school task, and what is worth investing in.

Purpose as Primary

Curriculum debates are important and need to be considered when examining the school's role in affecting student motivation for learning. Accepting that, our hypothesis goes beyond this definition of options. As anticipated in Chapter 3, we suggest that irrespective of content and cutting across a wide variety of ways of teaching, acting, and doing there is the pervasive issue of purpose. Purposiveness is basic to whether or how students will become invested in school and in learning. Different purposes affect the nature and quality of learning that will be exhibited when students invest. As students hold task rather than ability goals, they are more likely to exhibit adaptive learning patterns and develop a continuing investment in productive learning activities. That part of our argument should already be quite clear. What we add now is every bit as important and should be of special interest to those who teach, manage, or care about schools. The school—what it is, what it does, especially what it stands for—is a major factor in determining the goals that students will adopt. Ineluctably, schools reflect and convey a purpose for learning. Of course, purpose is clearer in some learning settings than others. Likewise, schools are known to vary in the purposes they stress. The purposes as well as the purposiveness of schools are not just other aspects of school culture. Rather, they are the very essence so far as determining how students will view schooling and invest in learning.

Of course, schools and what goes on there are not the only sources for the sense of purpose that students adopt. Individual students vary in how they view school. Family, peers, the media, and an array of experiences doubtless play some role. But schools play a fundamental role they must self-consciously act out. The school context in which the student finds herself at any given moment contributes significantly to the personal construction of purpose for school-related activities. If a school stresses ability goals, the student is more likely to adopt personal achievement goals that reflect an ability orientation, other things being equal. Possibly, school influence in this regard is greater in some circumstances than others; for example, at different grade levels and for individuals of different backgrounds. But across the board, school influence is pervasive and profound.

Student Perceptions as Cause

Basic to our understanding of how school cultures make a difference in the life and learning of students are assumptions about the subjective nature of cultures.

The Subjectivity of Culture

"Outsiders" can make observations about what is going on in schools; they can take note of signs, symbols, actions, and preferences exhibited. But the fundamental essence of schooling is not what is observed from the outside but what the full-time participants in the school observe from the inside. Most important to determining how motivation and learning will occur is how students perceive the persons, processes, and substance of schooling. In the final analysis, amidst all that might be seen as going on in schools, it is the student's grasp of what the school is, what the context of school presents, that determines what the student will do. The critical issue is how the student perceives the actions of the school, teachers, and staff. Especially, it is the reflected purpose and the definition of schooling that is presented in such saying and acting that is the crucial element. So students are likely to see a composite of actions, statements, and symbols as summing to differential stress on task and ability definitions of schooling. It is the perceptions of how a school context defines its being that is an immediate "cause," an occasion for the adoption of the student's own personal goals which are in turn associated with the action, affect, and thoughts they exhibit vis-à-vis school and schooling (see Chapter 2). It is not what the teacher or the researcher sees that is the immediate cause of the student's behavior. It is what the student sees that counts. Obvious perhaps, but much of the work on culture is more concerned with the observations of school leaders, teachers, and external observers than with the report of those who are the critical respondents to the school culture: students.

In a primary sense, then, culture is in an individual's mind and can rightly be treated as an individual difference that presumably is indexed by what people say (in interviews, on questionnaires, and so forth) about the context.[1] Aspects of the context are not equally salient to all, and such variation is not without interest, though it is not the whole story. The use of the word *subjective* apposite to culture is an appropriate reminder of that operating assumption. The use of the term *culture* makes the shared thoughts of individuals about a commonly recognized entity an issue. So in examining school cultures it is not only interesting but important to examine the degree to which any perceptions, particularly perceptions of purpose, are shared. One important objective in the study of school culture is to determine what specifiable and observable action taken by school leaders and staff enhances the probability that a substantial number of students focus on task rather than ability goals. Moreover, the weight of shared opinion, the cohesiveness of the school in acting to define schooling in a certain way, is likely to be an important factor in the goals that students actually adopt.

The assertion that culture is a cause translates into a view of culture as a group experience felt subjectively. Although individual perceptions can be aggregated to characterize a context, a group, or an organization, when treated as a cause, the individual's perception is preeminent.

Three major hypotheses are at the heart of this conception of school culture and student learning. First, students' perceptions of culture, such as those that formed the measures described and discussed in the preceding chapter, affect the personal goals that students adopt in pursuing academic work.[2] A second hypothesis is closely associated with this: When students adopt personal task or ability goals, their view of self and other thoughts, as well as actions are affected (cf. Chapter 2). The third hypothesis is that the perceptions students have about schooling are significantly affected by the action taken by schools. It seems logical to assume that what students perceive is necessarily related to a degree to what is "there." One can establish functional relationships between what is observed to be happening in a school and context and the perceptions that students hold. If this cannot be assumed, we have little hope of effecting changes in what goes on in schools so as to affect the perceptions of students (see Chapter 5).

Each of these hypotheses must be seen as an inseparable whole. In this chapter, we focus on the second hypothesis: Student perceptions of the goals emphasized in school (school culture) effect thoughts, beliefs, and attitudes associated with a personal investment in learning.

The Multiple Cultures of School
Associated with Student Motivation and Learning

In principle and in fact, any given school must be thought of as consisting of multiple cultures. There are both theoretical and practical reasons for conceptualizing the nature of school in this way. There is the culture associated with individual classrooms. There are the various subgroups that can be designated in terms of the perspective on schooling as well as the organizational context they share: the athletic department, the theater group, the math department, and so on. Then there are the various subgroups of students: at-risk students, the college-bound and academic types, the "jocks," the "nerds," and what have you. Finally, there is the world of the teachers or staff, one that is thought to be of primary importance in determining the culture of school that comes to be experienced by students. Our definition of school culture (cf. also Chapter 3) can, to a varying degree, apply to all of these designatable groups, presuming they are in fact distinguishable groups, especially as they are distinguishable in terms of the perspective and definition of schooling they hold in common. In principle the general model presented in Figure 4.1 is applicable to all these different groups. Although we have examined a number of such subcultures and will refer to such work here and there, our focus will be primarily on cultures associated with classrooms as well as schools as a whole. And, the bottom line in all this is how these cultures or subcultures relate to the motivation and learning of students.

Classroom Cultures

As noted earlier, teachers are thought to be the heart and soul of the instructional process—and they are. With that belief is a tendency to see individual classrooms as the heart and soul of school culture, as that which is most immediately influential in the life and learning of students. There is, of course, an important degree of truth in this, although it is not the whole truth. In the early grades especially, it appears that the child's view of classroom and school are virtually inseparable so far as the definition of the purpose and meaning of schooling are concerned. Our experiences helping out in elementary classrooms have made us even more aware of that fact. What goes on in grade school classrooms under the direction of the teacher seems to be overwhelmingly important so far as defining school is concerned. But even at the elementary level, there are the lunchroom experience, the trip to and from a bus, the playground activities, the awareness of something bigger and beyond their own self-contained classroom. Be that as it may, any examination of school cultures does well to consider the several cultures that likely exist in classrooms. For one thing, as a kind of microcosm of school it may be a convenient and more manageable venue for systematically testing the culture hypotheses we propose. Moreover, one cannot imagine changes occurring in the school as a whole without parallel changes in the multiple instructional contexts that make up the school.

Certainly, there is a strong precedent for viewing different classrooms as having different learning environments that influence the way students approach learning (cf. Chapter 3). When motivation began to figure prominently in educational research, interest in "personality" as a fairly fixed cause of student motivation moved quickly to school context. A focus on instruction and motivation led rather naturally to an examination of what teachers do to enhance motivation (for example, Blumenfeld & Meece, 1988; Blumenfeld et al., 1991). The emergence of achievement goal theory proved to be a catalyst for this emerging perspective. Making *thoughts* about purpose (goals) a major motivational variable opened up a new possibility. Such thoughts were easily viewed not only as changeable but as changing with context and circumstance. Indeed, one could actually view children's thoughts of purpose for school and learning as constructions made in the social context of classrooms (McCaslin & Murdock, 1991; Nicholls & Hazzard, 1993). All of this anticipated the possibility that goals were influenced by what happened in classrooms and were perhaps constructed there.

The work of Carole Ames and her colleagues (Ames & Ames, 1993; Ames & Archer, 1988; Ames, 1990) has been especially important in this regard. This work set the foundation for an empirical analysis directed specifically toward determining how something about the psychological environment of the classroom eventuated in different patterns of motivation and learning. Several elements in the model outlined in Figure 4.1 were implied or explicitly set forth by Carole Ames and Jennifer Archer (1987). First, they identified classroom environments in terms of their goal orientation, or the emphasis put on differential goals. Second, they placed the stress on the students' perceptions of these goal emphases as the immediate cause of motivation-related attitudes and orientations toward learning. Of course, what was especially important was that Ames and Archer not only set forth the hypotheses but operationalized the variables in a way that led to an early testing and confirmation. In brief, they found that students' perceptions of task and ability[3] goal emphases in the classroom are in fact related to qualitatively different motivational orientations and patterns. If and as students saw their classrooms as emphasizing task goals they were more likely to report that they used "effective" learning strategies, preferred challenging tasks, and held more positive attitudes toward learning. Interesting also was the differential view of self vis-à-vis doing well in school. When the classroom was seen as task-oriented, students were more likely to stress effort as a cause of achievement. Similarly interesting was that those who saw the classroom as stressing relative ability were more likely to lay the blame for failure on their own ability.

In summary, Ames's work was important in a number of different respects. It provided a preliminary outline of the model presented in Figure 4.1 and specified several of the major hypotheses basic to the theme of this chapter. Students sense something in the words and actions of teachers and in the nature of the tasks offered that affects not only whether they will invest but also *how* they will invest in learning. They observe differential goal emphases on whether schooling is about learning, progress, engagement in a task for its own worth (task goal), demonstrating performance and ability relative to others, or a competition to establish one's place in a hierarchy. These conceptions and the way they were operationalized remain instructive for further work on classroom cultures and also suggest a perspective for defining and analyzing the culture of the school as a whole.

Recent research has built on Ames's efforts and clarified and expanded the results and interpretations. For example, Anderman and Young (1994) conducted an instructive study of middle school science classrooms. As reported in Chapter 3, this study employed hierarchical linear modeling techniques to demonstrate the existence of essentially different classroom cultures so far as a stress on task and ability goals was concerned. Of special importance in the present context, they found that these differential cultures were associated with differential student motivation patterns. Briefly, instructional stress on the importance of high grades, competition, and more generally, ability goals was associated with lower levels of motivation. In interpreting their results, Eric Anderman and Allison Young make an interesting point about the likely cause of loss of interest in school science in the middle grades. It is not just that children are too busy with other things to be bothered with science; it is not simply that now science is "tough"; nor is it that science is too abstract, remote, and irrelevant to their lives. Rather, the way instruction is conducted and managed—the learning culture that is presented—is a critical factor. Specifically, Anderman and Young argue for the increased application of goal theory in designing instruction to create an optimal motivational culture for learning.

Anderman and Carol Midgley (1995) followed a sample of 341 students as they made the transition from 5th grade in elementary school to 6th grade in middle school. In this case the focus was on motivation associated with math and English classrooms. The transition to middle school was accompanied by a reduction in a task-goal orientation and with that also a lowering of self-efficacy and a greater use of surface level learning strategies (memorizing, rereading). Again, the case was made that the oft-noted middle school drop in motivation (for example, Anderman & Maehr, 1994; Eccles & Midgley, 1989) is likely a product of a change in learning environments (in this case, classrooms), not just an inevitable phase of development, the burden of adolescence.

One important point that was not pursued fully in the initial studies by Ames but which has emerged as increasingly important in subsequent studies relates to the mediating role played by the personal goals students hold or adapt in response to the school culture in which they find themselves. Our model stresses that individual goal adoption is likely to be an important mediating factor that can in principle be separated from the perception of school goal emphases. The point is that individuals not only view the classroom as stressing a certain view of the activities in which students are and should be engaged, they likely have their own view of what constitutes "success" and "failure" and what is worth striving for. Of course, the notion of personally held views has long been a part of the goal theory literature. Some attention has been given recently to separating perceived culture from these personal goals (Roeser, Midgley, & Urdan, in press) and to viewing culture as influencing students by changing not just their perception of how the "game is to be played" in a given situation, but their personally held and cross-situational view of learning.

There is a growing body of data that confirms the essential point that classrooms not only differ in the culture presented, but as children experience these different stresses on task and ability purposes for learning they respond accordingly. Children tend to adopt the goals that are stressed in the classroom as their own guiding purposes for how they invest in what is happening in that classroom. More accurately, their perceptions of what schools are stressing frame their own definitions of schooling and the degree to which they will adopt and be guided by task and ability goals. It is likely also that as students repeatedly experience classrooms as task- or ability-focused in nature, they will acquire a durable and widely generalizable view of schooling that will be hard to change. Their view of schooling will shape their investment in learning and schools.

School Culture

But what about the culture of the school as a whole? More precisely, do students act in terms of perceptions of the message that is sent through schoolwide policies and practices? In Chapter 3 we presented evidence that schools do appear to present different perspectives on learning—a different mission, if you will. What evidence do we have that the nature of schools as a whole, the tenor and thrust of schoolwide policies and practices, is an important factor in student motivation? Do students not only sense that their school stands for something but respond to this stand of the school in the way they go about learning? It is one thing to argue that a school is more than a sum of its classroom parts; it is quite another to show that something about the school as a whole makes a significant difference in the life and learning of students. Intuitively, it seems plausible. Common observations would suggest that it is so. But really, do students actually see the school organization as conveying a purpose, a rationale for schooling, that in turn is likely to affect how they participate in the schooling enterprise? That is a large and difficult question but obviously an important one. If the students' perception of a school's purpose can be associated not only with how they relate to that school but also to the act of learning, it points up the possibility of examining precisely how schools affect or lead to the construction of such purposes. Whether or how culture emphases of the school as a whole affect student investment should be of interest to school leaders and give new meaning to the regular routines of faculty meetings.

Early Preliminary Work

Our exploration of this central hypothesis began well over a decade ago. Motivational researchers were just beginning to attend to the concept of goals as now defined (Chapter 2), and that work was largely focused on a rather narrow range of observations of children, often in very controlled and sometimes artificial ("laboratory") settings. An opportunity presented itself to consider the role of motivation in the world of work. Scales were developed to assess essentially four basic goals and the opportunities to pursue these on the job (Braskamp & Maehr, 1986). Fortuitously, those in charge who invited us to test the scales and our notions of motivation in their organizations kept asking, "But what can we do about it (motivation)?" A few of them had been reading about "corporate culture," which was then becoming an increasingly popular concept. The possible determining role of corporate culture was forced upon us, as it were, by the practical demands "to motivate," not just to study individual differences.

Not incidentally, at the same time the teachers we were talking to about motivation for learning asked similar questions, so did their principals. Interestingly, teachers did not talk much about school culture or even classroom climate and neither, as we remember it, did their principals. But they did ask searching questions about what could be done in the classroom to make a difference. They didn't assume that motivation was the child's—or even the parent's—responsibility. Rather, they seemed to take it as given that teaching meant motivating. But how? The world of work provided a strong clue that the answer to motivation may lie in the context. The world of school seemed increasingly to concur in that assessment as options for doing something about "unmotivated kids" were discussed. In any event, we were nudged to look to context in the primary and secondary sense, to classrooms and to the wider context of school that seemed to shape, modify, and intrude on whatever happened in classrooms. This predilection was strongly encouraged by work focusing on motivation in the middle grades.

A body of literature was evolving that documented not only an apparent decline in motivation during the middles grades but which began to suggest that this decline could in part be attributed to what was going on in schools and classrooms during that period (Anderman & Maehr, 1994; Eccles & Midgley, 1989; Midgley, 1993). Simmons and her colleagues (1987), for example, determined that negative shifts in girls' self-esteem were rooted in the character of the school and other contexts that dominate adolescents' worlds during this stage. This possibility is reinforced and specified by the work of Jaque Eccles and Carol Midgley as they conducted extensive studies of adolescent development. In particular, Eccles and Midgley and their colleagues challenged the assumption that declines in motivation during early adolescence are related to psychological and physiological changes associated with puberty and are thus inevitable. They found a direct link between changes in the classroom context when children moved from elementary to middle level schools and expectancies and values in mathematics (for example, Midgley, Feldlaufer, & Eccles, 1989a, 1989b). Most children moved to a less facilitative environment after the transition and experienced the noted decline in motivation. But those children who moved to a more facilitative environment experienced an increase in motivation. The motivation of low-achieving children was particularly sensitive to positive or negative changes in the classroom environment. They described the root problem as a "mismatch" of student needs and environmental presses at this stage of life, but the argument was clearly emerging that the psychological environment of the learning environment in classrooms and schools was responsible for the kinds of motivational problems that were too readily evident.

At the same time, those working in the area of organizational behavior generally were in the forefront of pushing the case for considering the role of psychological facets of organizational life that might be at the heart of motivation. The popular literature on industrial malaise during the late 1970s and 1980s as well as research conducted by social scientists increasingly began to focus attention on organizational culture and how it might affect the nature and quality of worker engagement (Denison, 1984; Hof-

stede, 1991; Ouchi, 1986). In this regard, we have a degree of indebtedness
to a number of business executives with whom we've worked. As we focused on individual differences in personality, incentive systems, evaluation
practices, and task definition, it was they who kept bringing up the issue of
corporate culture. It wasn't always clear what they meant, but they kept
suggesting that if only they could change the culture of their organization, it
would make a motivational difference. Naively perhaps, the executives
thought they could do something about cultures and they wanted us to tell
them how to provide a culture in which workers would be motivated. We
didn't really respond to that but we did, somewhat incidentally, create an
organizational culture scale that was parallel in form and content to items
eliciting workers' personally held goals and beliefs. The scale "worked," that
is, it had reasonable levels of reliability and a degree of discriminant validity
in distinguishing different types of organizations as well as groups of people
within the organizations (executives, clerical, maintenance, and so forth). It
also seemed to relate to such measures of job investment as "job satisfaction" and "organizational commitment." As such, an organizational culture
scale became an attractive feature of a battery of items designed for the
analysis and prediction of work motivation (Braskamp & Maehr, 1986).

Increasingly this effort focused on schools (Maehr & Fyans, 1989; Maehr,
R. Ames, & Braskamp, 1988). Through the initiative of Dr. L. J. Fyans and
with the support of the State of Illinois Department of Education, items
adapted from the original organizational culture scale were inserted into
the periodic statewide school assessment program along with items on motivation, social background of students, and school achievement patterns.
Somewhat surprisingly, the items on culture explained a significant portion
of the variance in motivation and achievement scales. Students' perceptions
of the goals stressed by their schools were related to measures of student
motivation, which were in turn related to indices of school achievement.
The thought was inescapable: Maybe there was something about the concept of organizational culture as it applied to schools that could be readily
assessed and that related to the way children felt about learning. It seemed
to be as simple—and perhaps as profound—as the presence of beliefs about
what the school stood for, what it stressed, the purpose for education that it
presented—how school was defined. Such perceptions of purposiveness of
the school were something that students reliably reported and these
summed to a significant characterization of the school as a whole (cf. Chapter 3). But the work initiated in this regard indicated that students recognized something about the character of a school that in turn related to how

or whether they would invest in achievement. How students saw the school, so they invested. Most especially, how they saw the *purpose* of school, so they invested.

The most important of the school scales, collectively and to varying degree individually, related to measures of student motivation, and motivation was related in turn to standardized scores on reading, science, and math. Path analyses were conducted to clarify causal relations. These analyses yielded evidence in support of the model presented in Figure 4.2, especially at grades 6, 8, and 10.

That is the general finding and one of some significance in making a case for school culture as a factor in student motivation and achievement. Several comments on various facets of the results, however, are worth adding. The measure of motivation was an omnibus measure of motivational direction and did not reflect the quality of motivation, as is the case in more recent work. Nevertheless, it is noteworthy that, overall, school culture, as we have defined it, was associated with students' motivational orientation, which in turn was related to performance on standardized measures of achievement in major instructional domains. Of further interest is how the strength of the overall pattern, especially the importance of school culture in explaining motivation, increased as grade level increased; this is especially evident in Figure 4.3. Note there also the apparent importance of school culture for different ethnic groups.

Incidentally, measures of peer and family influences were taken along with measures of school culture to obtain a reading of relative influence of these three factors at successive grade levels. The results are a bit too complicated to portray graphically, but the general pattern of the results can be described briefly as follows. As one might expect, the patterns were least interpretable at the 4th grade; it seems that peers, family, and school effects were not as readily separable at this stage. At grades 6 and 8 family, peers, and school culture seemed to operate independently. However, it is interesting that school culture explained more of the variance in motivation for learning than either of the other two contextual influences. At grade 10,

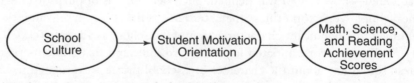

Figure 4.2 Summary portrayal of path analysis results

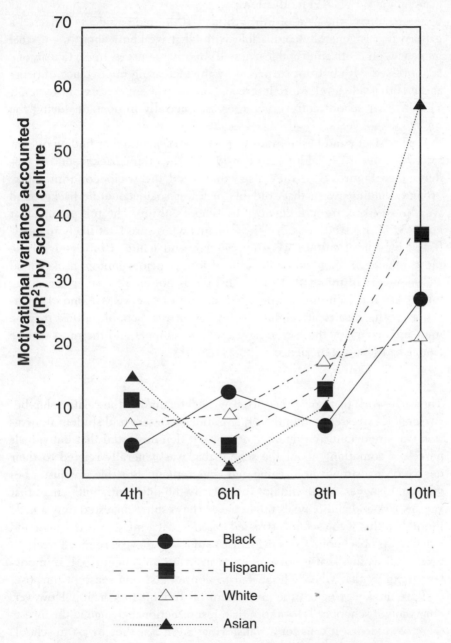

Figure 4.3 Motivational variance accounted for (R^2) by school culture at successive grade levels

however, peer influence emerged as an equally important variable in explaining the variance in motivation.

The results in the case of 6th, 8th, and 10th grade students reflected a pattern that is generally compatible with what we know about contextual influences on motivation and learning from other sources. In particular, one is impressed with but not surprised by the increasing importance of peers at the 10th grade level. More interesting in the present context, however, is the hint that school culture emerges as especially important during the middle school years.

Martin Maehr and Leslie Fyans (1989) report one further finding of considerable interest. In addition to considering the ethnic background of students (see Figure 4.3), they also considered the socioeconomic background. Findings were that students of lower socioeconomic background were most likely to be influenced by school culture. The full picture that emerged in this study was that the students who were least likely to be affected by school culture were upper class and white. Conversely, those most influenced for good or ill were of lower socioeconomic background and members of minority groups. This too is not an altogether surprising finding but it is an important one. Not only does it serve as a kind of verification of the results, it reinforces the notion that school culture may be most important for those who have the least support and the most to lose from a bad school experience.

Conclusions.

The early work that concerned itself with determining the relationship between goals stressed within the organizational context and student motivation was important in a number of ways. It demonstrated that individuals perceived something about the school that was generally related to their degree of investment in learning and achievement. But this was just a beginning. It suggested but did not fully clarify the differential influences that various task and ability goals might have. The results suggested only a little more than that if the schools stressed *something;* if a mission was salient and a definition of schooling was evident to students, they were more likely to invest in learning. That is not altogether insignificant, of course. It is important to know that when schools fail to convey a strong sense of purpose, they are unlikely to elicit the investment of students in learning. However, our vision of school calls for more than just directional change in the investment of students. It calls for a transformation in *how* they invest in schooling—the way students view schooling, pursue it as worthy in its own right, and see it as an adventure or as simply a job that has to be done.

Recent Research

More recent research conducted by us and by others has gone beyond the concern with the direction of investment to consider the nature of the investment. That is, it has refocused interest in the *quality* of motivation. In discussing the differences that the culture of the school as a totality makes, it is important to consider not just whether a person invests time and energy in learning. One must also consider the character of that investment. As we noted in looking at classroom cultures, learning strategies and possibly academic venturesomeness and creativity may vary depending on how the purpose of schooling is defined. Does the school as a whole also make that kind of difference? Cautiously, one senses that this might be the case. All of us can cite anecdotal evidence—usually about a specially focused and endowed school—where this does indeed happen: a magnet school for the arts, a chartered school serving the scientifically "gifted." But what about the common school, the school that serves students of diverse backgrounds who are not selected because of their special talents, motives, values, or backgrounds? Can these schools too exemplify a culture that fosters not just an enhanced work ethic but a qualitatively different and possibly superior approach to learning and an inclination to explore, to create, to grow, to understand? Our recent research provides a degree of support for hope that this can indeed be the case.

As we noted in Chapter 3, schools as well as classrooms can be characterized in terms of a purpose profile. It is not only that some schools are more purposeful than others—although that is important—there is the potential for schools to stress task goals more than ability goals. Students perceive this variation in the way schooling is presented not only at the level of classroom activities but also in the policies and practices that pervade the wide range of activities associated with school. If students can indeed see such differences in school, there is every reason to believe that—just as at the classroom level—they will adjust their purposes accordingly. Increasingly, we have focused our efforts on exploring this possibility, and the results hold strong promise that this is not only a hypothesis worth testing but a principle worth applying.

While it is logical to assume that perceptions of school goal emphases operate analogously to classroom goal stresses, we have in fact gathered data that confirm this logic. In an extensive study of perceptions of schools and classrooms and motivation patterns in four different schools over the course of a four-year period, we found the following basic results (Urdan, Hicks, & Anderman, 1994). Students' perceptions of the goals stressed by their schools have been regularly found to relate in expected ways to the personal goals that students hold for how they approach schooling and learning. Thus, if the school is seen as being socially competitive, focused on ability hierarchies, the chances are high that students will espouse similar personal goals. In short, when students see the school as stressing ability goals, they will first of all tend to adopt these goals in approaching school tasks. With that comes a strong tendency to go about the task of learning differently than if task goals are primary. Ability goals do not foster strategic learning, reflective thinking, and the "deep processing" of information. They promote shortcuts in learning and the achievement of short-term goals, memorization to do well on a test, for example. Ability goals do not foster understanding. They do not encourage the learner to apply what is learned in different contexts and circumstances to different problems. Not surprising also is that a school stress on ability has been associated with lower feelings of academic efficacy, a sense that one is not capable of doing what is expected in school, and with that a general feeling of not "belonging."

In short, the school culture as a whole is representative of the way students see learning being defined and has been shown to explain a considerable portion of the variation in students' orientation toward learning and to their place within the school. This may be of special importance in the case of children who—for a number of reasons—may be at risk for school failure.

That having been said, an important point must be added about the differential role of school and classroom cultures at different age and grade levels. Given the way schools are organized, it is not surprising that it is difficult to disentangle effects of school and classroom in the case of elementary school level children. It is at the middle school level and later that school definitions can be separated from individual classroom definitions of what schooling is about. And consequently, it is at these later levels where school level effects are most pronounced, statistically speaking.

Conclusion

School Cultures Make a Difference

School culture makes a significant difference in the bottom line of education, which is the investment of students in learning. Students recognize that classrooms and the school as a whole stress certain objectives, goals, purposes; these define what schooling is to be for students. Most important so far as our vision of school is concerned (see Chapter 2) is that if the school or classroom is seen as stressing ability goals, students are likely to follow suit. They will see school and education as essentially a competitive game of winners and losers. The focus will be on achievement hierarchies and external recognition and reward—not for learning and progressing in the gaining of knowledge and understanding but a venue for the demonstration of ability. Several predictable patterns of attitude and action are virtually inevitable in that case. Certainly, this orientation does not contribute to building community. It will inevitably "turn off" those who most need the school: those from backgrounds who start out with two or maybe even three strikes against them. Whether or not they progress in their growth and understanding, if what counts is relative performance, they will be losers—and inevitably come to view themselves as such. Above all, if the objective of education is not just to separate and categorize children but to optimize growth and understanding and develop life-long learners, a stress on relative ability in the school culture will fail. But there is a strong chance that if schools stress task goals, they will encourage students to view education quite differently, as something worth pursuing in its own right and as an opportunity for growth and improvement. The schools will be seen as accepting and facilitative, not as a place to be avoided. Because of the culture(s) they present, schools can in short be both a bane and a blessing for children and for the future that is theirs to create.

And yes, it is the school, teachers, staff, and all those who design the policies and practices that reflect the definition of schooling who can and will have a profound effect on students. Children, of course, may come into a school or any given classroom with this or that definition of the work to be done. Forces in the family and the world at large continue to affect how they view school and learning. But the school shapes this definition as well. Often for good, fortunately, but regrettably, all too often for ill.

Toward a Fully Facilitative School Culture

Our analysis of school culture culminates in an argument for the desirability of a certain course of action. Indeed, it lays the groundwork for the action to be taken. Much of the writing on school culture has not focused on what we believe to be the most fundamental fact: that school cultures define the purpose and meaning of schooling for students and thereby shape the kind of learners they will become. A cohesive culture has its value in conveying purpose: Clear messages are more likely to be effective than mixed ones. Certainly, the working culture experienced by teachers, the way they share and invest, cannot be ignored; it is absolutely critical. But our argument goes beyond simply establishing a coherent and cohesive culture or in simply being purposeful. It goes beyond simple empowerment. Our argument—sufficiently clear by now, we trust—is that a specific kind of culture must be created, a school culture where task goals are pervasive and preeminent.

The mechanisms for defining the school in different ways are, generally speaking, in place. They exist in the everyday policies and practices, the routines and the symbols that are substantially under the control of those who manage and teach. The problem with schools is that these mechanisms for defining learning and schooling are often misused or misdirected so that schooling is defined as a competitive game in which some win and some lose. In other words, the "problem with schools" so sorely decried and so seldom explained is misdefinition of learning. Schools and classrooms differ from each other in a variety of ways. So far as eliciting the investment of students in learning is concerned, they differ most critically in the way they define the task to be done and in a larger sense in the definition of schooling that they stress. Far too many schools—perhaps most schools—at best give mixed messages on schooling; at the worst they stress ability goals.

But this can change! In the ensuing chapters we describe how.

Notes

1. In this regard, we are generally guided by the tenor and thought of social cognitive theory. We have been particularly influenced by the work of Triandis (1994).

2. The issue of how, whether, and when students may follow what the school is seen as stressing is an interesting side issue which we will forego discussing at this point. Clearly, this issue can and should be discussed within the context of current social influence theory and research (for example, Cialdini, 1995).

3. Although Ames and Archer use the terms "mastery" and "performance," we retain consistency by continuing to use the labels that we find preferable. It is our view that little difference beyond labeling exists between the goals employed by Ames and Archer and those employed by us.

Part Three

Transforming School Cultures

5 Toward School Culture Change

> If we give culture its due, if we take an inquiring attitude toward the deci-
> phering of culture, if we respect what culture is and what functions it serves,
> we will find that it is a potentially friendly animal that can be tamed and made
> to work for us.
>
> —E. H. Schein, *Organizational Culture and Leadership*, p. 30

We could have concluded this book without embroiling ourselves in the messy business of school change. That is, the preceding chapters could well have served as the heart, soul, and substance of the book,
needing only a conclusion: *Here is what you must do—now do it!* Instead, we
decided to put theory to the test of practice. There are several reasons why
we risked such an effort. It is and was the only way that we could determine
the practicality of our vision. More important is that we learned something
about theory as well as application in the course of doing this—as, it is
hoped, will be evident in this and the remaining chapters. Denying ourselves the insights of practitioners would not only have made our words less
useful, it would have made them less truthful. And incidentally, we learned
something about school change in the process.

So it was that we decided to initiate a bold experiment. Actually, two experiments. With the necessary support of willing funders and a cooperative
school district, school leadership, and staff, we began an effort that gave all

our previous work special meaning and value. "We" is not used casually or with pretended modesty. For the work was and had to be the work of a complex collaboration of persons with many and diverse skills, interests, and motives. In addition to committed school staff, there were eager and willing undergraduate and graduate students. There was a small group of conscientious, supportive, and engaged parents who contributed time and insight. There were students who somehow weren't put off by talking to us about school and themselves. They taught us what we could learn in no other way. We were lucky that district administrators and members of the school board saw something valuable in what was happening and occasionally contributed dollars, as did two funding agencies.[1] What united this diverse collection of talent was a concern regarding the personal investment of children in learning. Although individual teachers and administrators each had their own way of articulating it, there was little question they saw this as a major challenge in their work, an aggravating problem facing their school. The university group, of course, expressed parallel interest and concern. But school staff and the university group hardly saw the issue and the answers in the same way at the outset. Not surprisingly, school staff was less inclined to point to school practices and policy and certainly did not spontaneously express a need to "transform school culture." The university group came with some rather strong assumptions about the importance of school contexts in determining motivation but a lack of ability to specify school sources of student motivation precisely. We had much to learn from each other and fortunately, learn we did. We learned how to cooperate and collaborate. Together we identified school policies and practices that should and could be changed. Collaboratively, we came to a realization regarding whether and how our vision could be embodied in the concrete events, processes, and day-to-day realities of school and schooling. It was a bold experiment but a necessary one.

Chapter 5 introduces our story of putting theory into practice. We describe our choice of schools: site, setting, district, and community context of which they are an integral part. Then we portray the entering assumptions about *what* had to be changed and *how* this could be accomplished. Following chapters will present a "thick description" of the processes that ensued and analyses of and reflections upon the results obtained.

Site and Setting

These schools were not chosen accidentally. In the fall of the 1990–1991 school year, we met with administrators in three neighboring school districts to describe our program and to determine if they would be interested in a long-term collaborative relationship focusing on school culture change. Two of these districts expressed an interest in collaborating with us. One seemed especially suited for the project we had in mind. In broad outline, this district was similar to the others in terms of demographic characteristics, locale, and character. All were part of the same metropolitan area. The chosen district was a relatively large district with a sizable blue-collar population. (Many parents worked in automobile factories and many at the time were on indefinite layoff or unemployed.) Approximately 16 percent of the student population were African-American, and 37 percent received reduced-fee or free lunches based on level of income. In the district there were six elementary schools, two middle schools, and one high school. Only after considerable deliberation, we decided to select Lakeside (a fictitious name) as the site of our demonstration project. The reasons included the apparent stability of the administration and staff, the accessibility of the school sites from Ann Arbor, the relative absence of major university projects that might conflict with our efforts and of course, the apparent receptivity of district administrators.

Community Context

It probably is not accurate to say that the schools were the "heart of the community" if that is meant to imply that they were fully appreciated and valued. As we began our work, school leadership and staff indicated that they felt that the community had not always been fully supportive. As evidence, a recent teachers' strike and the failure of a bond issue were mentioned along with other facts and anecdotes. Yet, the schools served to bind together and give some sense of unity to what we label a "community." Calling it that may in fact be a bit of an overstatement. The area served by the school district is a collection of housing areas amidst a sprinkling of assorted small businesses, interspersed among shopping centers—all dominated by the massive presence of large auto manufacturing and assembly plants. This exurbic jumble, curiously enough, exists within a naturally lovely setting: amidst rolling hills, a charming (if slightly polluted) river, and a small lake. The community is not really part of the large metro area it borders, but it is not separate from it either. Increasingly, it is dominated not only by urban economic exigencies but also population migration patterns. As a result, this once sleepy, rural-oriented area is being affected by all the problems that characterize urban life. The public housing that borders the highway reputedly reflects this trend in a most severe fashion. But more broadly, the schools here are no strangers to ethnic conflict, drugs, gangs, violence, abusiveness, poverty, and even hunger.

When we began our effort, the community was just beginning to experience the effects of a recent downturn in the economy, occasioned by a recent phase of adjustment or restructuring of the auto industry. This eventuated in the closing or relocation of plants, threatening the livelihood as well as the lives of many fathers, mothers, and children in the community. Those who were or would be losing their jobs may have lost them forever. Children who expected to follow their fathers and mothers to one or another manufacturing plant began to realize that they were living under a false expectation, especially if they chose not to become and remain invested in learning and the acquisition of the orientations, skills, and knowledge demanded by an increasingly high-tech world.

In sum, this was a community in adjustment. The problems were not just the problems of some poor children and certain impoverished, demoralized, and dysfunctional families. The problem was and remains more pervasive than that. And of course, the community problem was and is a school problem. Community leaders, the school board, parents, and school staff recognized this and worried about it. Not an atypical state of affairs in today's world. Not a set of problems or challenges unheard of by anyone willing to read and listen. But a serious and what must sometimes seem to be an almost overwhelming problem for those who are entrusted with assisting children to learn, to realize their potential, to aspire, to be responsible, and to feel good about themselves and their world.

School Selection

Of course, a choice of the district and the community was not tantamount to finding school staffs that would be able and willing to work with us in this somewhat grand effort. We could not set up our criteria and choose the "perfect school" for our purposes, expecting that somehow district administrators could command the school's cooperation. Any who have at least one foot in the real world of school would accept this as given. Yet, it is easy to glide over the obvious here and forget the importance of this observation. At the least, it should suggest something about distribution and locus of power, organizational processes, and how change does or does not, can or cannot, occur in these and probably most schools. Certainly change does not occur as the direct result of some hierarchy, if indeed one can even identify who that might be. Even before the emphasis on site-based management, individual schools exhibited a degree of independence and autonomy that characteristically made any change from the outside a compromise with those on the inside. What recent organizational theory has contributed is the insight that this may not only be inevitable, it can be desirable. There are strengths on the "inside" to be exploited. Indeed, desirable and sustained change is likely to eventuate if and only if those on the inside are instruments in that change. In any event, the importance of schools choosing us as well as our choosing them was a reality.

Parenthetically, this enhanced awareness of the "separateness" of the individual school increased our belief that the individual school must be reckoned with as a critical unit for educational change. It is more autonomous than organizational charts and public policy statements would lead one to believe. The school is, as we will show, sufficiently in control of its destiny to make choices critical to maintaining and enhancing a culture that defines schooling as learning or performing.

So our search for collaborators necessarily moved toward finding apparently willing schools with willing leaders, staff, and to some degree parents. After receiving the endorsement of the superintendent and the director of instruction, we met with the elementary and middle school principals to explain the proposed endeavor. Arrangements were then made to meet with the teachers in each of the schools to describe the program and answer questions. Following those meetings, the staff at three elementary schools indicated they were eager to collaborate with us, two said they were not interested at this time, and one was uncertain. Of the three schools that indicated they wanted to participate, we selected Riversedge (fictitious name) as the demonstration school and another school with relatively similar demographic characteristics to serve as a comparison. Both of the two middle schools in the district expressed an interest in participating. One, however, wished to wait a year in order to bring certain ongoing projects to conclusion. Thus, we chose the school (Plainview, also a fictitious name) that was ready to begin immediately and the other (N-School) served as the comparison school.

Obviously, our selection of schools was not random, being based largely on matters of expediency. We would strongly argue, however, that the choices were justified on grounds other than convenience. They were in fact very typical schools, not the best of schools or the worst. Indeed, they were in most ways representative of the many schools in which we have worked over the years, disturbingly so in some respects. That is, they faced daunting problems of funding. They were coping with children from families torn apart. They were under pressure to improve their test scores. They were worried about gangs, guns, and substance abuse, how to cope with needy children and parents. As we describe our experiences in these two schools in the context of their district and community this should become quite evident.

Entering Perspectives on *What* to Change

This was our opportunity and our challenge. Two not atypical schools who agreed that they wanted something, perhaps something like the culture change we had defined. Because these schools, like most, seldom met for more than a half hour or so on most any issue, the culture change had been defined only briefly. There was not a lot of time for dialogue, planning, and reflecting. The reasons are obvious and readily understandable: Schools are persistently faced with taking action. We were also somewhat vague, not only because we had to be brief but also because we had only an initial knowledge about what had to be changed. We did not know as much then as we now know, but we did know and believe something about what should be changed and how. We entered the schools ready to learn but also with a perspective. We had formulated the outlines of our vision of school change. We had also identified "pressure points" for effecting the desired change: a list of school policies and practices that likely affected student investment in learning.

Recalling the Vision

At the heart of our thinking was a vision of what a school ought to be. We outlined that vision in Chapter 2, but there are several fundamental elements of that vision worth repeating as we focus on how that vision can be put in place in the real world.

The objective is to enable, empower, and equip children to become life-long learners. Few will have problems with that. What follows, though no less important, may be less readily accepted or understood. Schools can promote and children can adopt two profoundly different definitions of what teaching, learning, and schooling are about: *task* and *ability* goals. Task goals relate essentially to the value of learning for its own sake, the desirability of each and every person progressing, growing in understanding and skill. Ability goals focus on learning and schooling primarily as a means to another end. That end may be extrinsic to and often actually undermine the pursuit of learning, as is often the case when the child is basically paid to study as if it were just a job to be done. Equally if not more problematic is the stress on social comparison, even fierce competition: a stress on outperforming others and establishing oneself in some sort of social hierarchy which ignores advantages and disadvantages, opportunities and hurdles, effort and progress. Schools stress and students consequently focus on these contrasting goals to varying degrees with enduring effects on learning. Our vision of school revolves around the nurturance and enhancement of a task focus, minimizing the emphasis on relative ability that may intrude.

That, in a nutshell, is the vision we wished to see realized in our selected schools. With some evidence, we concluded that these schools, like most schools, probably stressed ability goals more than task goals. Our task was to assist the schools in moving toward an increased emphasis on tasks goals. That was the "cultural transformation" that we sought.

What *Do You Change* to *Change School Cultures?*

But what does one change in order to obtain an enhanced emphasis on task goals? Broadly speaking, we are talking about realizing the purposes of school. And especially, defining what school is for children. All organizations exist for some purpose and to varying degrees stress or promote that purpose. Schools have been assigned functions and therewith purposes and objectives by persons and groups that establish and fund them. Often, the assigned purposes are somewhat vague: to educate, to enhance moral development, to train, and so forth. These purposes vary in the degree to which they are common to all or most schools. Private schools, such as the Groton that Franklin Roosevelt attended, have a special sense of themselves and their purpose that no student can ignore (Davis, 1972). Various case studies (for example Lightfoot, 1983) lead one to believe that a number of private schools today still maintain a sense of who they are, as do select magnet schools: schools with a special clientele and possibly unique reason for existing. From time to time one hears of certain inner city schools identified for their sense of mission and their pursuit of it (cf., Edmonds & Frederickson, 1979; Glenn & McLean, 1981; Weber, 1971). Maybe more than we know or believe, many schools are seen as special and purposive by the teachers, parents, and students who relate to them. But not all are, certainly, and that is likely a primary factor in their effectiveness or lack of it.

Without considering school culture per se, this rather basic point was taken particularly seriously by the "effective schools" movement (Brookover, Beady, Flood, Schweitzer, & Wisenbaker, 1979; Purkey & Smith, 1982; Rosenholtz, 1985; Rutter, Maughan, Mortimer & Ouston, 1979; Wynne, 1980). In the examination of schools that are deemed to be effective (compared to those deemed to be less so), a consistent finding has been that a shared sense of purpose is essential. Also stressed are actions that presumably make it possible for the organization to fulfill such purposes: creating a safe and clean environment; maintaining order, regularity, and predictability; specifying clear expectations and norms. Such instrumental objectives are of obvious importance. It is certainly true that no one can relate well to chaos. To the degree that these objectives are indeed instrumental to the pursuit of the larger mission of the school, they are not only desirable but absolutely necessary. Indeed, it is precisely in the routines that are followed in pursuing these instrumental objectives that the definition of the organization becomes evident. Students and teachers do not relate particularly to goal statements or missions as these are copied on sheets of paper or posted on walls. What they relate to are how these projected means and ends, these statements about objectives, purpose, and mission are embodied in action. In this case, as well as in many others, "Actions speak louder than words."

Doubtless in part because of the impact of the school effectiveness movement, it is common for schools to write objectives and develop mission statements. Some state laws require it. Those of us who have read countless such mission statements are varyingly amused and bemused by them. Sometimes they seem to be taken out of an ubiquitous administrator's handbook: The mission statement of the school in Sweetwater Township sounds curiously similar to the one developed in Thunder Bay on the other side of the state. That makes one wonder a bit about whether the school has really examined itself and set about defining purpose in a way that can be realized in practice or just fulfilled an assignment. Such curiosities aside, the definition of the purpose and goals, objectives and raison d'être, is nevertheless not to be taken lightly. And in no sense is the degree of commitment to the designated mission a matter of incidental concern. Purposes guide the life of organizations as well as persons. The clarity and coherence of the mission is critical. Where there is no mission, there is likely to be no commitment to the organization and little shared investment in a productive enterprise within the confines of that organization. Schools vary in the clarity and coherence of their mission, and this is recognized by students. When students see that the school has a mission, they are more likely also to take it seriously (see Chapter 4). The first step toward enhancing the effectiveness of any organization, including the school, is to establish, clarify, and gain a substantial degree of allegiance to some definition of purpose. That step must be complemented by action that reflects the definition. No organization can exist under the banner that "anything goes." Flexibility may be evident and individualism fostered, but certain basic formative and guiding beliefs are the essential groundwork of organizational existence and life. In order to change organizational culture, one has to attend to this feature from the very first as well as throughout the change process.

Given this set of understandings, our main concern was to assist the school in examining what it was, what it wanted to be, and particularly how it would define the purposes of schooling for students. As a result, we did not begin with programs, technology, and new methods but with beliefs, values, educational theory, and the issue of identity. Abstractions! But these abstractions can be quickly shown to take concrete form in policies and practices. Since we and others had done considerable work on how certain policies and practices were likely to lead to specific orientations toward schooling (Ames, 1990; Brophy, 1987; Epstein, 1989; Maehr & Midgley, 1991), it was relatively easy to make the abstract concrete and relevant to the day-to-day life of schools. We were prepared to show how a certain range of policy and practice choices were likely to make children believe that schooling was either about demonstrating relative ability or developing competency. Table 5.1 outlines areas in which action taken is particularly important in defining the purpose of schooling for students. But further elaboration is likely useful.

School Activities and Tasks

Schools, administrators, and teachers, collectively and individually, ask children to do many different things in school settings. A significant portion of these requests are associated with learning. The nature of these tasks; how they are described, defined, interpreted, managed, and given; and the priority assigned to them has a lot to do with how students come to view what school and learning is about. In particular, the choice and framing of tasks is likely to influence perceptions about the purpose of school. Is school predominantly "work" or "play"? Is it about "learning" or "performing"? Is it a "contest" or a "game"? Is it about "growth" or "self-actualization"?

Certainly, what is done and how it is done is not under the full and complete control of those who teach or manage the school. States and school districts have mandates regarding what children must do within school settings and how they must do it. Parents bring their opinions to bear as well. There are many forces at work to define what is to be done in school and why. But in spite of legislation, parental expectations, and district mandates, individual schools have considerable influence over what children actually do in school settings and especially over how they do it. Equally, if not of greater importance, school leadership and staff interpret the meaning of tasks that are to be done or not done within school settings: "This is

Table 5.1   Policies and Practices That Affect Definitions of Purpose

Area	Issues	Example
School Activities and Tasks	What is the student asked to do?	Memorize labels for plant phyla. Write a letter-critique in response to an editorial on the failure of schools.
Evaluation	What do assessment grading procedures imply about school objectives?	All students receive A's if they behave. Effort is the primary basis for grades. "Grading on the curve" The use of portfolios to assess student progress
Rewards and Recognition	What outcomes and behavior are especially attended to? What reward and recognition schedules are followed?	The predominance of athletic awards diminishes academics at the honors convocation. Students are given a $25 check for reading 25 books. Grades are posted for all to see.
Freedom, Autonomy, and Responsibility	Emphasis on staff control versus student autonomy—what kinds of choices are students given? How is student sense of responsibility enhanced?	Faculty makes the rules. Students obey—or else. School emphasizes student growth in handling freedom and responsibility. Conflict resolution programs that encourage student involvement are in place
Organizing Students into Groups	Is ability grouping an implicit or explicit policy?	Sixth graders who are thought to have "math potential" are taught in separate classes.

	Is learning viewed as an individual and/or social constructive process?	Cooperative learning, group projects, and learning opportunities are a regular part of instruction.
	Are interdisciplinary and thematic teaching encouraged?	
Scheduling	Is the 40- to 50-minute instructional period sacred?	"Blocking" and teaming are encouraged and practiced.
	What flexibility is there for accommodating the need for larger blocks of time?	After school and summer programs are promoted.
	How is the school building used throughout the full course of the day—and year?	The schedule is readily adjusted to accommodate needs for field trips.
Resources	What are the rules by which equipment, in-service opportunities, and supplies are distributed?	Computers are the exclusive property of advanced math classes. Seniority or equity determines who will receive a budget allotment.
	Who gets what—and for what reasons?	Programmatic efforts directed toward school improvement claim the lion's share of discretionary funds.

Source: Constructed by the authors from their own work as well as that of others, especially Carole Ames (1990), Jere Brophy (1987), and Joyce Epstein (1989).

important!" "Don't worry about this—it won't be on the test." "After you've completed this, we'll have some fun." "This is hard, but you won't get a job if you don't get it." But the meaning of school tasks is often more subtly defined not just by what the teacher or the school says but by the structure of the task itself.

We have been impressed with the many and varied ways in which administrators, teachers, and curriculum committees can translate state and local mandates into definitions of schoolwork as work—and boring work at that. On occasion, we have also been excited to see how the same externally imposed guidelines and expectations can be expressed as an opportunity for growth, as something fun and interesting and worth doing in its own right. Take the teaching of science, for example. Those who have spent some time observing science classrooms are aware that much of the teaching there boils down to developing a vocabulary. The predominant task set for students is memorizing, recalling, and reciting. Few would claim that this is very enjoyable for students. It is purely and simply *work,* something done for extrinsic reasons, such as retaining one's weekly allowance. Of course, many voices are calling for and putting into place a very different form of science instruction. Some of this occurs under the label of "project-based science" in which an attempt is made to have students engage in authentic tasks as authentic participants. The focus of the learning is on something that is meaningful to students, perhaps some facet of their own health or something about the environment. But most important, full advantage is taken of the fact that students are indeed captivated by the knowledge-building process, by making sense of their world. Creating sense out of nonsense is naturally not only "fun" but is in fact its own reward. It can be and is readily defined not as "work" but as "fun" even though it leads to learning something that has broad and continuing significance for making one's way in the world—next semester as well as into the next decade.

Most educators are aware of such approaches to making school tasks meaningful. Many would like to introduce them into their schools and classrooms but find it difficult to do so except perhaps in a piecemeal fashion. Unfortunately, introducing something like project-based science instruction often comes up against the strictures and constraints of school, district, and other operative policy (for example, McCaslin & Good, 1992). In support of this perception, teachers will cite example after example of rules they must follow, starting with the expectation that they must not only cover certain material but use a specific text. An exploratory approach to science is likely to come into conflict with rules about field trips and instruction outside the school grounds as well as the school schedule.

The design of school tasks and their meaning for children is affected by policy choices. Legislation foisted on schools by external groups cannot be disregarded, of course. But it is at the school level where broad mandates and general guidelines are translated into action. Legislatures, policy boards, and central administration officials may promote many policies and practices, but in the final analysis schools interpret and shape them, stress some more than others, and give greater or lesser latitude in fulfilling them. In particular, the interpretation of school activities in task or ability goal terms is not only possible but likely to occur at the school level, however the mandates on high may read. It is as leadership and staff set out to make school meaningful to students, to motivate them to learn, that they also make critical decisions about the specific tasks students should be asked to do. Are they going to force students to work methodically through a district-approved text or define the text as a sourcebook and choose and adapt activities that are meaningful for their students? Teachers typically make these choices. They can be facilitated or inhibited in making this or that choice by policies, practices, norms, and expectations that have a salient and daily presence in their school. What does the principal expect, allow, or encourage? What do colleagues do and value? What does the structure of organization allow?

Evaluation

Even when the task is interesting or attractive for its own sake, there are things that can be done to subvert the joy of learning, the natural inclination to invest in adaptive engagement. Among these, evaluation must be listed as primary. By evaluation we refer generally to the wide array of processes and means by which what is done is appraised. Teachers "grade" papers; schools administer tests that evaluate levels of performance. Critics assess the worth of a product. Evaluation is naturally and necessarily a part of the schooling process. But choices about *what* is evaluated as well as *how* serve to define the purpose and meaning of school for the student. Indeed, there is probably no facet of school life that stands out as more important in determining a task versus an ability goal orientation than evaluation policy and practice.

By choosing *what* is evaluated, school leadership and staff make clear statements regarding what school is really about. The regular assessment of student knowledge of science and math certainly points to the value placed on these areas. If a history teacher regularly includes many test items on dates and places, she is likely to convey the idea that history is about dates and places. Less obvious perhaps is how evaluation may define schooling as a process that is concerned with learning as opposed to selecting and sorting. Thus, schools may focus on general achievement outcomes, ignoring the levels of competence students bring to the situation.

But it is not only what is evaluated that is important but *how* it occurs. Over the years, the literature surrounding the negative effects of evaluation has been substantial. This literature has done much to confirm what many teachers have always felt in their hearts: Evaluation holds the strong potential of making children anxious and thereby reduces their performance levels. And certain children are likely to be more anxious than others (Hill, 1984; Hill & Wigfield, 1984; Covington, 1992). An emphasis on "objective" tests graded "on the curve" is known to enhance test anxiety and fear of failure and in many cases seriously underestimate the level of learning a student has reached. The introduction of portfolio assessment, on the other hand, appears to be a promising way in which students think less about "measuring up" and more about "progress along a path" (Moss et al., 1992). It is perhaps one of the better ways in which teachers can specify rather concretely that school is about learning and not just performing. Moreover, such individualized and progress-oriented approaches to assessment and evaluation will not so readily breed social comparisons that are endemic to typical assessment procedures: "Guess who did the best in the class?" "Look who got them all right." "Some of you simply didn't get it." (Paris, Lawton, Turner, & Roth, 1991).

Although we have illustrated our points by calling attention to testing practices in the main, it should be obvious that grading practices and the recognition that may be accorded for competitive performance can eventuate in similar, problematic effects. What and how we assess and evaluate affects how the student comes to understand school. Indeed, these policies and practices are among the most crucial for determining whether school is essentially a contest where there are winners or losers or a place where all can belong, participate, and benefit, a place that above all fosters the continuing investment in learning.

Rewards and Recognition

It is virtually impossible, of course, to separate the evaluation process from practices and policies of recognizing and rewarding students. Common sense and behaviorism have led many educators to believe that motivation for learning depends on the receiving of rewards, including rewards that are extrinsic to simply engaging in the task, discovering something, coming to new understandings, or developing a skill. It is still widely assumed that when children "get the right answers" they ought to be praised by the teacher and given an award of some kind. Even teachers who are philosophically committed to making learning interesting and fun for children at times find themselves adding an extra bonus that is extrinsic to the task— irrelevant to learning at best, detrimental at worst. This issue needs to be examined. Closely related is the form that reward often takes in a group setting, namely the social recognition and approval that is conveyed and the attention that is given.

It is common for schools to single out individuals for attention, perhaps as examples to others, sometimes simply to "reward" them. Inevitably, recognition defines and publicizes the values of the school, not only to students but to other constituencies as well. When a whole evening of festivities is devoted to recognizing the performance of athletes and the activities of the science club are noted only briefly in a few clippings tacked in a corner of an isolated bulletin board, a statement about values, purpose, and mission is there for all to read. Organizational theorists have made a point of emphasizing the symbolic value of recognition in reflecting the mission of an organization and subsequently urged leaders to take specific note of how they recognize as well as for what (for example, Deal and Kennedy, 1982). And in any event it is evident that the distribution of rewards (and sometimes punishment) as well as the use of recognition has been and continues to be perceived as a major mechanism for fostering a motivation for learning. As already implied, however, there are problems associated with the use of recognition and rewards. How they are used is likely to be a major factor in how the purpose of schooling is set forth.

And, of course, prior to initiating our collaborative effort we were aware of a large literature on this topic. That literature raises serious questions about reward and recognition practices common to schools and all too often depended upon by teachers (Csikszentmihalyi & Nakamura, 1989; Lepper & Hodell, 1989; Deci & Ryan, 1992; Fink, Boggiamo, & Barrett, 1990). It is not just that extrinsic rewards in and of themselves are so bad that they must never be used (for example, Lepper, Keavney, & Drake, in press). Rather, it is the fact that the use of extrinsic rewards and punishment to foster learning often carries extra baggage with it that can subvert the learning process. When the teacher feels constrained to give children a treat after having accomplished a task, it may imply that the learning itself cannot be a positive experience; it is only worth doing when it leads to an external reward. To adopt and paraphrase an apt expression coined by Mark Lepper and his colleagues (for example, Lepper & Greene, 1978), learning becomes work; something that must be paid for; something for which the motivation will be commensurate to the amount of the payment. One should not have to tell educators that learning is not exactly like work. Anyone deeply engaged in learning knows the intrinsic enjoyment that can be there in discovery and in the development of new knowledge and skills. One should not have to remind educators that the pursuit of knowledge will not predictably and invariably lead to large extrinsic rewards. But above all, we were well prepared at the outset to view an emphasis on extrinsic rewards and social recognition as problematic.

Thus, in searching for the sources of classroom or school culture, we were prepared to look closely at the reward and recognition systems in place. What is being rewarded and recognized? Who is being rewarded? Why is recognition and reward given? Through it all, the fundamental issue is what, through rewards and recognition, may be conveyed to students about schooling. It is as natural as anything for a teacher to express joy when a student does something that she likes and wants. Maybe that joy is expressed in a hug, in a smiling face, or even a special pleasure. Schools, like most organizations, are inclined to celebrate what they like to see happening. These celebrations inevitably involve reward and recognition. Is this bad? Not necessarily. The issue is the message that recognition, reward, and celebration carries.

Freedom, Autonomy, and Responsibility

The roles of freedom and choice in child rearing and education have been debated over the centuries. As we write these words, it remains a matter of singular significance in schools that are seemingly out of control. The increase of violence within school walls has almost replaced the reports of achievement scores in the popular media. Discussions of what is to be done range from the sublime to the ridiculous, from turning schools into what are essentially prisons through somewhat more modest proposals for increasing sanctions for violent acts, to worries regarding the effects of reduction of student freedom on development as responsible citizens.

Certainly, the objective of providing a safe and orderly environment (often written into the mission statement of schools) is not to be denied. Learning cannot effectively proceed where order, decency, civility and respect for others are absent. One has to feel safe in order to give thought to ideas, to concentrate on the development of skills, and to gain an appreciation of ways of expressing oneself in music, art, and writing. One cannot therefore argue with a first objective of many administrators to make the hallways safe, the classrooms free from fear, and each child a protected and valued member of a school community. One cannot argue with teachers who try to maintain order in their classrooms. Pandemonium is not a notable contributor to intellectual growth.

However, we were aware at the outset that policies and practices designed to provide safe and orderly environments can all too easily drift into becoming mechanisms of control for control's sake, reaching far beyond the preparatory role they were meant to serve. An emphasis on external control can subvert learning, perhaps by making it a task to be done for the sake of others or for other than learning reasons. About thirty years ago, the clinician and personality theorist Carl Rogers was noted for stressing the value of "freedom for learning" (1969). More recently, this point has been updated and the principles clarified by motivational researchers (for example, Deci & Ryan, 1985). One doesn't encourage intrinsic interest in learning when the experience is totally in the hands of others. The notion of learning as personally relevant, meaningful, and worth pursuing in its own right is hardly fostered when one engages in the process (almost literally) under a gun.

Organizing Students into Classes and Groups

The practices and policies grouping students have often been debated and recently subjected to special scrutiny (for example, Cohen, 1994; Qin, Johnson, & Johnson, 1995; Oakes, 1992; Gutierrez & Slavin, 1992). There are many facets to this issue just as there are in the case of each of the potential pressure points for school change that we initially considered. However, we suspected that grouping policy or practice might contribute in a special way to how the purpose and goals of schools were defined to students. Several examples came to us as we contemplated this potential.

Grouping students according to abilities is likely to suggest that relative ability is important. It may imply that the school is about selecting for and rewarding ability. The reasons for organizing children into ability groups that are often given stress desirable instructional goals. The evidence does not really justify this (for example, Oakes, 1992). Some teachers readily admit that the main reason is ease of instruction and that too may be justified. But in any event, the grouping of students into ability levels presents many hazards. In particular, it most often serves to reinforce the idea that school is concerned more with establishing ability hierarchies than fostering the personal and intellectual development of all students.

We also considered yet another facet of grouping. Placing students into forty- to fifty-minute classes for six or more periods a day is bound to put limitations on the tasks that can be done and therewith the definition of learning that will ensue. We have been impressed with how organizing teachers into teams and students into "small schools" at, for example, the middle school level has opened up new possibilities for instruction: interdisciplinary experiments and greater emphasis on contextualized learning and on relating what is done in one domain to that in another (thematic instruction) to name but a few. Many of these programmatic options have real potential for making learning meaningful and for defining it not just as a job to be done but as something interesting and worthy in its own right. In short, at the outset there was reason to expect that such approaches would serve to enhance a task goal stress.

It is also worth noting that typically as students are grouped, different resources are assigned. Consider a specific example in this regard. We have often observed that computer usage is not broadly distributed across classrooms nor equally available to all students. *Who* gets to use the computers and *for what* may effectively state what the school thinks about who can achieve and what that achievement is worth. Similarly, project-based science may be reserved for those in the "advanced" groups. Again, there is a message here. All children can presumably profit from seeing the relevance of science and technology in their daily lives. Opportunities to use science in the course of learning science should not be the province of an elite few if learning, not just competitive performance, is the preeminent goal of the school.

And so, we were immediately sensitive to the existence of school, classroom, and sometimes district-level policies (and practices) that generally had something to do with organizing students (and teachers) into groups.

Scheduling

As we reviewed issues of organization and grouping, we incidentally alluded to the matter of scheduling. It is difficult not to consider time when one thinks of ways in which the school is organized. Yet the important role of time and scheduling in framing purpose is seldom considered seriously. It dare not be ignored, however, if one wants to initiate educational change. It is potentially a primary pressure point for effecting culture change, particularly at the secondary level. Our examples may prime the reader to think of how issues of time impact both educational change and learning and schooling.

There are few things that are so inflexibly managed in the schools as schedules. Science teachers who wish to engage students in challenging projects quickly learn that the forty- or fifty-minute hour may interrupt activities at the point of real insight. The first part of the period (say ten minutes or so) has to be devoted to setting up the experiment as well as the usual housekeeping chores of checking on assignments and taking attendance. Only then can the real work of the day begin. There is perhaps thirty minutes left to conduct a particular experiment before students have to gather their materials and clean up. What this means is that often such experiments have to be preprogrammed, which is not all bad. Often they don't become the students' experiments but the teacher's illustrations. This too may have its place. But the primary issue is that it is difficult within the confines of a fifty-minute period to involve students thoroughly in *doing* science. As a result, many students do not really develop a thorough appreciation of the methods of science or acquire much if any knowledge about the processes through which it is conducted. It is just another "book" subject, characterized by words, formulae, and applications to memorize.

Science can justifiably relate to observing nature *outside* the classroom. If a teacher wishes to move instruction beyond school walls to a museum or to a garden on the edge of the school grounds, he will be bound by scheduling policies, sometimes to a forbidding degree. Such forays are likely to involve more than forty or fifty minutes and will impinge on the instruction in another area, creating a whole new set of problems. Students may have to miss band, football practice, or another class or two. Of course, there are bound to be school policies regarding how many field trips can be taken, constraints over where they will be taken, and with the ubiquitous forms to sign and letters to send out. It is almost always a hassle to go against the regular forty- to fifty-minute class. But of course, the limitations and constraints that scheduling presents not only inhibit what can and will be done, they will also shape or reshape the definition of the task to be done—the critically important issue. In brief, scheduling inevitably affects the nature of tasks that will be presented to students. It is, therefore, bound to contribute to a task or ability goal emphasis.

Our examples probably seem more relevant to secondary than elementary education. Superficially, it seems that elementary teachers are not faced with the same types of time constraints in their own self-contained classrooms. Perhaps. However, "special" classes and schoolwide assemblies can and often do intrude. Moreover, we have been struck by how many elementary classrooms have a fixed schedule posted on the front board. 9:00–9:42 reading, 9:45–10:30 math, and so forth. We suspect that this scheduling and its display has been encouraged by principals and school policy. Sometimes it is there to inform and impress parents that the teacher has a sense of organization. But rigidly followed, it may eventuate in some of the same effects in framing instruction to which we alluded in discussing secondary school teaching of science. In any event, one wonders how seriously the schedule is taken. Can one break it, for example, when the students are deeply engaged and excited about solving a problem, conducting an experiment, or completing a drawing?

Now we come to a fundamental point. Scheduling and the use of time is a matter of policy—usually school policy. Changing science instruction cannot be done solely by training teachers differently. Giving teachers a dose of project-based science teaching methods may whet their appetites, enhance their knowledge and skills, but the school policy on time and scheduling can still constrain and prevent anything really new from happening. We have sat in on too many meetings where instructional innovations have been seriously considered, only to be "shot down" by the argument that it simply couldn't be worked out in the schedule. Anyone who has taught, administered, or worked in the schools knows exactly what we mean. The use of time and how we schedule something is a basic entry point for making school change. It must not be considered a given, something ineluctably determined by bus schedules or district and state mandates, although these doubtless play some role. It is also a variable to be manipulated at the school level and ultimately at the classroom level as a factor that can contribute to a changed view of what schooling and learning are about.

Resources

There is also the matter of resources. Not a demand for more, but a recognition that the distribution and use of available resources must follow and underwrite the policy made and acted upon under the preceding areas.

We began this effort with the strong belief that the problem of schools is not just (or primarily) lack of resources. It lies in how these resources are distributed and exploited. In our experience, a form of equitable distribution is usually attempted. In one sense, it is hard to argue against the equal distribution across classrooms and teachers except it turns out that it never is quite equal. Some get computers, others do not. Maybe everyone gets to go to at least one "current educational technology" workshop and a few can manage to attend a special conference or two. Searching through what most schools do, one can only conclude that discretionary resources are not large but they exist. They can be used in ways that support a particular school mission or scattered about in a way that confuses or dissipates any statement about the purpose and meaning of schools and schooling. One should not attempt significant school culture change without also agreeing to substantially redirect whatever resources are available to support this change.

Workshops attended and materials purchased should be compatible with fostering the emergence of task versus ability goals.

The point, while simple, deserves repeating and merits the most serious reflection: Lofty mission statements mean little if the worthy thoughts, goals, hopes, and aspirations contained therein do not lead to action. Some of this action is associated directly with the preceding categories. Some must involve the distribution of resources—"putting one's money where one's mouth is." Even in the most centralized districts, schools have money to spend. Many schools have been specifically granted "school improvement money"; however, these resources are used in a variety of ways. Often resource allocation follows the equity rule: every program, staff member, or proposal put forward gets something, maybe even the same amount. That may keep the peace, but if the change we envision is to take place, resources must be targeted specifically at supporting the vision. The distribution and use of whatever resources are available must be related actually and symbolically to the objectives of creating a task-focused environment, even if that means breaking the equity funding rule.

Conclusion

There are a number of different areas in which policy is made at the school level by teachers individually, the staff as a whole, or principals. Collectively, policies make the school what it is and are crucial in creating what it can be. The policies are interwoven like a Persian carpet. Yet each policy represents a potentially important entry point for action. Is there something that can be done at the school level to frame a particular vision of school that will make a difference in the learning, growth, and development of students? Of course! We have given a few examples of decisions that can and will be made and which should be taken seriously. Maybe no single decision in any one of these areas is critical, but as action is taken in each of these areas in line with a task focus theme, a task focus culture is likely to evolve.

How Does One Realize Sustainable Change?

Identifying pressure points for school change does not in and of itself ensure substantive and sustainable school change. Policies and practices must be *changed!* That will not happen automatically. Even knowing what to do does not ensure that something will be done. Those who have tried to change the course and direction of a school, or just one or another feature, know that well. Achieving sustainable school change is a complex challenge, something sought with more hope than certainty. Commission reports, as well as professional journals and the popular media, regularly give us examples of the failure of efforts to change schools. Nevertheless, we ventured forth in the fond hope that the quest would not prove futile. To prepare ourselves, we reviewed the change literature. We reflected on our own experiences and consulted experts. We expected to count on the special knowledge that our school-based collaborators would bring to the task. As we distilled our thoughts, we found ourselves being guided by three major principles

System Change

There is a widely accepted truism that you can't have effective education without good teachers and teaching. It is, however, a half-truth. It implies that school change is a simple matter of getting the right teachers to do the right things. Sometimes, this half-truth has encouraged educators and policy makers to promise that pouring money into teacher education, credentialling, or assessment programs will save American education. As we argued earlier, it hasn't and it won't. Some who have questioned the personnel approach to educational change have often gone no further than focusing on getting the right materials to schools and into the hands of teachers, even arguing for a "teacher-proof" curriculum, an option that seems curiously out of place. The whole thrust of this book is that teachers, curriculum, students, leaders, and parents cannot be treated as readily separable components in effecting school change. The stress on school culture suggests a system approach to change, that one must deal with what happens in teaching and learning as part of an interlocking process involving the participation of multiple actors bound together for specifiable purposes. Since systems may exist on a continuum ranging from the microcosmic to the macrocosmic, one has to make some choices. Somewhat arbitrarily and without question based on a very American experience of educational change in recent years, we chose the individual school as the best place to begin. One probably should not go much smaller than that and reaching for all-encompassing change may prove overwhelming. In any event, the individual school became our focus. Our line of reasoning went something like this.

Working solely or primarily with individual teachers, often in isolation from their colleagues as is often the case in special workshops and programs of teacher continuing education and instructional enhancement, may serve to improve what happens in one classroom—for a time. However, major changes cannot be made without impacting the rest of the life of the school. When, for example, a whole language approach is introduced in kindergarten, it will affect the lives and efforts of 1st and later grade teachers (and their students) as well. Initially, it may just unnerve colleagues. But doing this in kindergarten and not in later grades will, to say the very least, unnerve students (and their parents). Moreover, any such innovation as whole language instruction can hardly be done without the blessing of school leadership and some redistribution of resources. More specifically in line with introducing our own vision of schooling, it seemed impossible to think of confining a goal theory approach to classroom instruction in 7th grade science, while forgetting that following 7th grade science, the student must enter the ability-dominated world of, for example, a math teacher. The kind of changes we proposed to pursue involved more than what happens to individual classrooms. Indeed, anyone who regularly visits schools will realize that school at any educational level is not just a collection of individual classrooms. Teachers at times may act and feel as if they each exist within their own little one room schoolhouse, but this is hardly the case. There is the hallway where important transactions take place. There are field trips and trips to the principal's office; athletic and playground events. The student's experience of school most certainly involves what teachers do in classrooms but also a lot more as well.

Obviously, there are policies that relate especially to some parts of the organization, such as kindergarten classrooms, more than others. Some policies are schoolwide in applicability but are likely to be translated into different forms in individual classrooms. In our early work we concentrated first on policies at the classroom level that the teacher seemed to follow in guiding the ebb and flow of events of the classroom following an example set by Carole Ames (1990). However, we found as did she that schoolwide policies often intrude on what can be done at the classroom level. In a number of instances it became dramatically evident to us that what happened in the classroom was not easily separable from school policies and practices. As we worked with classroom teachers to provide recognition on the basis of progress, improvement, and effort, teachers pointed out to us that recognition at the school level was often based on relative ability (school honor rolls, for example). In one school, the teachers were developing and employing classroom strategies that minimized social competition and extrinsic rewards for output, stressing progress in accomplishing individualized student goals. As this effort was being undertaken, the principal announced that the school would participate in the Pizza Hut program. This well-meaning effort rewards students—with pizza, no less—for the number of books they read. Students compete with each other, recognition is on the basis of relative ability, and the difficulty or challenge inherent in the task is ignored. The teachers were unhappy about this, of course. They saw it as undercutting their efforts—and they were right. Unfortunately, this is not an isolated example of what happens in schools. What is done by teachers in the classroom may be undermined at the school level. Schoolwide policies and actions invariably insert themselves into what is and can be done by teachers in the presumed isolation of their room.

In addition to recognizing that one has to work with the whole as well as parts of the whole, there are questions about how this can be approached. Ames and Ames (1993) described an approach that begins with teachers and the management policies they use to carry out instruction. It does not stop there, however. As they focus on classroom concerns, they support the inevitable need to confront schoolwide issues. This initiates a larger concern with the system as a whole and a sharing of concerns and ideas and the formulation of wider policy. This might be described as a kind of "bottom-up approach."

Alternatively, our work began with a "school leadership team" that included a principal or assistant principal and teachers who had been appointed (prior to our effort) to initiate plans for enhancing the effectiveness of the school. Such school leadership teams are, of course, not uncommon. Typically, they represent a broad segment of the faculty and are authorized to make recommendations but have little formal power beyond that. Sometimes they serve as missionaries for a given course of action. They can, of course, serve as inhibitors of change. The advantage of working with a team is that one begins with a small group while retaining a schoolwide focus. The advantage of beginning directly with individual teachers who want to change what they do in the classroom is that one is dealing with the immediacies of their life. Many teachers may approach schoolwide issues as an abstraction of little relevance. They may worry about seeming to restrict the freedom of teachers in carrying out their designated duties. The fact of the matter is, regardless of the entry point so far as working groups are concerned, one has to deal with schoolwide issues and treat them as relevant to what goes on in the classroom. Abstract discussions of school policy are likely to go nowhere. But there are issues that touch significantly on issues at the classroom level that can only be handled at the school level.

A Shared Theory of School

Our second operating principle was that sustainable school change is fostered by an integrating rationale for change. More specifically, we believed that school change in particular, and the operations of schools in general, should be guided by a "theory of school." There needs to be some set of shared understandings about the purpose of schools, the nature of the tasks to be done, and the means for doing them.

The Nature and Function of Theory

The notion that effective school functioning as well as school change involves some degree of shared understanding and acceptance of purpose is common. Susan Rosenholz (1985), for example, argued persuasively that a shared perspective and a degree of cohesiveness built around that perspective is at the heart of "effective schools." We accepted that basic principle but by explicitly using the term "theory" implied something more.

The Public Nature of Understandings

Individuals, groups, and organizations always hold and operate in terms of assumptions, beliefs, goals, and values. In using the term theory we wanted to suggest that the vision for school, whatever it might be, should be articulated, objectified, and subjected to some degree of testing and verification in a public arena. It isn't enough for one teacher or one principal to present a "vision" that is not objectifiable and testable. Responding "I just know this works" is not sufficient whether or not it is based on one or twenty years' professional experience. Public evidence, shareable and testable by all those who wish to put forth the effort, must be an explicit objective. So we based our effort on a particular theory.

The theory was informed by an accumulating body of empirical evidence. But it could and would be tested and refined further in the course of a collaborative school change effort. The concrete and objectifiable nature of the theory—its public nature—made it not only a target to shoot at, criticize, and argue about but a basis for generating specific concrete hypotheses regarding what should work to enhance task goals in the school

Definition of Means and Ends

A theory is concerned with causes and effects, means and ends. A theory of education must also accept, propose, and define objectives and outcomes and delineate possibilities regarding how they can be attained or achieved. Most of the argument about education seems to be about means: What textbooks should we choose? Should we initiate whole language methods? What about "math their way"? Who should run the school? How much time should be devoted to this or that? The means, the methods, the tactics, the strategies, and the resources to be applied in instruction are indeed important. However, choices here are determined and inevitably framed by the purposes that are adopted. Indeed, much of the futile argument over methods could be invigorated if underlying assumptions about purposes were first considered. In any event, we assumed that a theory of school was not only desirably but necessarily based on a definition of purpose.

A Framework for Talk, Action, and Understanding

Theory provides a basis for dialogue, action, and evaluation. Certainly no theory currently available provides the answers to each and every question of importance in the practice of education. It serves as a heuristic, a generator of hypotheses, a raiser of questions, perhaps occasionally a guide. Equally important, it provides the framework and language for discussion and shared planning within an organizational setting. Many, probably most, analyses of the state of the nation's schools call attention to the importance of an intellectual cohesiveness in creating an effective school. That is to say, the leadership and staff must be able to talk to each other, to plan, to share aspirations and goals, as well as understand from where the other is coming.

There are, of course, multiple "theories" of school. Arguably, each teacher, each parent, and each child approaches schooling with something like a theory. There are many formalized and widely shared theories of education and schooling available. One theory of school is embodied in the whole language approach to literacy education. A Montessori or a Dewey school has a different theory. Each book that suggests how schools should be reformed has a different theory. And, of course, we also have outlined a theory of school. But in no sense do we wish to imply that *any* theory of school will do. Rather, by using the term theory we stress that in confronting practice, educators do well to operate in terms of the best synthesis of knowledge available and applicable to their concerns. This knowledge can and must include the perspectives and experiences of practitioners as well as researchers. But it should be a product of tested and testable knowledge. As a product of *tested* knowledge, it should provide more than the "experiences" of a few; rather it must convey the replicated understandings of many. Even more important, it must remain an unfinished work; that is, it must be stated in such a way that others—practitioners as well as researchers—can test it, reject it, or improve it. In the final analysis, theory serves not just to summarize what we know or think we know at a certain point in time, but it enables us to grow in understanding and practice. Good theory makes it possible for the practitioner to improve on the work of the theorist.

Leadership Initiative

There has to be some impetus for change if change is to occur. There has to be some convergence of interest, belief, and value. For any change to last, the actions taken have to be nurtured and supported. We often think of "leadership" when we talk of sustainable school change, and it seems appropriate to introduce that point as we present an overall picture of what school change might entail.

Consideration of organizational change in general, as well as school change in particular, has regularly brought up the issue of leadership (Leithwood, 1994; Murphy & Seashore-Louis, 1994). People are usually found to be at the heart of change: what it will be, how or when it will get started, whether or the degree to which it will be supported. Although we will return to this important issue later, there are several points we wish to introduce now.

Formal and Informal Leadership Roles

Within any group some individuals have more power; these people tend to influence others more than they are influenced by them. Perhaps these individuals command certain resources, such as expertise, the ability to communicate and persuade, access to salient networks and support systems. Leaders emerge for different reasons and through different processes (for example, Hunt, 1991; Yukl, 1989). In schools, administrators are the formally designated leaders and they indeed have certain special responsibilities for making the school work. With these responsibilities comes authority to hire, evaluate, and reward other school staff. Administrators have a degree of control over resources: money to disperse and privileges to give (for example, nominating or selecting certain staff members for attendance at workshops, conferences or other special events). By virtue of a certain knowledge as well as assigned authority given to them, they have considerable influence over schedules and schoolwide events and activities. They can impede the introduction of this or that curricular change, maybe even stop it. In some cases, they can initiate, support, and nourish change. Administrators such as a building principal rarely do these things without the support, shared interest, and initiative of a number of other staff members who play what are often termed "informal" leadership roles. Leadership exists in many quarters of a school, but it is the potential for leadership that exists in the role of principal that is of special significance in bringing about school culture change.

Of course, simply being appointed to a principalship does not make one a leader in the sense that she will act effectively to transform school culture. But we believed at the outset that it would probably be impossible for schoolwide change to occur if the person who sits in the principal's chair wished to block it. Teachers and other staff members are not in a position to command resources housed in the school budget and do not usually have entree to upper administration or a network of policy makers in district and state offices. The leadership of teachers most often resides in the persuasiveness of their ideas and the respect they are accorded for their expertise. It is certainly important but different than the leadership role that can and must be played by the principal. That leadership may be exercised in a variety of ways, but it must be supportive of the course of change. The principal need not lead the parade, but she had better join it!

In many cases, "transformational leadership"(Bass, 1985; Howell & Avolio, 1993; Leithwood, 1994; Sashkin, 1988) and "venturesomeness" on the part of those in leadership roles (VanderStoep, Anderman, & Midgley, 1994) are needed. This is especially true in moving from a school that heavily stresses ability goals to one that stresses task goals. But for such important and dramatic changes to be made and sustained, it is clear that more than one person or one office or locus within the organization must be involved. Although the role of principal is critical in the culture change equation, we also recognized it as just one source of leadership for changing and sustaining a facilitative school culture. The crucial role of leadership in realizing our vision of school was fundamental in our thinking from the outset.

A Role for University Collaborators

These four guidelines were uppermost in our minds as we looked at the school, its leadership, and its staff. But this was to be a collaborative effort. What role would and should we (the University of Michigan team) play vis-à-vis the school leadership and staff? The literature on the role of change agents and organizational development specialists is voluminous. Currently, there is a running dialogue on how school-university relationships should be pursued. We were probably influenced by that literature more than we were aware as we initially considered our role. On the one hand, our mere presence reinforced latent motives to do something. If not the agent of change, we were certainly seen as the occasion for change We also brought in many of the ingredients for change such as new perspectives and a penchant for questioning what and why things were done. However, there is no real coherent way to describe how we thought of ourselves at the outset. One analogy that came up in our discussions was that we were like psychological counselors. We did a certain amount of diagnosis. We obviously brought a vision of what the school might be, and we saw ourselves as gently prodding and probing to stimulate the realization of that vision in the targeted schools. But the vision we brought was and had to be elaborated on by the school staff. The action had to be taken by the staff and they had to decide, act, explain, and be responsible for whatever course was followed. The policies and practices of the two schools targeted for change were by no means under the control of the university team. At best, we could suggest options to pursue and comment on the implications of taking one or another course of action. We were prepared to provide evaluative information regarding how changes might be influencing students. At times we probably were used to justify action to the central office and the school board. So what role did we really play? Not a simple one, as succeeding chapters will reveal.

Conclusion

We began this chapter with the words of Edgar Schein, a scholar of note who has had a distinguished career studying organizations and reflecting on change. His words deserve the attention of any who wish to reform schools. His words were comforting to us as we launched our uncertain effort. We wondered frequently about the possibility of initiating school change as fundamental and pervasive as we have proposed. Can school cultures be changed? More directly, could we expect schools to move willingly and effectively from an emphasis on ability goals to an overarching concern with task goals? There is first the hurdle of reaching agreement that a task-focused vision of school is worth the investment.

Inevitably, there were members of the school staff who held theories of learning and schooling alien to our vision of school. We were not so naive to think that everyone would quickly reject social competition and comparison as valid within a learning context. And rewarding some and punishing others in terms of the products they produce instead of the progress they exhibit is broadly accepted. Inevitably, there were those who tacitly assumed that learning is dull at worst, hard work at best, and must therefore be motivated by extrinsic rewards (Kohn, 1993). In sum, we were likely to confront a range of implicit, though probably not critically examined, theories of motivation that were diametrically opposed to ours. What made us think that our vision of school could and would be accepted and acted upon within a few short years of discussion and dialogue?

As if this were not enough, there was simply the problem of change per se. Change of any type is not easy to bring about, let alone the culture change we sought. After all, schools are complex organizations, composed of intelligent and sometimes very independent professionals, influenced by outside political and economic forces. The thought of "transforming" let alone changing school cultures assumes that somehow some of the actors within the system can, as it were, get outside the system a bit and act on it instead of just reacting to it. That requires reflection and a high degree of insight and focused effort at the very least. And there were numerous other factors that came to our mind that might sidetrack if not demolish the process.

Nevertheless, we proceeded, armed with a belief that we could ultimately frame our outline of a vision for school into a practical and valid reality. We had a few guidelines, a little knowledge, some experience, and a committed cadre of administrators and teachers who took the risk with us and made a commitment that must have been much harder and more courageous than ours. To that saga of hope, effort, frustration, some success, some outright failure, and much dedication and courage, we now turn.

Notes

1. In this regard we note our indebtedness to the U.S. Department of Education (OERI) and two grants: R215A00430 and R117C80003.

6 A Story of Riversedge: Recreating the Magic of Learning

Well, can we do this or not?

—A 1st grade teacher confronting the principal regarding
the first proposal for change

What really happens when one attempts to rectify the vision of schooling in a specific school at a specific time and place? To be sure, the vision of schooling we have portrayed thus far was built up out of countless hours of working in school settings—by us and many others. Yet, none have actually attempted to transform the culture of a school along the lines called for by our vision. So it was that we decided to initiate a bold experiment. Actually, two experiments. With the necessary support of willing funders and a cooperative school district and school leadership and staff, we began an effort that gave all our previous work special meaning and value. "We" is not used casually or with pretended modesty, for the work was a complex collaboration of persons with diverse skills, interests, and motives. In addition to the absolute necessity of willing schools and two University of Michigan researchers who were able to find money to partially underwrite the effort, there were the resources of (then) graduate and undergraduate students who not only were intrigued with the idea but were open and quick learners and talented young minds on their way to becoming professionals in their own right. What this diverse collection of talent held in common above all else was a commitment to school reform and to

135

the goal of determining how the personal investment of children in learning could be enhanced. What ensued was not only a bold experiment but a necessary one. In order to inform practicing educators on their way toward enhancing the task focus of schools, we had to learn not only what should but also what could be changed. We had to learn more about how schools go about defining their purposes. We had to learn more about the hurdles and pitfalls involved in rethinking these purposes. In the process we also learned something about the applicability and validity of the vision that could not have been learned in any other way.

In this and the next chapter we present a "thick description" of an elementary school and a middle school in the course of considering whether and how to adopt the vision of school presented in Chapter 2. We begin, then, with the fictitiously named Riversedge School, a real school facing some of the harshest realities schools today face.

Setting the Scene

Riversedge served children from kindergarten through grade 5. It was known throughout the district as the elementary school with the most "problem" children. Nearly half of the total student population of 485 received free or reduced-fee lunches. The principal, Mrs. T., had been at the school for twelve years and was by most accounts a dynamic and sensitive leader. Teachers called her by her first name, and she respected their ideas and encouraged their input but was very much in charge. During our first year of collaboration, there were two kindergarten teachers; four 1st grade teachers; three 2nd, 3rd, and 4th grade teachers; and two 5th grade teachers. There were also physical education, music, art, and special needs teachers. Riversedge was a primary feeder to the middle school selected for study.

It was evident to us at the outset that before we arrived there was already a strong awareness that something different had to be done, although there was a struggle to define "different." Indeed, this probably figured into their decision to invite us to initiate the discussion that culminated in a partnership. Initially at least, school leadership and staff were prone to express their expectation that our major contribution might not just be university "wisdom" but money as well. That was not a major part of our plan, of course, and it became increasingly clear to everyone that the problems faced by Riversedge would not be solved simply by extra money.

In our initial meetings, school leadership and staff expressed concern about student motivation (or lack thereof), discipline, student safety and well-being, lack of parental involvement, and of course, financial limitations. School staff had been working on solutions and many different ventures to improve the state of affairs. Special "self-esteem days" had been established in hopes of expanding students' horizons, showing them options that might be available, giving them new experiences, and enhancing their self-esteem. They made regular use of "motivational speakers," often individuals who described how they had overcome handicaps and achieved a full and satisfying life.

The Process

We entered this collaboration with some essential conceptions of how school-university collaborations could and should work (Chapter 5). We had a basic outline of what needed to be changed to enhance task goals as well as some notions of processes, although not as clear as they eventually became. This flexible framework served as a point of embarkment for our venture. The processes changed as our relationship with the school evolved and as we learned.

Our experiences yielded an enhanced conception of how collaboration might proceed. There were several obvious biases that guided our efforts initially and, though in somewhat revised form, figured strongly in our work to the end. Generally, we saw collaboration as just that, multiple individuals, perhaps in this case reasonably defined as two different groups, bringing separate biases, strengths, and weaknesses to the table. In an important sense, the school staff and leadership had the power to decide and to act. It was their school and they had to live with the results. Yet the university group brought something important to the collaboration as well. At the outset, we thought we provided a theoretical perspective and perhaps some expertise. Upon reflection, the theoretical perspective may have been our most important contribution, although it became that only as our school collaborators helped us fill in the details.

Since this was to be a collaborative effort, our actions had to fit the cul ture already in place when we arrived on the scene. We had to become acquainted with and respectful of the structures, processes, and values that had been operating at the school for some time. We had to try to understand why the school did what it did as we commented upon what we saw and sensed. But we did not assume that we had to remain silent and passive if and when we confronted policies and practices that appeared to be in conflict with enhancing task goals and minimizing ability goals. The fact that we entered this collaboration committed to a vision of school meant that we would not be satisfied with *any* change. We made it clear that our objective was change of a particular type. We stated and restated, clarified and amplified the essence and ramifications of the theory of school that was to guide the endeavor. This insistence on making changes in accord with a specific vision of school held potential for conflict. And conflict did occur. Fortunately, however, the parties involved not only held together but came to new understandings without sacrificing the basic principles on which the effort was based.

The story of Riversedge reflects persistence in pursuing a vision as well as dealing with the inevitable conflict. We surmise that it is representative of what might happen at any school that took our argument seriously and tried to change accordingly. Riversedge was not the best of schools; it was not the worst. From the beginning, it appeared to exhibit a degree of commitment to some form of shared or distributed leadership and teacher empowerment. At least there were structures and processes in place that signified such, and we accepted these for what they seemed to be.

Following statewide guidelines, a "school improvement team" had been appointed that seemed to be broadly representative of the staff as a whole. This team consisted of the principal, two 1st grade teachers, a 2nd grade teacher, two 4th grade teachers, and the compensatory education teacher. The team (with some change in membership) had been working together to suggest school improvements for five years. One of its proudest accomplishments was the "Wednesday folder" which was sent home to parents each week with work samples, school notices, and so forth. Parents expected that folder each Wednesday, and the teachers agreed that this had facilitated parent-school communication. The productive existence of this group provided the collaborative effort with a fitting mechanism for reaching out to all facets of the school in hope of engaging most if not all in the culture-change process. As we shall see, however, staff involvement in our effort was not universal even at the end.

Of course, one of our first tasks in the collaboration was to engage leadership and staff in a comprehensive dialogue about the definition of teaching and learning as task- or ability-oriented and what that meant in terms of policy and practice. Naturally, this would logically relate to and perhaps influence what teachers did in their individual classrooms. But we encouraged our collaborators to think about the school as a whole. After all, the child's experience of school is not just one classroom or one teacher; it is what happens in multiple places in and around the building, in the presence of and under the guidance of various actors. We continually stressed school culture much as we described it earlier, though at the time we didn't always recognize the concrete ways in which it would manifest itself.

Our school collaborators doubtless had their own expectations and biases. These were not as apparent to us at the outset, but they quickly became evident in the discussions that were the heart and soul of the effort. For example, there were two notions that were widely held by the school in spite of what was said in person or in document. First, there was an almost unshakable belief that through the university collaboration more resources would become available to the school, a belief that was to some degree confirmed, though not as fully as hoped or expected. Second, and in many ways more disconcerting to us, was the initial belief that somehow the university had a "program" that would be given to the school to put into practice. In its crudest sense, this was interpreted to mean that we would tell them what to do and they would (maybe) do it. We're not at all sure that this is what they really wanted, but it was clear that they had learned to expect this from university projects. In early conversations, school staff would ask, somewhat exasperated, "So, what do you want us to do?" It will become increasingly clear as we describe the dialogue that accompanied the ebb and flow of culture change that in the beginning we were both negotiating the terms of collaboration and confronting our respective assumptions and biases. Fortunately for the effort, we shared much early on and ultimately forged a joint working perspective; both groups changed though perhaps in slightly different ways.

It was inevitable that the major instrument for action would involve dialogue: exchanges of beliefs, attitudes, and ideas. Such dialogue ultimately occurred in many different ways, such as in casual encounters in the school office. A university person was on-site several days each week and took advantage of the opportunities for listening, learning, observing, and explaining. But all of these incidental encounters were centered in a regular weekly meeting—usually on Thursday afternoons from 4:00 to 5:15. At first the group consisted of a university "team" and the members of the Riversedge school improvement team. The university team was composed of two senior University of Michigan investigators and six graduate students. Two of these students had taught at the elementary level. During the three-year collaboration, two of the students graduated and were replaced with two other students. Four of the students were members of the team during the entire three-year period.

The agenda for the next meeting was always set by the group in attendance. The chairship alternated between members of the university and the Riversedge teams, but it became such an informal process that at times it was difficult to remember who the chair was or what the agenda had specified. The regular recording of the discussion on tape and in writing, however, was adhered to rather rigorously. Minutes based on these notes were prepared by the university team and shared with all participants. Later in the process they were also made available to the faculty as a whole.

The Ebb and Flow of the Dialogue

And so we met and met and met. Discussed. Visited. Listened to each other and to selected "experts," usually from other schools who had tried to implement various programs or innovations that were under discussion. Seldom did we call on persons from universities, at least during the first year.

Year One

During the first few meetings, we discussed the theory on which the project was based and the process that would be used to make changes. The university team essentially elaborated on the rationale for the project, which consisted of two parts. First, an outline of the motivation theory that would guide the effort (an early and briefer version of the exposition presented in Chapter 2). Second, a sketch of the complementary roles foreseen for the university and Riversedge teams: The university team was to describe theory and suggest possible implications for school change, but the Riversedge team and the school staff would be the final arbiters of what changes would be made.

Presumably, the Riversedge staff had accepted this rationale and procedure in agreeing to participate. Not surprisingly, they weren't altogether sure what this meant. The early discussion on theory seemed tedious to some at first. All had read the documents or heard the presentations. But it was when the theory was applied to policy and practice that the discussion took on meaning and at times proved problematic. The university team might have thought it understood the theory but sometimes stumbled in applying it to specific instances. Clearly, the theory had something to do with grading practices, learning materials, grouping practices, and so forth. But the university team's examples were not always apt and referred to practices that seemed remote to the Riversedge team. Occasionally at first, increasingly over time, someone from either team would stumble onto a metaphor or an example that seemed to stimulate discussion or crystallize understanding. For instance, to distinguish between a task-focused child and an ability-focused child, someone offered the example of a child coming home from school and telling her mother she had a great day because she got an A, did better than her best friend, or because she won the spelling bee. That was contrasted with a child saying she had a great day because she finally mastered long division, read a wonderful story about India, or tried to solve a really difficult problem. In discussing how one orientation or the other might influence a person's behavior, a lively discussion ensued on an apparently common educational experience: deciding not to take a course in college because it might lower one's grade point average. Many had experienced this. One teacher said, "I've always wanted to learn chemistry but I didn't take it. Wouldn't it be wonderful if we could just think about what we want to learn and not worry about how well we'll do?" That summed up much of what the university team had been struggling to sense and say not only in this instance but over the course of years of observations.

Some progress was also witnessed in the definition of the task and our roles. At the end of one meeting a teacher said, "I'm beginning to get the idea. You are helping us to think about things differently so that the children will think about them differently." Clearly this person sensed that culture change might reside in thought change. That certainly was an idea with which we entered the collaboration, but we doubt whether we could have expressed it fully and clearly up to this point in the dialogue. Even if we had, it probably would not have been something that would have become the operative principle for the working of the group. It was the insight of this teacher and the way she expressed it and similar statements by others that gave form to the relationship that was emerging.

These were examples of many positive moments of insight and progress in collaboration; but not everything was that positive, especially in the early stages of the endeavor. At a meeting shortly after these expressions of insight occurred, the university team was jolted by a rather aggressively stated complaint by one teacher, echoed to varying degree by others: "I'm tired of talking about theory and want to get on with it—to do something more concrete." This need to move quickly was a recurring theme during the first year. In this case, the agenda for the next meeting was designed to set "action alternatives." A brainstorming session was planned at which, it was hoped, needed changes could be identified. In the course of the discussion that followed over several meetings, someone from the university team suggested that it would be helpful to select one of the possible changes for extended discussion, developing it as a prototype of the kind of change that would be in accord with the theory. This was agreed to and the Riversedge staff team selected the design and operation of their educational fair as a case—not just for discussion, as it turned out, but also for action. In this way, the perspectives of the university team and the Riversedge team were both served. Moreover, a series of decisions, actions, and events followed that emerged as an important marker in the endeavor as a whole.

The education fair was similar in form and design to a science fair and in fact had once been that. Most of the displays were still science-oriented. The annual event was a major school function. Parents were strongly encouraged to help their children develop a project but not to do the work for them. Projects were judged and those deemed best were placed in the hall; the remaining projects were displayed in the classrooms. The team began by discussing the strengths and weaknesses of the fair. Teachers talked about the role of parents and noted that some parents, in spite of guidelines, did the work for their child because they wanted their child to win; other parents did not become involved in any way so some children were unable to participate. Teachers spoke about the disappointment many children experienced when they didn't win and the tendency of parents and other visitors to pay attention only to the winning projects on the night of the fair.

From the university team's perspective, the education fair provided an excellent case for prompting an examination of the rationale for the project. For the Riversedge team it very quickly became more than that, and the university team was swept along in a current of discussion aimed at direct and immediate school policy change. Questions of "What if?" became "Why not?" This was something the Riversedge team really identified with and the discussions were not only lively but electric, with sparks almost visibly evident as disagreements or frustrations or anticipated roadblocks were sensed. There were no more yawns or early departures. Collectively, we were on to something real and important. Theory was chasing practice. The Riversedge team talked about eliminating the judging and giving all participants a ribbon. One teacher offered to contact the high school to see if students could be recruited to provide guidance to Riversedge students whose parents were unable to help. Other ideas were suggested for making parents feel more comfortable about getting involved and providing support for students who needed it. They suggested putting the 4th and 5th grade students' projects in the hallways and the other projects in the classrooms. At that point, someone from the university team dared to mention that we were discussing this as a way to illustrate and understand the theory. This was quickly brushed aside. Certainly, much of the action discussed was moving in a direction that was compatible with the theory. Reflecting on that fact might have proven helpful, but that was not high on the agendas of most of the members of the Riversedge team. This was not an illustrative case. This was their school in action. They were beginning to converge on ideas about what should be done—and they wanted to do it now! At one point, a 5th grade teacher turned to the principal and said, "Well, can we do this or not?" The answer was incomplete at best; equivocal at worst. Clearly the principal as well as some of the university team members were energized by the discussion but a bit unsure of where it would lead. Nevertheless, the thrust toward action was not to be denied. After the meeting, decisions were made, plans were drawn, and action taken which in fact did change many essential features of the education fair. In particular, changes were made that were substantially in accord with what the university team believed would enhance a task goal orientation. Competition was minimized. All children were encouraged to try and to take on a challenging project; all were given an opportunity to demonstrate what they had accomplished. The policy changes, as it ultimately turned out, were not only an immediate success with the teachers, they were well received by students and their parents. Few complained that standards had been lowered, that this was not fair, or that it would reduce student motivation. This first policy change was by all accounts a success.

At the team meeting immediately following the extended discussion of the education fair, members of the university team suggested spending some time thinking about the changes they were making and how these changes were consistent with the theory. There was not a lot of enthusiasm for this. Pushing theory and the need for reflective action, a member of the university team suggested that it would be useful to think about how this decision might be viewed by the rest of the staff and by the parents. Teachers on the Riversedge team began to express impatience, saying that the rest of the staff and the parents would be no problem and the teachers knew how to handle them in any event.

But it was not at all clear to the university team that theory was fully grasped or where it might be next applied. We tried to use the changes in the education fair as a prototype, a model that might prompt the examination of other policies and practices. Making school a contest was not just limited to school fairs or extracurricular events. What the staff team rejected in the case of the fair were practices that in slightly different form were found in many other places and processes at Riversedge. We knew that and the school staff did too, but there was little inclination to discuss theory or how it might be applied. Riversedge staff wanted action. As one of the team members, obviously exasperated, said, "This is taking so long. How are we going to make all those changes we listed on the board [at an earlier meeting] if we move this slowly? We talked about the education fair last week. Why are we talking about it again this week?" We soon learned that this need "to get on with it" was a feeling shared by most of the teachers on the team and also by the principal. As one teacher said, "I have a lot of at-risk children in my classroom who need help immediately!"

This need for action was not as surprising as the situation that followed. Increasingly, we became aware that the Riversedge team members believed the university team had answers to their problems and we were somehow holding back. Our surprise centered on a couple of points. First, we had emphasized at the outset that this was a collaborative project in which the leadership group and the university team initially and the school staff as a whole ultimately would search for answers as we framed theory for practice. Second, we wondered why they expected us to have the answers. It is no secret that school practitioners are frequently wary of university "experts" and how much they know and can accomplish. The situation became tense. The exchanges were sharp. The emotion was palpable. We were really testing the relationship and what it meant to collaborate let alone get a job done.

Somehow the topic changed. Perhaps someone from the university team said something like, "Well, what problems do *you want* to solve?" The response was quick: "The retention problem." Later, one of the university team members admitted she had not the slightest idea of what that meant, and one admitted privately that the first thing that came to his mind were issues related to memory or the enduring quality of learning. There was no real context for this within the collaborative group. But the teachers on the team had something very specific in mind, a problem that was widely known and shared in discussions they had had before: the retention of students in a grade when their work was deemed unsatisfactory. Clearly, there was unhappiness with the current policy to retain students, and they wanted to examine alternatives. Most seemed quite convinced, by what they had read and what they had experienced, that retention was not a good answer to problems of underachievement. All had a story to tell that more or less spoke to the validity of the practice. Most stories revolved around students they knew who had or had not profited from being retained in grade.

But what could be done to address the "retention problem"? Two teachers suggested that some kind of ungraded classroom might be useful to consider as an alternative to retention, at least in the lower grades. They confessed that they had always wanted to team teach and that combining students of more than one grade might give them this opportunity. This change in structure might make fewer retention decisions necessary. All agreed that an ungraded structure would allow an immature child time to "blossom" at a later age and to then undertake work commensurate with his age. What was at first a structural change quickly prompted a set of instructional issues. What and how do you teach in an ungraded or multiage classroom? To some, this was clearly a problem with no easy solution; to others, it was a challenge to solve. And the latter group really got to work: reading, brainstorming, discussing, and occasionally visiting other schools where multiage grouping practices were in place. Much of this work occurred outside the context of the weekly meetings, but the results made for some interesting discussions for a considerable period of time.

Teachers committed to or at least interested in the idea began envisioning not only grouping children differently but organizing and conducting instruction differently. The university team purchased and distributed materials on the topic, including especially John Goodlad's book on the ungraded classroom (1984). It became obvious that most of the teachers interested in multiage grouping were reading that book from cover to cover and were discussing the contents with each other. They seemed to be "sold" on the idea and began to believe it was something they could indeed put into practice. Several teachers began to talk about the possibility of team teaching. They became serious about rethinking how they would meet district and state curriculum objectives and increasingly leaned toward cross-disciplinary and thematic instruction, blurring traditional ways of categorizing learning. Those at the primary level exhibited an increasing interest in "whole language instruction," and a number at all levels took a cue from selected math (for example, "math their way") and science (for example, "project-based science") programs that they had run across. In this process, the university team played an important facilitative role searching out information; identifying sites, teachers, and schools where some of these options were being tried; locating workshop opportunities; and sometimes contacting an "expert." Other than that, the university team's role was increasingly interpretive: Team members persistently asked how the considered practice related to, embodied, and enhanced the theory. We stressed that multiage grouping did not automatically translate into a more task-focused school culture; rather it could provide a mechanism within which a task-focused culture can flourish.

It is not surprising that the principal initially raised serious questions about the direction in which the discussion was going. She could sense that her faculty would be split on this issue. Not all would be prepared to go in this direction and some would likely be upset if two, three, or more teachers pursued this presumably innovative course. And realistically, there was reason to pause before acting. As the principal reminded the teachers, "For years, I have heard how you hate 'splits,' and now you want multiage grouping?" She and others discussed and described how multiage classes would be different. How would teachers handle the curricula for two or three grades? On what basis would students be assigned to these classrooms? Would students of different ages and ability levels get along socially? Would all teachers be required to take part? How would art, music, gym, and library teachers handle multiage groupings? What would be the cost of setting up and maintaining multiage classrooms? Would it be necessary to reduce the class size or hire extra support staff? Would parents accept or understand the goals of these classrooms? What kind of physical space would be required? Would the school board allow such a change? It soon became clear that more than just the ages of students would be different in these classrooms. All areas of schooling including curriculum, materials, instructional techniques, classroom management, and evaluation would have to be reconsidered. A daunting task. At the least, the principal had to worry about whether the commitment was really there. Could it really be done? Also in the back of her mind had to be the issue of what parents would say. Then there was the matter of the district and the school board, which had little experience with this kind of innovation. Her concerns were real and understandable.

But as the discussions proceeded, Mrs. T. listened, remained engaged, and read more than she ever had before (her words). And she tilted just a little toward supporting and encouraging this venture. Within weeks she made it clear that she was ready to encourage experimentation with multiage classrooms. The serious planning and hard work began. There were four major parts to this: learning, planning, preparing, and reaching out to others.

Learning

Much had been learned already. Much more knowledge had to be absorbed. Now the Riversedge team was not just evaluating options. Something was going to be done and most admitted to some uncertainty as to how it could and would be accomplished. Team members, in particular, wanted to hear how teachers who had taught in multiage classrooms solved problems. Two experienced multiage teachers from other districts were invited to meet with the teams. They spoke about their philosophies and methods and how they handled the diversity of ages in their classrooms. Teachers on the team also visited two elementary schools that utilized multiage classrooms. Parenthetically, one teacher commented that it was the first time she had been in another elementary school in over twenty years.

Planning

By the end of March, a decision was made to break up into four smaller working groups, each focusing on a particular set of issues that would be involved in the move to multiage classrooms. One group considered the curriculum, materials, and planning time. The second looked at possible configurations of students within and across classrooms. A third examined classroom management and changes in the roles of teachers and students. The final group considered how to communicate the program's goals and involve parents and community members.

Preparing

By May, four teachers had decided to participate in the first year of the multiage classroom program. Other teachers were interested but wanted to observe the classrooms in practice. The multiage classrooms acquired a name, Multi-Age Grouped and Individualized Classrooms (MAGIC). On weekends and over the summer, the MAGIC teachers spent countless hours together planning. They attended "whole language," "thematic teaching," and "math their way" workshops to learn new teaching methods. They purchased books, educational materials, and professional literature. They designed a brochure to describe these classrooms to parents. Significantly, this brochure described the classrooms as "helping to put emphasis on self-improvement not competition." Theory was finding its way into practice: The objective of working toward a task-focused environment seemed to be making its way into the thinking of the Riversedge team.

What became increasingly evident was that introducing multiage classrooms was more than an organizational innovation. It provided an agenda for reconsidering the nature of teaching and learning processes. In a real sense, the organizational change was not really important; what was significant was the fact that it presented new challenges, produced new thinking, and gave an opportunity for putting theory into practice. Increasingly, the teachers argued and talked about what they were doing in terms of concepts and terms that were compatible with, if not always directly derived from, the theory that was to guide the project. Integral to the change was providing opportunities to focus on student progress and improvement at their own developmental pace. In addition, instead of being retained, children would be given time to catch up by continuing in the same class with the same teacher the following year. They envisioned pairs of teachers working together and suggested that an interdisciplinary approach to instruction would be appropriate. Students would be focused on meeting learning objectives not following a strict curriculum. Instead of separating students by grade and within grades into ability groups, the multiage classrooms would take advantage of the variety of skill levels with peer tutoring and cooperative learning.

It is interesting to note that later in the process teachers seemed to believe that the idea for multiage classrooms came from the university team and that it represented one of the items on our "agenda." The idea of multiage grouping as a way to facilitate the move to a more task-focused school culture had never entered our thinking. Quite frankly, when this idea was first introduced by several of the Riversedge staff, some on the university team greeted it with skepticism. We were more than a little concerned regarding where this would lead. How did it relate to establishing task goals? How did it relate to changing school culture? Was the multiage classroom just one of a number of educational quick fixes? But certain of the teachers committed to the idea patiently taught the rest of us that organizational change, specifically this type of organizational change, could be an avenue for culture change. In any event, all those closely involved soon became excited about how this structural change seemed to encourage and support the move to a more task-focused learning environment.

Reaching Out

Since the university team saw only about eight to ten teachers and the principal at meetings focusing on school change, we understandably worried about communication with the rest of the staff and increasingly asked questions about this in the regular weekly meetings. It had always been in the university team's thinking that while deliberations and planning might appropriately begin within the context of a smaller group, it must as soon as feasible engage more and more members of the staff as a whole. The principal and teachers exhibited less concern, probably in part because they had the benefit of many formal and informal contacts that were not available or experienced by the university team members. In any event, the Riversedge staff tended to minimize the university team's concerns, stressing that other teachers knew they were welcome to participate and that they learned about the team discussions from the teachers who attended the meetings. This was not an unreasonable assumption to make since Riversedge teachers prided themselves on being a very warm and open staff and seemed universally to like and respect their principal. However, midway through May, four teachers came to the meeting to say that they felt excluded from the decisions that were being made and were wary of the implications. They had heard many rumors about changes that were being considered and did not know which were actually going to be implemented. The principal was surprised at this reaction and emphasized that all had been encouraged to participate. Ironically, these four teachers and others thought the pace of change, especially the implementation of the MAGIC classrooms, was moving too quickly.

To increase communication with the entire staff, professional literature and minutes from coalition meetings were distributed to all teachers. The principal emphasized in staff meetings that all teachers were welcome to participate and that all teachers on the team should share information with the rest of the staff. A half-day in-service in May was used to present the plans and philosophy of the MAGIC classrooms to the rest of the staff and as the principal put it, "to let the staff know we are not just out in left field." The in-service included a brief overview of the theoretical framework, a discussion with the principal of a multiage school, and a presentation by the MAGIC teachers of their vision of multiage classrooms. Most of the teachers in the school expressed excitement and were very supportive of the MAGIC teachers. A handful of parents also attended the in-service.

Riversedge and other school improvement teams from the district were asked to make a brief presentation to the board of education in the late spring. The teachers on the team played a central role in the Riversedge presentation and delivered an enthusiastic report, emphasizing in particular the changes that centered on the emerging MAGIC program. The university team looked on with scarcely veiled pleasure as the board responded with enthusiasm, encouragement, and a 5,000-dollar appropriation for expenses.

Year Two

Riversedge School opened in the fall of year two with four MAGIC classrooms; two consisted of 1st, 2nd, and 3rd graders and two consisted of 3rd, 4th, and 5th graders. The composition of each of the classrooms was approximately one third lower achieving, one-third at grade level, and one-third higher achieving students. The goal was to enrich the curriculum; integrate the subject matter areas by developing themes, group children according to interest and to promote cooperation; and emphasize task mastery, skills development, and real understanding of the work. At first the MAGIC teachers talked about feeling overwhelmed. They were exhausted from long hours of planning and the myriad of practical details that had to be worked out. By November, however, the classes were functioning reasonably well. The teachers' frustrations changed to cautious optimism as they saw the benefits of their new approach reflected in their students' motivation and learning. In practice, these classrooms represented a significant move toward a more task-focused learning environment.

Meanwhile, the university team and school staff began to meet again on a regular basis, with a commitment to focus on the school as a whole not just on the MAGIC classrooms. The trend toward fully open meetings was now accepted operating procedure. Moreover, there was an increased blurring of distinction between what we have been terming the university and Riversedge teams. Certainly, university participants were still not staff, but there was a growing acceptance of their presence and contributions. This was evident from the perspectives taken in the meetings: The "we versus they" mentality was beginning to break down. There were strong signs that *one* team was beginning to emerge. "We" was now a heterogeneous group of university people, school principal and staff, and an occasional parent. While the original Riversedge school improvement committee continued to play an important role, the group had widened considerably. This permitted and encouraged the expansion of the topics of discussion. It also changed the nature of the discussion.

Student Assessment

The first issue to be considered was student assessment. The discussions were wide-ranging, with questions raised about defining learning objectives; setting goals; and assessing, reporting, and recognizing student progress. We, the group as a whole, agreed that for our discussions to be productive, we needed to separate the issues. A pressing concern for the teachers in the MAGIC classrooms was the approaching "marking period" and how to report to parents. While this was certainly the main concern of the MAGIC teachers, it was recognized as a school issue. The principal had to explain and justify whatever was done and there was increasing recognition that whatever was done might serve to change policy for the school as a whole. As is perhaps more generally true, an innovation can prompt wider discussions and ultimately serve as a stimulus to rethinking the whole process of schooling.

Teachers in the multiage classrooms had decided that report cards using letter grades emphasized differences in ability among children and were not appropriate in classrooms with children of different ages. Teachers were certain that both students and parents interpreted grades as measures of relative performance rather than measures of effort and progress. One teacher noted that her efforts to emphasize to children the importance of effort and improvement would be undermined if grades were interpreted as indicators of relative ability. Teachers also pointed out that letter grades convey very little information about what the student has mastered and where improvement needs to be made. They agreed that this type of reporting can be particularly devastating for low achievers who consistently receive low grades. A group of teachers began meeting to develop a new report card for the MAGIC classrooms. They collected report cards from other schools and adapted them to suit their objectives. They were pleasantly surprised when the assistant superintendent for curriculum and instruction helped them design the new report card on his portable computer, because they had been very apprehensive about approval for this change from central administration. It was evident that the resulting report card represented a move toward an emphasis on task goals. The principal made it clear, however, that the school as a whole was not yet ready to adopt the new report card.

In contrast, alternative approaches to assessment and new ideas regarding ways to recognize student achievement were seen as affecting not just the MAGIC classrooms but the school as a whole. A very visible change in schoolwide policy was the removal of the honor roll which had been conspicuously displayed in the main corridor. In this case, the principal made a unilateral decision not only to remove the honor roll from its prominent place in the front hall but to eliminate the practice of honoring children for their grades. She had come to realize that the honor roll defined the goal of learning as outperforming others rather than in terms of effort and improvement. Each term only a small group of students received honor roll certificates. The principal explained that she had not before considered how the awards served as a disincentive for the children who never received them, as well as the wrong incentive for higher achieving students. Her feelings were echoed by the parents of an all-A student. They had begun attending the team meetings during the previous spring, and the mother, with great emotion, told the group that she felt she had done her son a great disservice. She had been very proud to see his name on the honor roll, had praised him at length for having achieved this recognition, and had encouraged him to work for top grades. Now he was very focused on grades, was devastated if he received any grade lower than an A, and worst of all, would not take on challenging work in school unless he was sure of success. But not all parents and teachers agreed with the decision! Some teachers believed that an extrinsic reward of some kind was essential to get children to do their work. Some parents mentioned that they had taken pride in the certificates students brought home and displayed them prominently. In response to this pressure, the principal promised that the honor roll, at least for a time, would be replaced with a new form of recognition.

Four small groups were formed to focus on recognition, alternative approaches to assessment, parent relations, and community involvement. Riversedge staff again wanted some guidance from outside experts. Two speakers were brought in to speak about assessment in general and portfolios of students' work in particular. Both emphasized the link between learning objectives and assessment. They stressed that the teachers needed to have a clear idea of their learning objectives and needed to be able to convey to students both what "hitting" and "missing" those learning objectives would look like. They pointed out that students needed to be involved in the evaluation process to encourage self-monitoring and ownership. The teachers seemed interested in these ideas but also expressed frustration with not being told exactly what they were to do. They were very critical of one speaker who had not been particularly organized and said they learned very little from her presentation. Several teachers began experimenting with alternative forms of assessment such as reaction journals, portfolios, and tapes of students reading at various points in the year.

Recognition

The discussions about recognition were driven by the principal's promise to replace the honor roll and recognize as many children as possible. The group agreed that recognition in and of itself is not harmful and that the important issue is the basis for recognition. The group labored long and hard to come up with a list of "principles of recognition." In developing this list, teachers debated important issues relevant to goal theory. They frequently asked, "What kind of message will that give to students about how success is defined in this school and what is valued here?" One of the parents who had been attending the meetings said that the articulation of the principles of recognition was a turning point for him and that he now clearly understood the difference between an ability focus and a task focus. He became a strong advocate for the changes, and since he was also a member of the school board, his endorsement was especially valuable. The principles of recognition that were developed are presented in Table 6.1.

Parents

The parent subgroup discussed ways to make parents feel welcome in the school. Teachers believed that many Riversedge parents had experienced limited success when they were in school and thus were wary of attending school events and getting involved with their children's schooling. Only a

Table 6.1   Principles for Recognizing Students

1   Recognize individual student effort, accomplishment, and improvement.

2   Give all students opportunities to be recognized.

3   Give recognition privately whenever possible.

4   Avoid using "most" or "best" for recognizing or rewarding—as in "best project" or "most improved." These words usually convey comparisons with others.

5   Avoid recognizing on the basis of absence of mistakes. For example, avoid giving awards for students who get "less than five words wrong on a spelling test."

6   Avoid using the same criteria for all students. For example, avoid giving an award to "all students who get an A on the science test" or "all students who do four out of five projects."

7   Recognize students for taking on challenging work or for stretching their own abilities (even if they make mistakes). This gives them a powerful message about what is valued in the classroom.

8   Recognize students for coming up with different and unusual ways to solve a problem or a novel way to approach a task. Again, you are telling students what you value.

9   Try to involve students in the recognition process. What is of value to them? How much effort do they feel they put in? Where do they feel they need improvement? When do they feel successful? How do they know when they have reached their goals?

10   It's okay to recognize students in various domains (behavior, athletics, attendance, etc.), but every student should have the opportunity to be recognized *academically*.

11   Try to recognize the quality of students' work rather than the quantity. For example, recognizing students for reading a lot of books could encourage them to read easy books.

12   Avoid recognizing grades and test scores. This takes the emphasis away from learning and problem solving.

13   Recognition must be real. Do not recognize students for accomplishing something they have not really accomplished, for improving if they have not improved, or for trying hard if that is not the case. The important factor is letting students know that they have the opportunity to be recognized in these areas.

few parents (usually fewer than ten) attended Parent-Teacher Organization (PTO) meetings. The first goal of the parent subgroup was to get parents "in the door" and to make them feel comfortable about being there. The group sent home a letter asking parents if they would be interested in coming to workshops where they could discuss issues of concern to them. They asked parents to list their concerns and to indicate what topics they would like to discuss. Parents were told that activities would be provided for children in the gym. Based on the responses from the parents, workshops were planned. At first, this approach seemed to be working. Attendance at the first workshop was high, and parents participated actively in the discussion. At the end of the session, parents were enthusiastic about continuing the sessions and said they would take the initiative to invite other parents to attend. The subsequent workshops were not as well attended, however. The subgroup continued to meet and to discuss ways to reach out to parents.

Community Involvement

The subgroup formed to discuss community involvement composed a letter to businesses. Because the effects of the recession had been pervasive in Michigan, the group decided not to ask businesses for financial resources. Instead the letter asked companies to support Riversedge by providing tours of plants and staff who could talk about jobs and become role models for students. There was also a desire to garner community support for the changes that were going on in the school. For the most part, the letters went unanswered. The subgroup talked about the need to make personal contacts, but this did not happen.

Expanding Staff Participation and Commitment

In spite of serious attempts to widen participation in the discussions, the need for persistent effort toward this end remained. Communication among the entire school staff was a continuing concern. During the previous summer, a letter had been sent to all of the teachers in the school discussing the changes that had been made the first year and encouraging them to participate in the after-school meetings. Because some teachers had commitments that prevented them from attending meetings after school, the decision was made to meet before school one week and after school the next week. After two months, it became obvious that this approach was not working. Many more teachers attended the after-school meetings than the before-school meetings. Much of each meeting was spent updating teachers on what had happened at the previous meeting. Finally, at a morning meeting attended only by the principal and two teachers (who, incidentally, had also attended many of the after-school meetings), the decision was made to revert to the previous afternoon-only schedule. More teachers began to attend the after-school meetings, with approximately two-thirds of the staff attending each meeting until attendance dwindled near the end of the year. Still, communication with the teachers who did not attend continued to be a problem, particularly as changes were made that had an impact on the school as a whole. It also became obvious that some teachers believed that the MAGIC teachers were receiving a disproportionate amount of the resources available for school improvement. In order to ensure that resources were available for all teachers who were taking steps to move toward a more task-focused learning environment, a funding committee was set up to review proposals. In addition, researchers attended several staff meetings to answer questions, address concerns, and promote better relations.

Engaging the Support of a Wider Community

Riversedge was asked to make a second presentation before the school board. Purposely, the MAGIC classrooms that had been discussed at a board meeting the previous spring were not the focus of this presentation. Instead, a five-year plan was described. Although some aspects of the plan did not relate specifically to enhancing task goals per se, teachers capitalized on the opportunity to convey their emerging vision of school where the emphasis was not on performance, categorization, or control but on valuing all children as worthy in their own right and as capable of becoming life-long learners. They did not talk of school culture as such, but they did accept the responsibility of providing the context and the opportunity for children to "become all that they could be." Their enthusiasm was palpable and catching. Several board members did not conceal their pleasure. It was a good moment and elicited an additional appropriation of 5,000 dollars. The board's motive was apparent. In no real sense had they been converted to the theory of school culture change; they were simply responding to a persuasive presentation on the part of a committed school staff. They were hopeful that the promises made would be fulfilled. They believed in the staff and trusted the leadership of the principal. This was their primary though not exclusive reason for action. Several school board members expressed some interest in what they had gleaned in this and previous encounters regarding the driving rationale for the effort. A heavy agenda undercut any possibility of such a discussion and in the final analysis it was probably the semblance of action and progress—and the lack of complaints—that were supported.

Year Three

The Evolving MAGIC Program

During the third year of the project, the MAGIC program was expanded. One lower elementary multiage teacher continued with grades 1, 2, and 3. Another teacher decided to move to a grouping of grades 1 and 2. A similar change was made in the upper elementary multiage classrooms with one of the two teachers moving to a grades 4 and 5 grouping, while the other stayed with the grades 3, 4, and 5 combination. In addition, two new multiage classrooms were added, one including grades 1 and 2, the other including grades 3 and 4. Thus, there were now six multiage classrooms in the school, all dedicated to moving toward a more task-focused learning environment. Parents who had children in the multiage classrooms the previous year were quite vocal in their support so other parents were willing to give it a try. Recruiting children for these classrooms was no longer a problem.

Beyond MAGIC

A special effort was made to inform all the teachers in the school that it was not necessary to teach multiage classrooms in order to move toward a learning environment that stressed mastery, effort, and improvement rather than relative ability and comparative performance. Some teachers had concluded that the principal would not allow them to make some of the changes that had been made in the multiage classrooms, such as moving to a whole language approach to reading or eliminating homogeneous ability grouping in reading. The principal assured her staff that although it had been necessary to focus a lot of attention on the multiage classrooms in the beginning, she was now committed to supporting changes in the "single-age" classrooms and that these teachers could indeed move in similar directions.

At the after-school meetings, a number of topics were discussed and some substantive changes were made in approaches to discipline, the young authors program, the annual field day, and the 5th grade awards ceremony (described later). In general, however, an awareness emerged that there was a need to reflect on and to consolidate the changes that had been made rather than to move in new directions. The discussions regarding approaches to testing and assessment continued, some of which included outside consultants; but in general there was little in the way of substantive change in this area. In particular, Riversedge staff spent many sessions describing the negative effects on children of standardized testing, but they seemed to feel that there was nothing they could do to change this situation. The university team urged them to communicate with central administrators and the school board and to investigate alternative ways of assessing student progress. A consultant from the University of Michigan involved in "work sampling" approaches to assessment was invited to make a presentation at a meeting. There was an interest among the staff but also an awareness that this would involve a major commitment of time and energy. They simply couldn't take this on in addition to all the other changes that were underway. In one of the meetings the principal said, "Someone else will have to fight that battle."

During the third year, some major changes did occur in the area of discipline. It was not at first clear how this issue was related to the theoretical framework that was guiding the change efforts, but it became evident that the topic needed to be considered. Several years earlier, Riversedge had implemented an "assertive discipline" policy that rewarded students for good behavior. Students received "pink slips" if they misbehaved in the lunchroom, hallways, or on the playground. At the end of each month, students who had not received a pink slip were rewarded for their good behavior by being allowed to attend a "no pink slip" assembly, while those who had received one or more pink slips sat in a "holding" room. Although the idea of rewarding students for good behavior had some appeal, the teachers were aware that the system had a number of drawbacks. Teachers complained that the responsibility for planning the assemblies was burdensome and kept them from more important teaching and learning activities. Teachers noticed that some students asked what the assembly would be that month, so they could decide whether it was "worth it" to behave. Students came to expect a reward for good behavior. Others who had received pink slips could not remember by the end of the month what it was they had done wrong. Moreover, the same group of students received pink slips again and again. Clearly, this discipline system did not teach children how to solve problems and resolve conflicts; the focus was on rewards and punishments rather than on learning and improving. After lengthy discussions, the teachers decided to create a new discipline program using "problem-resolution" sheets instead of pink slips. Modeled on "conflict resolution," students were given opportunities to examine actively the school rules, their own behaviors, and methods for resolving difficulties. Within two months, teachers noticed a drop in inappropriate student behavior. They also reported that some students were beginning to think about the reasons for their misbehavior and to generate appropriate alternatives. That is not to say that inappropriate behavior was no longer a problem at Riversedge, but the changes seemed to be having a positive effect.

Changes in the annual field day, the 5th grade awards ceremony, and the young authors program focused on recognizing student effort and improvement and promoting cooperation and positive interactions among students. For years, teachers had been somewhat dissatisfied with the field day. At this heavily competitive event, a few outstanding athletes won most of the awards. Students who were destined to be "losers" lost interest and some misbehaved. The teachers had continued with the field day, even with these problems, because some of the top athletes were also poor students and thus did not have the opportunity to be recognized for their academic accomplishments. But with the new recognition system, they hoped that all children were being recognized for their accomplishments in the classroom. The physical education teacher visited a local school where the field day was not based on competition among individuals but included a variety of group games that all children seemed to enjoy. For many of the games, students were grouped together on multiage teams. The new field day at Riversedge was modeled after this program, with an emphasis on positive social interaction, cooperation, and the recognition of students' personal best. Although there were still some competitive activities for the older children, teachers reported that the new field day was an improvement over the old one. Several of the teachers who had not been involved in the after-school meetings made it clear to their colleagues (though not to us) that they thought the move away from athletic competition was foolish. They strongly believed that competition is healthy and that children thrive on it. The teachers on the team did not want to further alienate these teachers, and thus the field day continued to include some events in which students competed against one another and received prizes for winning based on their ability relative to others.

Changes were also made to the annual 5th grade awards ceremony. This event was established to recognize the accomplishments of "graduating" students. Previously, a small number of students were recognized, and often the same students received several awards. Teachers reported that after the same student had been recognized several times, students in the audience would sometimes boo rather than applaud. Students who knew that they would not receive an award became restless and some caused problems. Many teachers did not look forward to this event. The teachers decided to change the emphasis from recognition to celebration. Refreshments were served and the principals from the two middle schools were invited to attend. Each 5th grader received recognition for one area of improvement, accomplishment, or effort. These changes were perceived as positive by most students, teachers, and parents.

Some changes were made to the young authors program. Students in this program produce their own bound books complete with an original story and illustrations. In previous years, the books were judged and the "best" authors were sent to a district-wide young authors conference. The teachers decided instead to base the selection of those who would attend the conference on evidence of hard work and interest in writing. The message they wanted students to receive is that they can all be authors and that they have a chance to go to the conference if they try hard. After the conference, teachers expressed some dissatisfaction with these changes. Their students' books had not stood out among the many books that were there. Those who viewed the books had no way of knowing how much effort the children had put into them or how interested they were; they could only see the product. The teachers had been put in an environment where relative performance was highlighted and it made them question the decisions they had made.

Teachers began to talk about having a vision for their school, knowing now where they were headed and what they wanted for their students. A few teachers still expressed their belief that competition is what makes the world go around and that students need to have rewards for which to strive. But in general, the staff seemed to be pulling together. At the end of one meeting, the principal reminded the staff that the annual contest to select the best essay on the history of Riversedge School was coming up, and they should convey this information to their students and remind them that they could win the trophy. One of the teachers looked at her in amazement and said, "That's not what this school is all about. How can we make all these changes and then do something like that? It makes no sense. No. We can't do that."

The staff and the principal recognized that there was still much to be done, but they also understood that they did not need the university team's participation to make additional changes. Not only had relations among the teachers improved somewhat, but there was a change in the relationship between the researchers and the staff at Riversedge. A genuine feeling of mutual respect and affection had developed. The year ended with a celebration of our efforts and successes at the home of one of the teachers.

Afterword

When one reads any story such as this one wonders about the school a year or more later. We are no different in this regard and so have gone back to find out, although in a less intense and systematic way than when we were collaborators. In addition to wanting to see old friends—and many of us had become that—we felt some responsibility for whatever happened in that school, having urged and encouraged leadership and staff to take risks, venture in new directions, and "stick out their necks." And so we have made a point of visiting from time to time, helping out as volunteer teacher aides, and generally showing interest and attention. As a result, we have some knowledge of what may be happening now. Our impressions are not quantified, and what we observe is more anecdotal than systematic. Given that there have been multiple observations and observers as well as multiple conversations as well as conversers, what we say in this regard probably is not too far from what we might have learned in a more scientific way.

Two types of observations are warranted. First, Riversedge is currently experiencing a change in context and the clientele it serves. We are referring first of all to the school's neighborhood. It was not a particularly good place for children when we started work at Riversedge. It is now worse. There had always been some sense of pride in Riversedge; although the school was in a "tough" neighborhood, those at the school seldom if ever had to deal with vandalism, break-ins, and thefts. There was a sense that the school was valued by the neighbors and that the staff was "trusted." Principal, social worker, and teachers regularly walked across the street to "the project" when there was a need. At the least, they think seriously now about the wisdom of making these visits. Violence in the neighborhood has increased, with shootings occurring during the day while children are walking to and from school. The school has experienced a series of major burglaries, eventuating in the loss of computers and other equipment of which they were most proud. We have not sensed that school staff members are worried about personal safety but concern is growing. Most of all, families who formed the heart of the school and provided support and stability are beginning to leave the area served by the school, and this has begun to seriously affect morale.

A second observation is of a different order and related more specifically to our earlier work. The staff members most involved in the earlier project seem to remain committed to the ideals they framed during our joint effort, under sometimes difficult circumstances. They welcome us back whenever we return and seize the opportunity to talk about what they are doing. They frequently refer to our collaboration as a high point when they could discuss issues that were of vital importance to them. They report that discussions of this type are increasingly rare, but they seem to be carrying on quite well—we think. Some express worries regarding the division that occurred between staff who were at the core of the changes made by the school and the rest. One commented that "open wounds" remain. Most agree that Mrs. T. remains a positive force and that she has not forgotten the hard-earned conclusions hammered out in the course of the collaborative effort. So the sense of purpose at the heart of the vision of school we constructed together has not been lost. It is there though probably not as salient as it once was.

7   A Story of Plainview: Establishing a Learning Community by Thinking Small

I can't waste any more time planning for change when nothing happens.

   —a school improvement team member expressing frustration

I will never be able to go back to teaching the old way.

   —a teacher who "converted to the vision"

Not an Atypical School

Plainview is one of two middle schools that serve the district. Many of the children attending Riversedge Elementary School expect to proceed to Plainview. Whereas Riversedge was known as the school with the largest number of poor children, Plainview, as it drew from Riversedge as well as several other elementary schools, was more heterogeneous. Also, whereas Riversedge was located on the edge of the district off the interstate and near a large public housing project, Plainview was located on the border of the village that was the center of the district. Plainview Middle School was built several decades ago, more or less along the "California plan" with many windows and multiple corridors all on one floor. The building was generally inviting, attractive, and clean. It had housed all the junior high school students in the district until 1974 when a second junior high school was built.

In the early 1980s the 9th grade was moved to the high school and the 6th grade was assigned to Plainview in line with the nationwide movement to middle schools. The associate superintendent of the school district had played a major role in that transformation, and said candidly that he had been disappointed that the move to the middle school model represented changes in the composition of grades in the school and little else. Ten years later, during our tenure, one could still sense a division between the 6th grade (formerly in the elementary schools) and the 7th and 8th grades. Some of this was purposeful, intended to provide a bridge to the upper grades. Sixth grade staff tended to have had experience teaching at the elementary level and leaned toward an "elementary education orientation." They were less identified with a subject matter area, thus less inclined to describe themselves as science, math, or language and literature specialists than simply as teachers of children. In comparison, those who taught 7th and 8th grade classes had not only in some instances been "brought down" from the high school during the earlier reorganization but saw themselves as teachers of a specific subject matter. Not surprisingly, they were more sensitive to what would likely be expected of students when they reached high school. And their arguments for and against school change turned more on notions of "standards, coverage, and correlation of content and curriculum." In sum, issues that have been debated in reconstituted middle schools almost anywhere were always near the surface in the many interactions that composed the life of the school as we came to know it, a fact that will become increasingly evident as our story unfolds.

Demographically, there were approximately 750 students in regular attendance at Plainview Middle School, more or less equally distributed among 6th, 7th, and 8th grades. About 12 percent of the students were African-American, with the rest being virtually all Euro-American. As in Riversedge, parents were largely working class, employed in various jobs related to the automotive industry. Some parents lived in the more affluent areas and were engaged in varied community businesses. The school staff was composed of a principal, an assistant principal, 45 teachers, a full-time counselor, and several paraprofessionals.

In our initial meetings with staff and administrators, we received two somewhat contradictory messages. On the one hand, there were statements about the special collegial relationships among the staff. The assistant principal, for example, emphasized his delight at having been given the chance to return to this school after a tenure at the high school chiefly, he said, because of the fine spirit among the staff. At the same time, there were expressions of cynicism about the support that would be forthcoming from central admin-

istration and the district as a whole if anything worthwhile in the way of educational innovation was ventured. Moreover, as the discussion ensued it became clear that whatever collegiality might have existed could quickly be
broken down when serious discussions of change occurred.

Perhaps even more problematic were the mixed messages we received
about the school's interest in collaborating with us. Central administration
had clearly wanted the other middle school to work with us. We made a
presentation to the staff at that school and were told that they were interested in collaborating but were involved in other school change plans and
would have to postpone their involvement for a year. At that point, we approached Plainview. The staff knew that we had been "turned down" at the
other school, and they also knew that we were already actively working at
Riversedge Elementary School. There was a sense that they were being the
"good guys" who would hold up the district's bargain. At that point, they
didn't talk about problems at the school, the need for change, or their optimism that we could help; it was almost as if they were feeling that someone
had to do it and so they would volunteer.

Our depiction in this chapter of the process of collaboration and change
at Plainview is based on a naturalistic-descriptive approach that interprets
what is written, heard, and seen through our active participation in meetings with their team, our observations in the school, our interviews with
key informants, and our review of documents produced during the
process.[1] We attended a variety of special and regularly scheduled events including monthly "fun nights," Parent, Teacher, Student Organization
(PTSO) meetings, school board meetings, open houses, and staff meetings.
Additional informal conversations occurred during the school day in the
teachers' lounge, hallways, classrooms, and in the principal's office.

We taped the weekly after-school meetings between the university team
and the Plainview team and reviewed them to get a sense of the teachers'
and administrators' understandings of the school change process, their perceptions of their role and ours, and the emerging role of the theoretical
framework. Tapes of the first five months of meetings guided the questions
that were asked of eleven members of the Plainview team at the beginning
of our second year of collaboration. These interviews were structured to
tap explicitly their developing understanding of the theoretical framework
and its subsequent effect on the school change process. We interviewed the
assistant principal, a parent, and nine teachers who were active members of
the team.

During our early meetings, Plainview team members discussed aspects of
school life they found troubling. They knew that the school was experiencing

problems, but there was a tendency to blame parents, students, or a lack of resources. They knew that students weren't doing well in some cases; they recognized that too many students were being sent to the principal's office for disciplinary action; they were bothered by the level of achievement test scores, complaints from parents, and the occasional serious instance of a student misbehaving. At the same time, there was a clear uncertainty regarding what the university team could and would do. The Plainview team members read our documents and listened to our plans—we think. In any event, during the initial discussions notions of "school culture change" seemed to be far from anyone's mind. They needed and probably wanted help, but as with Riversedge, the Plainview team came to accept us fairly much on faith and perhaps we accepted them in a similar manner and for the same reasons. And thus the collaboration with Plainview began, not auspiciously but perhaps with a secret hope that something good might happen.

Middle Schools Are Different from Elementary Schools

We expected that the process of change at the middle school would differ from that of the elementary school. Indeed, one cannot get too far into the daily life of middle and elementary schools without realizing that there are differences in the concerns, expectations, and attitudes of parents, teachers, and society as a whole with regard to students and education at this age. Obviously, the students are confronting different "developmental tasks" (Havighurst, 1952) and consequently pose different challenges for instruction, interpersonal relationships, and management. As a result, different conceptions of teaching and learning and different organizational structures and processes are readily evident even to the most inexperienced observers. In the broader sense, the school culture at the elementary and middle levels is likely to be quite different and the path to culture change may not be the same. This was substantiality confirmed and validated in the course of our work. Several central observations in this regard deserve mention as we introduce our story of culture change in a typical middle school (Urdan, Midgley, & Wood, 1995).

A Volatile Stage

Striking physical, psychological, and social changes occur during early adolescence. Observations regarding these changes and their implications are likely to figure strongly in any discussion of the purposes and practices of schooling. Sometimes middle school students are described as "victims of their raging hormones," and therefore unable to behave and to learn as well as children of other ages. One junior high school principal told us that, at this stage, children are all "brain dead." During public interviews to select a new superintendent in a nearby school district, one of the finalists for the position described the early adolescent years as "happily psychotic," a characterization that did little to hurt his chances of getting the job. This perception is so widely held that it is usually not seen as an inhibitor to school reform. Yet it probably is. Many of the characterizations suggest that middle grade schools are little better than "holding pens." As a result, the stress is often on control rather than on personal, social, and intellectual growth. We were confronted with some of these conceptions at Plainview. The first time we met the assistant principal, he referred to the "happy hormones" of middle school students and expressed his belief that "their hormones interfere with brain growth." In their responses to an open-ended survey question about whether children's attitudes toward learning change upon entering middle school, several teachers referred to physical, psychological, and emotional changes associated with puberty as the reasons for these changes in attitudes.

Established Patterns

A different but commonly held belief about early adolescent students is that they are already too old and set in their patterns of learning by the time they reach middle school to be influenced positively by teachers and schools. Several teachers at Plainview mentioned that they believed it was a good idea to get students focused on their own progress in learning instead of worrying about how they compare with other students (that is, to develop a task-focused goal orientation). However, these teachers tempered this by saying that it would be difficult to do this with middle school students because they already had years of experience in elementary schools and at home where relative ability and competition among students is the norm. In an interview, one teacher said that three years in middle school is not enough time to offset the previous years of socialization toward competition that the student brings to the middle school: "I don't think in the three years that we see these students we're going to change their way of thinking against that. It's got to come from the home front, it's got to start at home if you want to change that. And we're not going to change it."

Family Support

Teachers at all levels are typically concerned with family involvement in their children's education. But it is commonly noted that parental participation in school-related functions falls off when children move to middle school. James Comer describes his own experiences as a parent at the elementary and middle school levels in this way: "When we went off to the PTA meeting or to the open house every year (in elementary school), we had to go very early or you could not find a parking space. It was just packed.

"When we went to middle school, you did not have to go early because there were plenty of spaces." (*Carnegie Quarterly,* 1992, p. 4).

One of the parents on the Riversedge team also had a child at Plainview. She was a visible, active presence in the elementary school, volunteering her time and working energetically with teachers and students. She told us that she had also volunteered to help out at Plainview, but they never seemed to be able to find anything for her to do. She said quite candidly that she felt distant from the teachers and administrators at the middle school.

We also noted that the team members at Riversedge and Plainview expressed somewhat different attitudes about their students' parents. Certainly, in both schools team members spoke glowingly about parents who provided active support for their children's learning. The different tones emerged when discussing parents who were unwilling or unable to provide such support and the impact this lack of support had on children's learning and development. One Plainview teacher consistently referred to the effect that parents and home life have on student performance, making such statements as, "Good kids come from good parents or at least parents who care," and "But I guess the point I'm trying to get across is that this area is not real gung-ho about going out and getting a good job. I am sure there are some parents who say, 'We're living on ADC just fine and you'll do the same thing when you get older.'" Teachers at Riversedge also discussed the home life of their students but often emphasized the need to improve the life chances for these students. Moreover, the elementary teachers talked about personal interactions with parents, whereas discussions at the middle school often centered on the lack of parental interest and involvement.

Logistical Barriers

Middle schools present different logistical and organizational barriers to change than do elementary schools. One example here concerns policies and practices associated with scheduling the school day. At the elementary school level, the daily schedule is relatively simple. For the most part, students are under the supervision of one teacher throughout the day. These teachers have considerable control over how they structure the school day and can use time flexibly if they are willing. At Plainview, the daily schedule requires the complex assignment of hundreds of students and all the teachers to six different class periods. Special programs, such as band or the "gifted and talented program" may serve only a fraction of the school's students yet have the power to dictate constraints for the school schedule as a whole. Teachers have almost no control over scheduling.

Another logistical barrier encountered at the middle school level involves teacher certification. Many middle level schools house 6th, 7th, and 8th grade students. Often it is the case, in Michigan at least, that teachers are certified to teach kindergarten through grade 6 or grades 7 through 12. On one significant occasion, this arose as a potential obstacle to change at Plainview. Early in our endeavor, attention was devoted to the possibility of reorganizing the school into several smaller subschools or "small houses," each of which would have its own faculty and a representative sample of students. Reasonably enough, there was hesitation about immediately moving to reorganizing the school as a whole along these lines. However, there was a strong interest on the part of some faculty members to experiment with the idea on a smaller scale. The experiment would probably have been enacted and become a visible example that "something could be done" except that none of the math teachers was interested in participating in this program at the 8th grade level. One teacher in the school, who was not certified to teach math at this level but who had taught math to 6th graders, volunteered to participate in this innovative program. Because of her lack of certification for teaching upper grade math—not because of her judged competence—administrators were reluctant to allow her to participate in the program. In addition, there was the fact that if she did participate, she would need to be replaced in 6th grade math and a relatively small number of teachers were certified at that level. In this instance and others, state and district requirements, such as certification, were seen as stumbling blocks preventing administrators and teachers from moving in new and potentially fruitful directions.

An issue similar to that of credentials is the training of secondary teachers as subject matter specialists and the departmentalized organization of many middle level schools. Departmentalization may lead to different school "subcultures" and to competing views of teaching and learning. The department heads at Plainview had considerable power. For example, we observed early on that the chair of the math department, as well as his colleagues in math, had a different view of teaching and learning than did many of the teachers in the other departments. At the outset, at least, the math department was adamant that its subject was different from others. The argument was that a math teacher could not be guided by the theory of instruction we presented to them. And most important, math could not be taught in heterogeneously grouped classrooms. As a result, math scheduling virtually determined how students could and would be grouped, regardless of how the rest of the teachers felt—at least for a while.

One of the common differences between elementary and middle schools is in the area of leadership. At Riversedge, there was only one formally designated leader, a principal. At Plainview, as with many middle grade schools, there were a number of formally designated leaders in addition to the principal: an assistant principal and various department heads, each with their own resources, prerogatives, perspectives, and allegiances. This certainly influences the politics of the school, possibly inhibiting school-wide changes in school culture if there is disagreement among the parties.

In sum, middle grade schools are different kinds of organizations than are elementary schools. They are typically much larger than elementary schools. There are more teachers to resist the changes and more students and parents who may be affected. Moreover, middle schools are regularly faced with integrating students who have experienced a number of different school cultures at the elementary school level. This in itself could contribute to the increased bureaucracy common to middle schools. Add to that the increasing application of curriculum guidelines, certification requirements, and statewide achievement standards and you typically get very different organizational processes and structures. Even though we began our collaboration with the middle school with basically the same general conceptions regarding the purposes of education and how these could be achieved, the road to change was bound to be different.

The Process

As we had done at Riversedge, we assured the staff that this would be a collaborative project. We, the university team, had a framework, and, of course, the Plainview team knew schools, especially its school. The school staff could help us see how that framework was or was not embodied in the life and work of its school. Together we could identify what did or did not facilitate a task goal orientation and discuss options. But staff members would have to decide what could be changed, perhaps with some degree of help from the university team but certainly only as a function of their choice. Additionally, our team would record and analyze the course of change for them and others in the professional community who might be interested. It could not have escaped the Plainview staff that there was the potential here of emerging as a kind of demonstration school, although that implied a complex of meanings, not all positive.

The Ebb and Flow of the Dialogue

As in the case of Riversedge, the primary instrument for change was dialogue. That dialogue began within the context of a formally designated school improvement team composed of several faculty members and chaired initially by the assistant principal. The school improvement team had been in operation for several years and had already produced a statement of school objectives that had been approved by the staff as a whole. It clearly was a group with whom the principal and assistant principal chose to work on this and other matters. The university team was composed of the same two senior investigators who were working with Riversedge staff but with a different group of graduate students, many of whom had experience in the middle grades as teachers or in related work. The membership tended to vary slightly through the course of the experiment, especially as graduate students left for other venues and others replaced them. A parent representative was a regular participant in the hour-long meetings held once a week after school.

Informal discussion began in late fall 1990 but took a systematic and regularized form after the first of the year. It continued thereafter through June 1993, or a period of two and one-half years, a somewhat shorter period than was the case at Riversedge. The length of the period was not planned but necessitated by funding and the opportunity presented by the school. School leaders simply felt that they could not manage to begin the project in the fall of 1990 because of other commitments. And the university team found it difficult to continue the effort when the funding period was over.

Year One

The beginning of our conversation was inauspicious. The first meetings were with a relatively small group. Alhough the group was composed of teachers and the university team members, the assistant principal was in charge. Occasionally, other teachers would join our discussions. Only rarely did the principal participate. Most of the time in these few early meetings was spent in sorting out what Plainview could expect from the university team and what we in turn wanted from them. It was apparent at the outset that the assistant principal saw the university team as primarily involved in the evaluation of whatever the Plainview team decided to do. As a result, early in the endeavor we spent considerable time describing the kind of data we might gather, how we could analyze data that were already available at the school, and how this might be useful to school planning. Plainview representatives were wary of sharing school improvement responsibilities with the university team, and the university team was struggling to explain itself in a way that was diplomatic and engaging but not overpowering or demanding. It was a delicate dance, converging at some early point on the precise membership of the group that would be meeting with the university team: Would it be the current school improvement group or a specially appointed one? We're not exactly sure how this was decided, but a certain group began attending weekly meetings somewhat regularly. With that, a routine of varying the chair (usually a volunteer, alternatively from Plainview or the university team), taking notes and writing up minutes (usually a university team responsibility), and setting the next meeting's agenda (largely determined by Plainview staff) became established.

In addition to the weekly planning meetings, we often visited during the school day and took the opportunity as an occasion for learning from informal encounters in the hall or the central office. We attended cocurricular activities held after school hours, as well as more academically focused "open house" nights. It was at a PTSO meeting that we and our project were introduced to a sampling of parents. Interestingly, one father seemed somewhat concerned about whether we were advocating the teaching of "values" to the students. He was rather summarily dealt with and the primary expression was one of appreciation and pride that Plainview had been "chosen" to be a part of this project. Both administrators were present at this meeting which was in fact attended by fewer than ten parents. The principal clearly played the dominant role in the discussion. We were accepted, but there was no discussion of what that acceptance might mean for the school. Most of the meeting centered on setting criteria and providing funding for a student "citizenship" award.

Several of the early team meetings were spent working out the details of administering the preintervention surveys. Permission slips would need to be sent home and collected and times for administering surveys in the classroom would need to be scheduled. All of this was also done at the elementary level, but again size, bureaucracy, and scheduling at the middle school level made for a more complex process and more lengthy discussion. By the time these details were worked out, both the Plainview team and the university team were eager to get into more substantive issues. There was a discussion on the purpose of the collaborative project starting with the theory that was to drive it. Appropriately or not, what was happening at Riversedge was brought into the discussion to illustrate the theory. Not surprisingly, the discussion switched quickly to specific and concrete concerns facing the school at the moment. Concerns about grading, both the merits of the use of letter grades and the basis on which grades were assigned, figured prominently. Another concern centered on the homework policy. Should there be a schoolwide policy consistent across grade levels and subject domains? A number of issues surfaced regarding control and tolerance of student misbehavior along with more general concerns about social and personal development. Special instructional concerns were brought up often and repeatedly by the principal, for example, the need to upgrade study skills and the need for instruction to match the "learning styles" of students.

None of this was unusual given the circumstances. Neither was it totally unexpected that some of the discussions were punctuated by personally felt problems. The school's mission statement was brought up early in the discussion and the reference to the belief that "every child is valued" prompted the exasperated question, "Some kids don't care about themselves—what do I do about them?" Someone added, "Some kids believe that they're 'dummies.'" There was conversation about what the school could do to improve self-esteem among students, an apparently widely recognized problem with few obvious solutions. There was a quick convergence on the value of a PTSO-sponsored program of recognizing one student a month or rewarding students for various good things by taking them out to dinner at a cooperating restaurant. There was disagreement and confusion over whether rewards should be given and for what reasons. For everyone for some good reason? For special behavior demonstrating citizenship or scholarship? For improvement? For comparative achievement? The discussion revealed an unease with the end of the year "awards assembly" but also despair in not knowing what to do about it. Some members of the school team were clearly worried about kids who were out of the loop as far as awards and recognition were concerned. There was some expression of fatalism about this, but there were also those who weren't going to give up on those students. A few thought the school itself might, at least in part, be at fault. We were only one month into the process and beginning to hit what we thought might be pay dirt.

The university team tried to inject the school culture theory into the discussion as much as possible. By hooking the theory to concrete issues and problems, we hoped to make it "live" for them. Teachers, in many cases, were more successful than we were in providing a bridge between theory and practice. When we were talking about the difference between defining success in terms of effort and mastery, and defining success in terms of relative ability, one teacher became very animated and provided this example: "When we teach a child to ride a bike, we don't say 'You did okay, but your brother did better.' That would be stupid, and we know that. We would say,

'Pedal faster, hold on to the handle bars, keep trying, you'll get it.' Why don't we do that in school?"

Somewhere around the middle of February two rather important things happened. First, a number of Plainview staff in addition to the original core group began to show up at the meetings. This was specifically encouraged by the university team, but it also represented a feeling among the staff that the discussion taking place in these sessions was important to the school as a whole. Second, a necessary review and discussion of the nature of the survey that was to be administered to all students and teachers went beyond a pedestrian conversation about form and format and focused on broader issues: What is meant by at-risk students? Who are they and how do we know them? The discussion progressed into areas of labeling and sorting students. For example, there were strong feelings for and against the "gifted and talented program." These sensitive issues on grouping students according to their "abilities" remained important throughout the course of the collaboration.

In the early part of March, we decided to hold a brainstorming session to become more systematic and thorough in identifying issues on which we could work. During this period, staff members were beginning to talk to us about what was bothering them as well as about their hopes for what we might be able to accomplish. As one member of the university team who spent considerable time at Plainview put it, "I'm amazed at how much teachers want to talk to me." The brainstorming was initially structured around the general question, "What would you like to change about school?" This question was expanded to: "What's really bothering you about what's 'out there'?" "What do you want to work on?" Ground rules were laid. All ideas and concerns would be respected. The merits of the ideas or the magnitude of the concern would not be debated. At the end of the meeting some attempt would be made to group ideas into themes and to prioritize. The chair and a couple of members from the original team provided some prompts: "like grades" and "like put downs." (Earlier, some teachers had expressed concerns with how students demeaned one another through deprecatory language.) One of the university team members stood in front of the blackboard and wrote down all of the ideas that were articulated. What ensued was a jumble of diverse thoughts, proposals, and reflections. Figure 7.1 reflects pictorially the way the ideas tumbled out in the course of the conversation.

The concerns raised and contained in Figure 7.1 probably would not vary much from middle school to middle school. The spontaneous and energized way in which they came into the conversation made it clear that they represented issues about which this school had strong concerns.

Shortly after this brainstorming session, someone from the Plainview staff introduced the idea of a "small house concept" for middle schools. That is, dividing teachers and students into small units in a way that would promote teaming and interdisciplinary teaching, ensure that students did not "fall through the cracks," give teachers more control over scheduling, and provide time for common planning. We recognized this as an "enabling mechanism," similar to the concept of multiage classrooms at the elementary level. In and of themselves these structural mechanisms do not represent a move to a more task-focused school culture; however, they provide a supportive structure in which these changes can take place. They also provide some interruption of the typical routine so that teachers are encouraged to rethink what they are doing. In the university team, we frequently

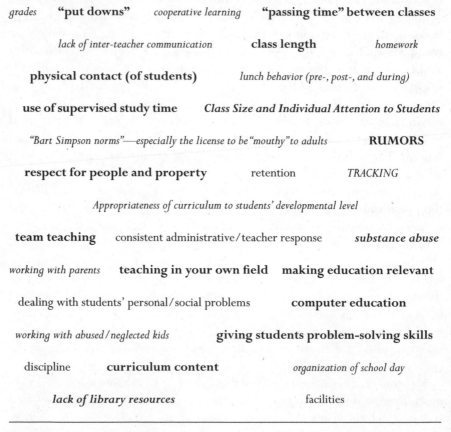

Figure 7.1   Proposed agenda items

discussed the merits of "enabling structures." Most of us saw these structural changes as positive. From our experience at Riversedge, we were very much aware of the potential that organizational change could have for building beliefs and redirecting purposes and goals. At least one member of the university team viewed these structural changes as "competing" with understanding and implementating the theory (e.g., Beck, Urdan, & Midgley, 1992). Over the course of our collaboration, more time was spent discussing team teaching, small houses, and block scheduling than any other issues. Discussions of what those mechanisms could enable were initiated only when the university team asked the teachers to reflect on why they might want to make those changes and how those changes might affect the students in their school. When the possibility of moving toward some type of school-within-a-school or small house was first raised at Plainview, many teachers were unfamiliar with these terms and unaware of how this structure was used in schools. Some mistakenly referred to it as "open house." Others had heard of this possibility and were attracted to it. But it was clear from the beginning that some were less than enthusiastic about what implications this structural change might have for their daily lives as teachers.

But the idea began to grow. With the university team's help, a visit to a school that had established a small house concept was arranged. Weekly sessions were punctuated first with questions about whether this was acceptable and possible at Plainview. From these discussions there evolved a plan to hold a workshop or retreat before the end of the school year to discuss the small house concept. The university team suggested the workshop be held at a university conference center and offered to provide a catered lunch. The Plainview staff was not receptive to this idea. They wanted to plan the retreat and decided it should take place locally. It was clearly their meeting and they would do it their way. They were taking over the reins in a positive way and we were very pleased!

As it turned out, the retreat was held in the school on a Saturday in early May. The planning team reported to the faculty as a whole, attempted to get a wider circle of staff involved and began serious planning for the changes—and more importantly, really took over the whole process. The tenor of the time was optimistic and hopeful.

After the retreat, the dialogue at the team meetings revolved around the nuts and bolts of establishing such a program: Would this be a small experiment involving a limited number of students and teachers? Or would it be a bolder step involving teachers at all grade levels? Worries about scheduling were punctuated with concerns about how to handle the math department's dedication to ability grouping. There were worries about how to communicate the changes to parents and about whether central administration would go along with the plans. In spite of these questions, the feeling persisted through the end of the year that some approximation of a small house venture would be initiated in the fall. In retrospect, there were also signs that plans were moving too rapidly for some and that all was not what it seemed. As we will see, the innovation did not quite occur as those involved had hoped.

And so the first phase of our effort was concluded. On the positive side, there seemed to be the possibility of structural change (small house) that could provide the same impetus for culture change that we saw happening at Riversedge. But there were lingering concerns. We sensed that the theory we held dear was not really a functioning part of the discussions. School staff did not describe problems or frame their solutions in terms of the theory. This was in part attributable to our inability to insert a theoretical perspective into the discussions. More troublesome perhaps was the role of the leaders at Plainview. We saw the assistant principal as an innovator and as an advocate of the kinds of changes that were being discussed. But our contacts with the principal were much less frequent and rarely centered around discussions of theory. Since the principal was not an active participant in the discussions, teachers regularly wondered aloud whether it would be possible to enact the plans under consideration. Plainview presented differences in leadership that served to affect the dynamic of change in significant ways throughout the period of collaboration.

Year Two

Year two began with the acknowledgment by the principals that they had been unable to rearrange the schedule in a way that would facilitate the plans that had been formulated the previous spring. The teachers, particularly those who had done some planning over the summer, were more resigned than angry. There was an "I told you so" undertone to early meetings that year. Teachers expressed disappointment that the principals had been unable to come up with the scheduling that was needed, but some acknowledged that scheduling is very complex and many factors must be taken into account. In truth, the university team seemed more disappointed and discouraged than did the teachers. We noted that issues discussed at length during the first year were dominating discussions again without any acknowledgment that they had been discussed in detail before and without any real effort to consider how these issues might be addressed by school change. Meetings sometimes degenerated into gripe sessions with teachers giving examples of the latest problem they had been called upon to handle. The number of times that "discipline problems" was brought up for discussion increased.

Occasionally a change was proposed that seemed quite distant from the problems that existed or from any real attempt to change the culture of the school. The principals decided to cut down on the number of bells that rang to signal movement from one class to another. They reasoned that students could move from one class to another with one bell as a guide. This was pointed to as a sign of progress. A new bumper sticker was designed and distributed that read "Proud Parent of a Plainview Middle School Student" to replace the old one that read "Proud Parent of a Plainview Honor Roll Student." We had not suggested these changes, but at that point we were pleased to see any sign of positive change, even these relatively superficial changes. We hoped they were the outward manifestations of some shift in thinking.

The teachers had not given up on the idea of some sort of structural change and conversations about teaming and small house persisted. At the same time, it was decided that the discussion should be expanded to include other areas of school life that needed examination and reform. In addition to expansion of the small house, items set for discussion included organization of the school day, student recognition, developing advisor-advisee programs, and again, homework policy and student evaluation. Subgroups were formed to bring back recommendations to the group as a whole and eventually to the entire faculty. The link to a more task-focused school culture was not obvious in all cases to the university team. We felt it was important for change to be driven by school needs as seen by the staff and retained a certain degree of confidence that the link could ultimately be made. In both small groups and in the larger sessions, the discussion was serious and although often repetitive, it was at times truly energized. All of this prompted this observation by the principal: "Change is going to occur. There is a new spirit."

At a fall meeting of the board of education, Riversedge and Plainview principals were asked to describe their programs and the changes that were underway. The elementary school principal described programmatic changes that were specifically related to an overall theoretical framework and to long-term goals. In contrast, the assistant principal at Plainview described what was a "laundry list" of changes that were on the table, some of which had little or nothing to do with enhancing a task goal emphasis. The assistant superintendent remarked that he was pleased to hear about the changes being contemplated at the middle school level, and he noted that some of these changes had been recommended years ago but never implemented. What was bothersome to the university team was that the presentation at best paid lip service to the framework that we brought to the endeavor. It was clear that our role and that of the guiding theory were much less pivotal to school change at Plainview than was the case at Riversedge.

Some members of the Plainview team began to take a more active role, perhaps out of frustration with the slow pace of change. We hoped that this was a sign that they were beginning to take "ownership" of the process in a productive and creative way. As one teacher put it, "I thought the U of M was going to tell us what to do, but they won't." Then she proceeded to suggest that the staff had to take the initiative. They visited schools that had inaugurated a number of programs that Plainview was considering and reported back to the group. Although they were enthusiastic about what they saw and heard, they often commented on the different financial situation in these other schools and the problems they would have implementing similar programs with limited resources. One middle school they visited had within a very brief period of time put into place a schoolwide small house system, with heterogeneous grouping in all subjects, thematic approaches to the curriculum, and advisory groups. When one teacher asked those who had visited how these changes had been implemented so quickly, the answer was: "The principal just decided it was going to happen and it did." Although we oppose a top-down approach to change and believe that thinking has to change in order for reform to be sustained, we were frustrated enough to wish that some dramatic action would be taken by the leadership at Plainview.

What became evident was that the weekly meetings reflected just a small part of what was happening. Some teachers were beginning to experiment in their approaches to teaching and classroom management. Here and there groups of teachers began talking to each other about teaming and about thematic instruction involving several content areas, such as social studies, literature, and science. Especially interesting in this regard was a teacher who had been given a self-contained 6th grade class, at his request, after the first year of the project. He had been energized by an array of sources, including a workshop he had attended on promoting self-esteem and by his wife who happened to be a member of the Riversedge team. He was enthusiastic about what was happening at Riversedge and constructed his own version of the vision we had been discussing. While he admitted that he wasn't always sure of what to do, he was convinced that something had to be done to enhance the self-esteem of all students. He saw classroom and school as places that could indeed make a difference. As a self-confessed former foot-dragger on educational innovation, he became an articulate activist for school reform. He served as a kind of counterforce to those who were congenitally skeptical of change whatever the form. His new motivation was a subject of regular comment, sometimes in humor, but often with a sense of intrigue if not outright approbation.

Increasingly, there seemed to be agreement that teaming, flexible block scheduling, and perhaps some version of a small house were in the school's future. Teachers were talking to each other about organizing teams. Questions were raised about whether everyone who wanted to be part of a team would be granted that prerogative. There were questions about who could teach what, and consequently, questions of credentials and competence emerged. There were discussions about how it might work out for an English teacher to team with someone in social studies or science. And there was always that lingering concern, "What about math?"

Teachers heard reports of what the high school staff had to say about all this, and at this phase these reports were presented as a caution in pursuing change if not as an outright barrier to change. After all, the high school expected that a standard curriculum would be followed—and how could that be assured under the circumstances? Then, there were side issues of importance: How would band, music, and art be handled? What about algebra? And what would be done about the "gifted and talented program"? It was becoming clear that even if a smaller portion of the school got the go-ahead to experiment with teaming and some version of small house, virtually every facet of the school and every faculty member would somehow feel the effects. What would these effects be? Teachers wondered if they would get a different type of student. Would they have to teach something they didn't want to teach? Would they be pushed aside as not part of a "progressive movement"? Would they have to work harder and in ways they didn't want to work and felt they shouldn't have to work?

As such feelings approached a kind of boiling point in some quarters, an outside official representing the Michigan Education Association (MEA) showed up unannounced at one of the group meetings. She obviously had been called to action by a disgruntled member (or members) of the school staff. Her main message was that change could not be undertaken unless it was "negotiated." She seemed to be minimally informed about what had been transpiring at Plainview and was not aware until after the meeting that some of the participants were from the university. But she inserted herself into the discussion forcefully with a flat statement that the teaming and other plans for reorganization that were being discussed absolutely could not be carried out: They violated the agreed-upon work rules. The changes would have to be negotiated. The university team remained silent, but a strong oppositional response came from the teachers who were present at the meeting. They made it quite clear that they were talking about things they *wanted* to do. They also made it quite clear that if they wanted to do it they *would* do it, whether or not the union supported it. The assistant principal, himself a former bargaining representative in the district, remained silent, probably the right tactical move under the circumstances. And, at a subsequent meeting, upon reading a letter from the MEA demanding that bargaining be reopened on work rules before any action was taken, he announced flatly, "I'm moving ahead."

March was a period of working in small groups, planning what would be done in the teams. There was a feeling that change was really going to happen and at times an expression of being "overwhelmed" by it all. Teachers developed outlines for carrying out thematic instruction within the teams. The assistant principal remarked, "This is the first time this kind of planning has happened this early." Amidst the activity and enthusiasm, the university team from time to time felt compelled to ask how the teachers' activities related to the overall theoretical framework or how they would lead to a greater emphasis on task rather than ability goals? These were generally accepted as valid questions and satisfactory answers were usually worked out.

It is interesting to note that during this period of time an incidental event became a "defining moment." Several members of the university team sent a note to the prospective small house teachers suggesting that it might be necessary to recruit a math teacher from the other middle school if one did not volunteer at Plainview. The note was placed in the school mailboxes of prospective small house teachers only. But someone copied it and distributed it to *all* the teachers. There was a huge and largely negative reaction from most of the staff. The reasons for this reaction are hard to fathom even now in retrospect. The suggestion that a teacher from another school might need to be recruited may have been seen as a negative statement about the quality of the staff at Plainview. Or perhaps the note made the inevitability of change salient. In any event, the ultimate result was positive. Increasingly, teachers began to express the feeling that changes would indeed occur. Some who had not been participating in the discussions may have assumed, based on past experience, that in the end nothing would happen. Suddenly, the issues were being discussed by the whole school and not just by a small group. One teacher told us that this was the first time she really understood or cared about what was going on in the after-school meetings; not only did she join the discussions after school but volunteered to teach math in the 7th grade small house. Others also came forward to express their interest or at least their willingness to listen. No one involved enjoyed

the conflict and the emotional outbursts, but maybe it all contributed positively to change in the long run.

Others were stimulated as well—not to become involved but to become
more organized in their opposition to change. In April it became apparent
that many of the members of the math department were still actively op-
posing change, not just in math classes but throughout the school. If they
refused to participate in the small houses, there was a major problem in
scheduling to accommodate them. Moreover, if they refused to budge on
ability grouping, they prevented any chance of obtaining heterogeneous
grouping in the teams, a concept that was fundamental to the thinking of
the planning group. The latter had many reasons for not wishing to separate
students of different ability levels. It was not just a matter of theory; they
agreed that the separation of students by ability sometimes contributed to
lowered self-esteem. They also believed that those assigned to the low
groups were difficult to teach. Generally, they just seemed to value the
ideal of integration of students of different type and background. The parent representative expressed concern about all the negative feelings she
sensed were surfacing. The conflict was out in the open and people were
taking sides. The process of incorporating the 6th, 7th, and 8th grades into
teams and subschools was brought to a temporary halt.

At this point, the principal and assistant principal approached two faculty
members regarding the possibility of teaching heterogeneously grouped 7th
grade math. One was the math teacher we alluded to previously. The other
was a vocational education teacher who was also certified to teach math. It
seemed as though one or the other would volunteer to teach in the 7th
grade small house. A 7th grade science teacher, language arts teacher, and
social studies teacher had already expressed interest in the new structure. It
also seemed as though the principals supported the concept. Possibly, at
long last, something was going to happen. The year ended with the expectation that a 7th grade small house would be in place in the fall.

Year Three

We were looking forward to the beginning of year three with great anticipa-
tion. Our positive experiences at Riversedge led us to believe that a structural change would be in place at Plainview that would enable teachers, at
least at the 7th grade level, to move toward a more task-focused learning environment for their students. We had already seen evidence that the 6th
grade teachers were experimenting with some new organizational structures and ideas. Thus, we were particularly disappointed and frustrated when

we learned that the principals had been unable to come up with a schedule that would facilitate the small house. We heard a number of different scenarios about what had happened. We were told that male teachers were needed to supervise the lunchroom and that this had complicated scheduling. Then we were told that scheduling band during the school day had been a priority, evidently higher than the small house. Finally, we were told that the gifted and talented program was sacrosanct and made the scheduling of heterogeneously grouped small house classes virtually impossible.

The university team seriously considered withdrawing from the project. "Why are we going over all this old ground?" "What we're saying now we were saying last year at this time." "Nothing's changed." Some suggested a change in strategy, working on smaller issues that might bring quicker evidence of "success," such as changing student evaluation practices. But we had tried that before with minimal results. It was a critical time for the project as a whole and we had to make a decision. "This seems like a time for us to decide if we are willing to devote some energy and enthusiasm to this effort, or give up," is the way one member summed it up. He quickly added, "But I notice we still make that trip to Plainview every Friday afternoon, so we haven't stopped trying and will probably keep trying." And so the project continued.

The 7th grade teachers who had expected to be planning and teaming together were resigned and also somewhat angry. Some of the teachers who had come to the after-school planning meetings regularly during the first year and one-half stopped attending. One who had been particularly pessimistic about bringing about change stated quite bluntly, "I can't waste any more time planning for change when nothing happens." In a hallway conversation, one teacher indicated that it simply was not worth putting any more of her time into the effort unless and until there was more commitment "from the top." At one particularly memorable meeting the assistant principal looked around the room at the six university team members and one parent and said, "It looks like there aren't many teachers here today." Our rejoinder was, "There aren't *any* teachers here today." By the end of the meeting three teachers had arrived, but we sensed that they came out of duty rather than out of enthusiasm or hope for the change process.

At the same time, the principal and the assistant principal were unexpectedly optimistic. They assured us that many changes had been made and would continue to be made. They urged us to be patient. The *Plainview News,* a publication sent home to parents at the beginning of the year included this upbeat statement:

Many of the changes that we have discussed at our School Improvement, U of M Coalition, PTSO, and staff meetings during the last one and a half years are finally in place. The majority of our students are grouped heterogeneously (tracking of students has been eliminated except for mathematics courses and the GT program) in their classes so that we can utilize our cooperative learning strategies in tandem with thematic instruction and interdisciplinary models. With these approaches, we are attempting to create a learning environment which is less stressful, risk-free, and more conducive for our students to learn in. Additionally, several sections of classes in the seventh and eighth grade are blocked so that the students move as a group from class to class and consequently form a support system within the learning environment. We are also focusing on teaching students "how to learn and retain information" researched or presented. We are constructing our curriculum to combine both the State of Michigan's Core Curriculum and our course goals and objectives.

This upbeat announcement glossed over the conflicts, struggles, and failures of the previous year. Not surprisingly so. Public communications to parents are not meant to show the underside of school change. But careful reading reveals that the school had only moved so far in effecting change—not far enough to satisfy a significant portion of the staff, many of whom were quite discouraged. On the other hand, we read this piece and wondered if we were being overly pessimistic. We knew that a few more teachers were working together in ways that they hadn't before. There was some reason to believe that instructional approaches had been rethought. Significant numbers of school staff now saw the problems as school problems to be solved by reforming what they were and did. Of course, they still wanted "support" for this, not so much money as commitment from leadership at the school and district level. And they were hesitant to move if they did not sense this support.

It's fair to say that meetings and the venues for interaction between Plainview and university team members widened and became more varied. Unlike the regularity of a weekly meeting at Riversedge, there were more often meetings in smaller groups with continually varying membership. There were some "regulars" and some who clearly seemed to have the potential for leadership, but the operative rule this year was multiple meetings, but not only with the "school improvement team" membership. And besides, some of the most important encounters were informal, such as an unplanned encounter with a teacher in the hallway. Additionally, we initiated a number of meetings with the principal and assistant principal to encourage action and to understand inaction. Most of the conversation through December was minimally concerned with organizational change and more concerned with general policies and principles that might encourage student investment in schooling. Evaluation came up as it had many times before, and again there were no clear directions articulated. The assistant principal announced that portfolios were probably going to be mandated by the district, and therefore some discussion was probably warranted. There was little response.

The focus turned to "recognition." We described how the development of the principles of recognition (see Table 6.1) at Riversedge had been a turning point in understanding for many. The decision was made to develop a similar list at Plainview. One member of the team asked us to bring in the list from Riversedge as a starting point. We were somewhat reluctant but agreed that this would stimulate conversation. In retrospect, it was a mistake. The Plainview team selected three or four of the principles they felt would be accepted by the staff as a whole and endorsed them with some minor changes in the wording. There was little in the way of debate, and although we continually referred to the theory and how the principles reflected that framework, this was essentially a lost opportunity. The staff as a whole agreed to the principles, but we had no evidence that any recognition practices changed as a result.

The teachers at Plainview were very much aware of the changes that were underway at Riversedge, not from our comments but through the school grapevine. One sensed that students who had come from Riversedge, especially their parents, were beginning to pass the word as did a board member or two. There was in fact some reason to believe that whereas Riversedge was gaining the reputation of the school that was "moving," Plainview was "stuck in the mud." In no sense did the university team make these kinds of social comparisons. We did not want to act in a way contrary to our own theory, of course. But the social comparisons were being made and to a degree they were being exploited in a positive way, as evidence of what could be done and as encouragement for trying something new.

Interspersed here and there were incidents and examples that showed change, although not dramatic, was occurring. One of the university team members was walking in the school hall one morning when a teacher who had been quite hostile to change of any kind opened his door and pulled him in: "Take a look at this!" Inside, students were reading in groups of various sizes. "They pick their own groups. They can work wherever they want—and they're all into it," the teacher stated emphatically. "I just wanted to let you know that although I know I haven't been very supportive of your efforts in the past, the work you've done here has definitely changed my career. As a matter of fact, if it weren't for what you've done, my career would probably have ended by now." That was enough to convince one university team member to keep at it, although there did not seem to be a lot going on in that classroom that one would characterize as task-focused. But perhaps it was a start. As it was shared with the university team as a whole, a few became less skeptical.

Conversations about the small house continued and began to sound repetitious. The same issues were discussed; the same hurdles were faced. It was now, as perhaps it had always been, a political issue involving power and control of resources. Those who wanted to create a small house were openly accused of trying to garner more than their fair share of resources. There were counter charges about the veto power that certain math teachers were wielding for what were deemed "selfish" purposes. It was a time full of conflict. Collegiality did not seem to be the order of the day. Emotions ran high. The university team was accused of forcing the school to make organizational changes that would undermine teaching. One teacher flatly refused to complete the annually administered survey, stating that if he had his way, the school would be rid of the university team.

The end of the school year and our period of collaboration with Plainview was approaching. The university team decided to put all its energies into the development of a 7th and 8th grade small house. A meeting was arranged that included both the principal and the assistant principal. They assured us this could and would happen the next fall if the teachers supported the concept. One of the teachers who had been the most articulate spokesperson for the small house had stopped coming to meetings. We called him and arranged a private meeting after school. We recounted our meeting with the principals and asked him if he would be willing to poll the teachers regarding their interest in and support for the small house concept. He expressed again his enthusiasm for the small house structure and what it would enable teachers to do and agreed to invite teachers to a meeting. He selected two times, one before school and one after so that all teachers would have a chance to attend if they desired. The meetings were held in his classroom and without the principals in attendance. Many teachers attended one or the other meeting and some attended both. A few of the teachers who attended had never participated in the after-school meetings. The teachers were determined to bring the plan to fruition. "Just give us a block of time and some students and we'll do the scheduling ourselves." Two math teachers volunteered to give the house plan a try, even though they expressed doubts about heterogeneous ability grouping in math. A highly respected 8th grade English teacher described how he had always been given the "best" students and stated adamantly that he no longer wanted to teach that way: He said he no longer believed in it and looked forward to being part of an 8th grade team.

We tried to understand this seemingly dramatic change in attitude. Perhaps the teachers recognized that the opportunity for reform was coming to an end, and it was a now or never situation. Perhaps they sensed that teachers had been given more control over the destiny of the school than they had ever been given before. Perhaps this was a sign that the many, many hours of dialogue and debate had changed some thinking and inspired action.

In the end, the principal announced that small house would be initiated at the 7th grade level in the fall and if that proved successful, in the eighth grade the following year. The teachers felt this was a fair and prudent decision. Arrangements were initiated for sharing this proposal with parents and the process of recruitment and planning began. A meeting was held in which parents of prospective 6th grade students were invited to hear about the program. The teacher who led the orientation session was particularly effective, but everyone who spoke expressed enthusiasm and excitement for what was to happen. A defining moment occurred when the parent of a Riversedge child asked, "Will this be something like the MAGIC program at Riversedge?" Not knowing exactly how to respond, the teachers essentially said "yes," and the parent proceeded to explain what a difference the Riversedge program had made in the life of her child. This was a moving testimonial by a parent who confessed to having been a less than stellar student herself. But the conclusion she reached was if this is something like the MAGIC program, she was for it and wanted her child in it. We were somewhat surprised that this was the majority opinion of the parents present. They definitely wanted this change. Teachers present were emboldened, even though much had to be done to bring the organizational ideas into existence.

At the end of the year, which also marked the conclusion of the university team's formal involvement, it could be said that something was started. Emphatically, an unfinished experiment. No one offered to celebrate what had been accomplished. There wasn't a party in which Plainview staff and university team members could bid fond farewell as there was at Riversedge. The parting was hardly noted; it certainly was welcomed in some quarters, it probably was not in others. We hoped that a few would remember and carry on.

Afterword

Our work in Plainview certainly did not come to a grand conclusion. But we did have a sense that something might have happened concurrent with our presence there, perhaps as the result of our encouragement. We re-called statements here and there that reinforced our feeling that change had indeed happened. Not a "sea change," certainly, but some movement in the direction of emphasizing task and minimizing ability goals was evident.

Contrary to this, of course, was an awareness that the commitment to the effort was not unanimous. All of this created a certain ambivalence on our part as to whether what had happened in small ways here and there would be sustained. We resolved to revisit Plainview after our project was offi-cially concluded. Periodically during the next year we called the assistant principal and suggested that we visit the small house team. Each time he as-sured us that the house was functioning well, that plans were in place for moving ahead with the 8th grade house but concluded that this was a par-ticularly busy time for them and not a good time for us to drop by. We did get permission to give surveys a final time in the spring, and one of the small house teachers included a blistering note: "Where were you this year? We've been hard at work, but you disappeared. All you want from us is data." We responded with a note that described our efforts to meet with school staff and resolved that we would continue to seek contacts with in-terested staff. The principal retired and although the assistant principal was expected to take his place, that did not happen. Many felt that he deserved the position. We wondered if the changes at Plainview were being viewed less than enthusiastically by central administration.

Subsequent visits did yield evidence of continuing effort directed toward enhancing the emphasis on task rather than ability goals in the school. The small house that was established at the 7th grade level appeared to be hold-ing its own. In a meeting with the teachers involved, one could not help but feel positive. As they discussed what they had done and what they were planning to do, their enthusiasm and commitment were palpable. The member of the team responsible for teaching math admitted that she had not expected to stick with the program for more than a year, but now she was no longer a hesitant participant but an advocate. Unquestionably, these teachers bonded as they pursued a unifying purpose which eventuated in the realization of many of the objectives discussed during our collaboration. Of particular interest was the way teachers discussed their commitment to heterogeneous grouping; their description of attempts at thematic instruc-tion, flexible scheduling, and cooperative learning; and their efforts to rec-ognize students for a variety of efforts and talents. One by one they told us, "I will never be able to go back to teaching the old way."

And, just as we were putting the finishing touches on this book, we learned of several interesting happenings that all bode well for the continuation of the culture change that was begun with our effort. Plainview has now also established an 8th grade small house. The local paper had an article about a thematic unit on the middle ages that was recently undertaken. And the assistant principal who assisted in the collaboration has now been made principal. We sense a heightened mood of optimism among those at Plainview who have struggled to transform the culture of their school. We share that optimism.

Notes

1. In this regard, we are especially indebted to former graduate students Jamie Beck Jensen, Tim Urdan, and Stewart Wood (for example, Beck, Urdan, & Midgley, 1992; Urdan, Wood, & Midgley, 1995; Wood & Midgley, 1995).

8 So, What Did We Learn?

There is nothing so practical as a good theory.

—**Kurt Lewin,** *Field Theory in Social Science,* **p. 169**

For Lewin, at least, there was nothing so theoretical as a good practical problem.

—**Dorwin Cartwright,** *Journal of Social Issue,* **p. 178**[1]

The immediately preceding chapters present our view of two on-going experiments in school culture change. We initiated these experiments to learn something. First, we hoped to enrich our vision of school and frame it more accurately in terms of the real world. Second, we wanted to test the practicality of what we were proposing. Can one really hope to change, let alone transform, school cultures? And more specifically, how does this change affect those who experience it—the students and the teachers? We hoped that pursuing both of those questions would contribute to the "truth" of the vision as well as its practicality. Thus, we set out on this venture guided by the spirit of Kurt Lewin, in the hope that we might not only learn something of theoretical interest but discover something that might be useful for practicing educators and something that would prove consequential in the lives of students. So, in retrospect, what did we learn?

Can School Cultures Be Changed?

Chapters 6 and 7 have already indicated that something like a shift, possibly a change, in school culture was beginning to occur in Riversedge and Plainview. It was not happening in every quarter of these two schools or as pro-

189

foundly and pervasively as some of those involved might have hoped. But in both schools there was tangible evidence of change. Changes in recognition and "grading" policies occurred. Individuals and small groups of teachers began to examine new approaches to instruction that might change student focus on learning—introducing whole language teaching methods and "math their way," as examples. Some began discussing reforming into small schools and proceeded to experiment with thematic instruction and team teaching. These schools were doing different things after less than three years. They were doing things that possibly were a part of refocusing purposes and goals. Along with this, principals and some members of staff were talking about children and teaching in quite different ways. Notably, the topics of their conversation and the language they used reflected a perspective that was becoming increasingly compatible with the vision for schooling presented in Chapter 2. Briefly and specifically, task goals were stressed more, ability goals less. Overall, this was most obvious in the case of Riversedge; less obvious with Plainview. But there was evidence of change in both cases.

Concrete examples of changed policies, the impressions of participants (students, teachers, parents, and researchers), and the anecdotes and stories that reflect changed thinking provide compelling documentation that something was happening.[2] Yet, we were also committed to searching for evidence of change using methods less tied to our participant-observer role. Importantly, Riversedge and Plainview were each paired with a "comparison" school in the same district that was not engaged in the same or a similar process. Surveys were administered to students and teachers in both the demonstration and comparison schools before the period of collaboration began and at the conclusion of our involvement. Rigorous analyses were performed to determine if the perceptions, beliefs, and behaviors of students and teachers in the demonstration schools became distinctively different. Specifically, we focused on changes toward and increased focus on task as opposed to ability goals and on beliefs and behaviors that should be related to holding these goals.

Our preference would have been to conduct this quantitative investigation at the end of five or even seven years rather than at the end of two or three. We were well aware that the first year of collaboration had been spent, for the most part, discussing theory and establishing a trusting relationship between researchers and school staff. We were also cognizant that significant changes were still in the planning stage, particularly at the middle school, when the post-collaboration data were collected. We were especially mindful of the literature on school change that warns against premature evaluation. Given the time frame in which we had to work, however, we did not have the option of a leisurely wait for things to happen in due course. Thus, after only about two years of serious effort to effect change we proceeded with a rather rigorous, quantitatively based evaluation of changes in teachers and their students. In spite of the time limitations, we were nevertheless curious to learn whether the changes as noted were powerful and pervasive enough to begin having effects on the thoughts and reported behavior of students and staff. Thus, we proceeded to conduct a series of studies based on established survey procedures. The items were framed so as to elicit reliable information from teachers and students regarding the school cultures in which they taught and learned. The studies were specifically designed to determine further and in what ways the demonstration schools changed over the intervention period relative to the comparison schools.

Detailed descriptions of these studies have been presented elsewhere (for example, Anderman, Maehr, & Midgley, 1995; Midgley, Maehr, Collopy, & Roeser, 1994; Wood & Midgley, 1995). Our purpose here is not to describe these studies in detail but rather to indicate how these studies contributed to a fuller picture of school culture change and its effect on those who participated in the process. We begin by summarizing findings based on data collected from *teachers*. Teachers' beliefs and behaviors are doubtless an important factor in determining what the school is like that will be experienced by students. Teacher change is a prerequisite for student change. It is likely that teacher change will antedate by some significant time period the evidence of change in students. In any event, we carefully examined the questionnaire filled out by school staff for further evidence of what did or did not happen in the case of the teachers in Riversedge and Plainview that did not happen in the comparison schools.

Changes in School Culture: The Teachers' View[3]

At various stages in the collaboration, all teachers at the elementary and middle school levels in both demonstration and comparison schools responded to surveys focusing on two central issues. The first issue concerned the teachers' view of their school, especially the "work culture" that existed. This assessment focused especially on perceptions held by teachers that they were in fact experiencing the kind of work environment that would encourage them to step back, think about what they were doing, and be venturesome. In other words, we wondered if teachers were experiencing the kind of environment that they were being urged to create for their students. Was there a stress on task goals and a deemphasis on ability goals in their work lives? Did they see the leadership and organizational structure of the school as leading to and encouraging them to pursue excellence, to innovate and put forth their best effort, and to grow and learn? Or did they see their work life as framed in terms of power, status, and competition, with emphases on winning certain rewards and recognition, wielding power, demonstrating superiority, and focusing on how good they were (or weren't) instead of on how good they were *becoming?* In referring to the task-goal emphasis in the work life, or culture, of teachers we use the term accomplishment. We label the ability-goal emphasis in the work context as power (Maehr and Braskamp, 1986; Braskamp & Maehr, 1985).

In addition to considering the work life of teachers, we looked specifically and rather extensively at teachers' orientations toward teaching and learning: their instructional goals, their beliefs about students, and their reported instructional practices. One issue of importance, of course, was what they considered the purposes of schooling to be. Essentially, they responded to items which asked them about whether they in fact believed that the school was not only *for children* but *for learning,* as oriented toward task rather than ability. They were also queried about their beliefs about ability: How stable or malleable was it? Could one expect that all children could learn? Was it the teacher's responsibility to stress progress, growth, and continuing investment in learning? They were also queried about certain specific strategies they deemed desirable and acceptable, all of which could be designated as contributing to or detracting from a task-focused classroom culture.[4]

We began our analysis by comparing responses of teachers in demonstration and comparison schools at the "start" and at the "end" of the collaborative intervention, following accepted statistical procedures. At both the elementary and middle school level, after controlling for initial differences, demonstration teachers perceived that the school culture was more focused on accomplishment than did comparison school teachers. There was also an indication that elementary demonstration teachers increased their use of task-focused instructional practices (such as using cooperative learning and encouraging students to monitor their own progress) more than did comparison school teachers. But the results were not strong or pervasive. They were at best marginal in terms of accepted statistical standards of significance.

Knowing what we did about the two demonstration schools, however, we were certain that this first overall analysis missed the point a bit. We knew that certain teachers were not participating at all in the process. They filled out the forms and cooperated in the administration of surveys to students, but they seldom if ever attended meetings associated with the collaboration. Their uninvolvement in, sometimes outright rejection of, the nature and direction of the change efforts was made known to their colleagues and sometimes directly to us. Given this reality, we decided to look at the survey results again, comparing the patterns of change of "involved" and "uninvolved" teachers. As we suspected, these two groups presented distinctly different profiles. The involved group did exhibited evidence of the kind of change that the collaborative activities were designed to bring about. Highly involved elementary teachers exhibited more change over time toward a task focus and away from an ability focus than did comparison school teachers. This was exhibited in their reported changes in instructional practices and pedagogical beliefs. It was also evident in the goals they held for their students. Similar findings were obtained at the middle school level, but the effects were less pervasive. As at the elementary level, highly involved teachers showed a greater movement away from ability-focused instruction and pedagogical beliefs than did comparison teachers.

In summary, systematic comparisons of data derived from an established survey instrument (Midgley, Maehr, et al., 1996; see Appendix) as well as informal and formal observations and interviews converged on a central point: Change had occurred, at least for those teachers who were highly involved in the process. At the end of less than three years, there was a basis for concluding that at least a certain portion of the teachers had shifted toward bringing a task-focused vision of school into being. They not only increasingly held a task-focused view of schooling and expressed themselves in different language but were apparently also redesigning their teaching and classroom management accordingly. All of this held promise for the ultimate emergence of a task-focused school culture for students. It is not surprising that these changes were particularly evident in teachers who were more involved in the discussions, the planning, and the implementation. It is, however, worth adding that subsequent to the time these data were gathered, there was a sense that at least some of the less involved teachers were beginning to see the positive effects of the changes their colleagues were making and also of schoolwide changes that had been implemented. Moreover, as we return from time to time, it is evident that the ideas that emerged in the course of several years' effort have not been forgotten just because the university is no longer heavily involved. The dialogue regarding task and ability goals continues at Riversedge and Plainview.

Changes in School Culture: The Students' View

There was reason to believe that there had been a cultural shift in the staff of the two demonstration schools. Each school had made changes in policies and practices that could influence the culture of school experienced by students. Teachers were talking among themselves and to us differently about teaching and learning. They were experimenting in their conducting, organizing, and scheduling of instruction. They were talking about students and viewing the purposes of schooling in ways we had not seen before. The changes were not dramatic, but they were there. But might these changes as well as the thinking, talking, and doing of some of the teachers, even in this short time period, trickle down to the experiences of students? To explore this, we also conducted two major studies with students. One study focused especially on Riversedge; the second on Plainview. In both cases, we examined the same basic set of variables, employing an individual- (early grades) or group- (upper grades) administered survey instrument.[5] Briefly, the variables we examined included the achievement goals held by students, their sense of self-efficacy, and their reported use of various learning strategies (for example, effort avoidance and deep processing). Of course, we also elicited students' views of their classrooms and the school as a whole: What were the regnant purposes? How was schooling defined? Both studies were longitudinal in nature and were designed to tease out possible effects over time that could be attributed to the culture change that might have occurred at the two demonstration schools.

Change in Students at Riversedge[6]

Surveys were administered to 1st through 5th grade students in both the demonstration and comparison elementary schools before the project began and shortly before our involvement in the project was terminated. Two general sets of analyses were conducted. First, we looked at the overall effects of school type (demonstration versus comparison) and grade level on student outcomes both within and across measurement times (that is, data collected before and after the collaborative intervention). In an effort to refine these analyses, we also compared students who had teachers who were highly involved in the change project in the demonstration school with students of teachers in the comparison school. In the second general series of analyses, we included student characteristics, including achievement level, gender, and ethnicity to see if different types of students were affected differently by the collaborative intervention.

As it turned out, there was no meaningful pattern of evidence indicating that Riversedge students experienced a greater task-oriented school environment than their peers at the comparison school, and they did not as yet exhibit different patterns of motivation and learning. This was disappointing but in hindsight understandable. The fact of the matter is that we experienced considerable difficulties in obtaining valid survey inventory data, especially from the youngest of the students. This was not for want of trying. Indeed, we took every step that we could to ensure that the survey inventory would be valid. We worded the items very carefully so that they would be within the vocabulary range of young children; we used sample items to familiarize children with the scales; we read all of the items out loud; and we administered the surveys to children in the 1st and 2nd grades on a one-to-one basis (one researcher to one child). Nevertheless, many of the scales that emerged from the data collected from children in the 1st, 2nd, and 3rd grades were found to be of questionable reliability. The reasons were partially clarified as we queried the children. For example, the children told us that they "liked the high end of the scale." They were eager to answer each question positively, even if that did not reflect their true opinion. Other researchers have had similar experiences with young children. Yet, we initially thought that the special care we were taking would overcome the expected problems. It did not and thus the attempt to assess change longitudinally during the course of the intervention was undermined. Therefore, it is not at all surprising that the "objective methods" we employed did not yield clear evidence of student change.

Of course, there also was the likelihood that changes noted in the case of teachers would not yet begin showing up in the perceptions of students in a powerful enough way that they could be assessed through surveys, especially with the young sample. In earlier work (Maehr & Fyans, 1989), we found that concepts of school culture are not clearly differentiated until after the 4th grade. In any event, the survey approach was insufficient for the purposes of providing an independent, perhaps more objective, reading on whether the changes that we could sense were occurring actually reached down in a significant way to the school world of the child. While in many ways understandable, it remains disappointing.

Did Plainview Make a Difference in the School Experience of Students?

While the survey results in the case of Riversedge students were noncommittal, a study conducted at Plainview[7] proved to be much more revealing. By the very nature of its clientele and the type of school it was, one could expect to obtain more reliable survey information. But we could also conduct a study that was more extensive in scope as well as more powerful in analysis.

Early adolescence in general and the transition from elementary to middle school in particular represents a particularly problematic period in the life of the child (Anderman & Maehr, 1994; Carnegie, 1989; Eccles & Midgley, 1989; Eccles et al., 1993). We keyed on that accepted finding in introducing our story of Plainview and pointed out further that an important characteristic of this problematic period is the disturbing decline in motivation for school achievement. Even "good" students may come to dislike school and avoid studying. Adolescents who like school will often like it for reasons that have little or nothing to do with the core curriculum. It may be the nonacademic side of school that seems to flourish—social relationships, sports—*not* learning or acquiring new academic knowledge or technical and vocational skills. We and others (for example, Harter, Whitesell, & Kowalski, 1992; Simmons & Blyth, 1987; Seidman, Allen, Aber, Mitchell, & Feinman, 1994) called attention not only to this disturbing decline in motivation but especially to the very real possibility that the cultures of middle grade schools are at fault. The point of our Plainview intervention, of course, was to see if our perspective on school held promise for turning this situation around. Specifically, we wondered if we could stop the slide toward a debilitating ability goal stress and possibly keep the task focus salient even during the middle grades period when many forces are at work to do just the opposite. Thus, the focus of our study was whether Plainview showed fewer signs of allowing this slide to occur than did the comparison school.

During the second year of our involvement, we collected survey data from a sample of 5th grade students from all six elementary schools in the district. At that point, little in the way of concrete change had occurred at Riversedge, and we did not expect that there would be any differences between Riversedge students and those in the other elementary schools. We then collected a second year of data from these students after they moved to 6th grade in either the demonstration (Plainview) or comparison middle school (there were only two middle schools in the district) and a final time after they had moved to the 7th grade. We measured students' personal goal orientations as well as their perceptions of the goals that were emphasized in their math and English classrooms.

We first checked the 5th grade data to see if students who were headed for the demonstration middle school (Plainview) differed from students who were headed for the comparison school. There were no differences between these two groups of students on any of the variables at the 5th grade level. We then looked at the trajectories of these students after they moved from 5th grade to either the demonstration (Plainview) or the comparison middle school. If changes were occurring in Plainview that were beginning to touch the lives of students, perhaps it would show up in how students expressed themselves about their schooling experiences. That is, the focus was on the different trajectories of their thoughts and feelings as they moved from elementary through the middle grades school.

Briefly, the results proved interesting and overall were supportive of the conclusion that something different was happening in the two schools. Over a three-year period, differences in orientations toward learning and achievement began to appear. Students who moved to the comparison middle school increased in their orientation toward demonstrating ability relative to others after the transition, whereas students who attended the demonstration school became less focused on demonstrating their ability after the transition. This is particularly interesting in light of previous studies that indicated that middle school students are more ability oriented than are elementary students (Midgley, Anderman, & Hicks, 1995). In addition, students who attended the comparison middle school perceived an increased emphasis on ability goals and extrinsic reasons for doing work in the classroom after the transition, whereas the students who attended the demonstration school did not.

Over the three-year period, middle school students enrolled in Plainview and the comparison school showed different patterns of orientation. One cannot say absolutely that these patterns were a result of the collaborative intervention that was taking place in Plainview but apparently something quite different was influencing the transition to and the experience of middle school. Perhaps the policy changes were having an effect. More likely, we believe, it was that the viability and value of a "task goal" became salient in the thinking of a certain cadre of teachers. They thought about this possibility, probably not just for the first time, but perhaps in a new way and with some new degree of confidence. And they began on occasion, increasingly, to teach, counsel, and relate to students accordingly. Maybe this would have happened without the collaboration, but this is doubtful. At the very least, what happened in the short period in which staff and university researchers worked together was that a certain direction—or theory of school—was given support, its saliency for practice was enhanced. And just possibly, that was beginning to be experienced by students in the classrooms as their teachers were seen as communicating something different about teaching and school than was communicated by those at a comparable school.

So, What *Did* We Learn—and So What?

What can be learned from this attempt to put theory into practice? Much, we think, and this book could not have been written had these lessons not been taken to heart. These results, as well as the more qualitative evidence described earlier, serve as the reference point for the rest of the chapters. More specifically, we single out several different types of understandings that emerged in the course of our effort and that gave life to theory we espoused at the outset and invigorated and informed the cultural transformations we propose.

The Validity and Practicality of the Vision

As we initiated this endeavor, our theory was built largely on the artifacts of focused research conducted sometimes in artificial settings. Certainly, we were aware of some ways in which the theory might apply to schools, but our knowledge was fragmented and incomplete. It is one thing to talk about possible "pressure points" for school change; it is quite different to experience firsthand the forms these take, the roles they play, and the interdependence that exists among them. If nothing else, the work we have reported should enhance the understanding of how schools define schooling for their students. As we learned, some of the simplest of things turned out to have the profoundest of effects. Who thinks about the fact that when the principal posts an honor role in a prominent place outside her office and makes a point of taking the honorees to lunch, it may be detrimental to instructional processes? And how often do researchers or practitioners pay attention to how schools are trapped by time, that by dividing up instruction into forty- to fifty-minute chunks of time they foreordain how courses will be taught and sorely limit the kind of innovations that can be tried? But these and other seemingly minor "facts" jumped out at us as we endeavored to understand and change school cultures.

So our vision did in fact lead us to learn more about schools: how they are constrained as well as how they can be reformed. It enabled us to find sources for framing purpose that are a root cause of student motivation and learning and that to no small degree validated our vision, at least as an outline for thought and action. But it was only through involvement in the daily working life of two schools that the outline could be fleshed out and thereby become practical. We now know, as we could not have known before, that task and ability goals are not mere abstractions. They are embodied in specifiable practices and policies. They follow from these practices — and they relate to the culture of school that will be experienced by students. At the very least, our experiences should make it easier for others to take this path. And we sincerely hope they will.

School Culture Can Change!

Of course, we also set off on this venture anticipating that we could find a way to change schools, especially school *cultures*. At the least, we believe we have evidence that the schools where the change process was undertaken were different at the conclusion of the collaboration than they were prior to it. More than that, we have described both in qualitative and quantitative terms, evidence that these schools were indeed different after the intervention and, generally speaking, moving in the direction of enhancing task (and minimizing ability) goals. All the evidence did not speak with one tongue, but we reported more than just vague impressions that a culture shift was beginning to occur in both schools. It was not a revolution in either case. Teachers in Riversedge and Plainview one by one, in this sector or that, simply began to think, act, and feel differently. A few policies were changed. In addition, there was evidence that children were beginning to receive the benefits of this. At the very least, the stories of Riversedge and Plainview indicate that it is not foolish or impractical to envision the emergence of task-focused schools. There are ways to bring this about that are under substantial control by those who teach and administer.

Reflections on Processes for School Change

We certainly did not set out to write a treatise on school change processes though such is certainly merited. We did, however, devote extensive effort to understanding how and under what circumstances changes may occur. And in particular, our in-depth experience with culture change in the case of Riversedge and Plainview provided us with plenty of opportunity to reflect on how schools change.

We began our two experiments in school change with certain basic notions regarding critical ingredients for school change (see Chapter 5). Change must be systemic. It is, desirably, guided by a shared theory of what school and schooling are about: Leadership is a necessity. Outside forces, including change agents, may serve to occasion reform. We discovered nothing in the course of this endeavor that would argue against those essential, albeit somewhat general, principles. However, in completing the collaborative intervention we were prompted to reflect further on what happened and why. Now in retrospect, what can we say further about school culture change?

Occasions for Change

In the final analysis, change may be inevitable—in things, in people, and in schools. Whether or not there are eternal verities, Heraclitus seems to have had the final word: *Semper flux.* In today's world, in particular, it is hard to imagine anything important not changing. An organization that does not move with the times or adapt to challenges inevitably ends up having a different function or place within its sphere of action: a loss of market or clientele or lack of audience. The cynic may argue that "The more things change, the more they stay the same." But one may also make the case that the less things change the more likely things will be different. In any event, it is difficult to deny the reality and the necessity for school change. Without question, schools and the context for schooling are currently in flux. The issue is not whether to change. For researchers and theorists, the issue is to understand the process. For school reformers, the problem is to control and direct the process, to have it occur in a certain way at a specific place and point in time. For both as well as for all those educators who are merely attempting to make it from one day to the next in a school, office, or classroom, there is no avoiding the reality and the inevitability of change. So a pause to reflect a bit on the processes of change has merit.

Those who have worked as change agents in schools and other organizations have called attention to a wide array of circumstances that serve as opportunities for change, including a change in organizational culture (for example, Kilmann, Saxton, Serpa et al., 1985; Hunt, 1991; Kanter, 1983, 1989; Schein, 1984, 1985, 1990). The opportunities arise in different ways at various stages in the life of an organization: They are likely to be different in new versus established organizations. Internal as well as external events condition the nature of the opportunities: loss of key personnel, rapid expansion of the organization, external pressures for survival. And of course, they may take various forms in different types of schools and organizations. The work on organizational change and development provides a general background and basis for our reflection, but so does the work on cognitive change processes. After all, thoughts, perceptions, and beliefs are at the core of school culture. These have to change if culture is to change.

Culture Change as a Shift in Thinking

At the essence of culture change, whenever it occurs and by whatever means it is occasioned, is a fundamental transformation in persons, especially in the way they think of themselves, their choices, their actions, and their purposes in acting. We propose that culture change occurs as a function of an alteration of thinking that occurs in people who make up an organization. In schools, administrators, teachers, and ultimately and primarily students need to think differently about schooling. They must consider their tasks and roles differently. They must view their schools in a different light, reconstruct the meaning of schooling and the purposes of teaching and learning. And most basic of all, individuals must change how they see themselves—their competencies and possibilities, their purposes and values, their deepest beliefs about themselves, their intentions and their practices. Examining and reconstructing beliefs and ways of thinking is at the root of culture change.

Thoughts That Make a Difference

More analytically, there are three categories of thought that are of primary significance in understanding why people do what they do and when and how they are likely to change.

Perceptions of options and alternatives.

People's actions are largely a result of the options they think they have. Enrolling in a particular class or course of study is highly dependent on what is perceived to be available. You don't choose to take a course in physics or in macramé unless you know that such options are available. Moreover, even if you know that such options exist in theory, you don't elect such options unless they are *experientially available,* that is, they are not just abstractions but options that individuals perceive to be there for them. "Cold cognitions" (Brown, Bransford, Ferrara, & Campione, 1983; Pintrich, Marx, & Boyle, 1993) do not determine actions. Actions evolve from and are inextricably interwoven with the sociocultural context in which the individual exists. What is or is not an option depends also upon the norms and patterns of the groups to which the individual belongs and of which she wishes to remain a member. One's options depend upon the roles one plays, the expectations that exist within a sociocultural matrix in which one lives. A sixteen-year-old "dropout" perhaps knows well that the continuing pursuit of an education is an option—in the abstract. But within the concrete realm of her experience it is not the most salient or attractive option, hardly a major competitor to a minimum-wage job that contributes to some sense of independence and a degree of survival and retains access to one's friends.

Administrators and staff are really no different in this regard as they contemplate what their school is and could become. The importance of options in determining what they do is paramount not only in their personal life but also in their work life. Teachers select and exhibit courses of action from alternatives that are not only known but that seem both reasonable and acceptable. Teachers organize classrooms, evaluate and discipline students, and present information according to their mental models of what can and should be done. When we arrived at Riversedge, although greatly troubled by the impact of the state testing program on their teaching and on the depth of learning and quality of motivation of their students, teachers were firm in their belief that they could do little to change the situation. It was only as they began to see new ways to act that their world—and Riversedge—changed. To change, teachers and staff must be aware of and ultimately embrace another realistic option that is viewed not only as acceptable but in some sense better.

Of course, this fundamental principle is the framing force in most preservice and in-service educational programs. We have, as we suspect the reader has too, sat in on many programs designed to prepare educational professionals. In particular, we have been most intrigued with the nature of presentations designed to promote any innovation. Demonstrations have ranged from "a whole language approach to reading" to "computer literacy." In the main, the thrust of the presentation has been to describe an alternative to what probably is currently being done. The alternative is often described vividly enough; however, little account is taken of the fact that the choice of any alternative is first of all a choice to reject what one is doing, to perhaps try what one has not done. Certainly, thoughts that emerge in considering practice and policy options are hardly "cold cognitions." The experience of others and the citing of research reports may make the new option viable—but only if the individuals involved view an option as realistic and acceptable within their own work world. How would my students respond? How would I have to change things and by how much? Would I risk too much in the way of my status within the organization, in my acceptance by parents? Do I have the energy, the competence, the will to pull this off? These thoughts consist of a person's feelings, hopes, aspirations, and sense of being. This is one reason change is not easy, and the more foreign an idea seems to be, the more likely it will be rejected.

Thoughts about self.

Obviously, one can hardly talk about perceived options without mentioning thoughts about self that reinforce at the outset that cognitions in each of these categories are all inextricably intertwined. They are all part of a whole that we can only separate out for purpose of analysis and discussion. Clearly, one's sense of competence is heavily involved in choosing action alternatives. One has to believe that there is a reasonable chance of success if one is to invest in a particular course of action. It is interesting to note that in the study of more involved and less involved teachers, the only variable on which they differed before the intervention was sense of teaching efficacy. That is, teachers who became more involved in the change process felt more efficacious than teachers who were less involved. The importance of such sense of competence varies drastically depending on circumstances, however. Contexts can be framed to make one's competence less a salient issue. That is an important objective in ensuring optimal learning experiences for all students. But it is equally important for school staff members who are risking innovation by considering a new path, a new program, or the transformation of school culture.

It is not only a sense of competence that is at stake; it is also one's professional, social, and personal identity. Change for good or for ill involves changes in relationships with others—how people will think of us, how we will relate to each other, what our place will be in a social scheme. Recall the portrayal of changes in Riversedge and Plainview. When a few teachers ventured to create multiage classrooms or small houses, they not only worried about their ability to succeed, they also had concerns about how others would feel about what they were doing. During the meetings at Riversedge, teachers who were experimenting with multiage classrooms were told by the principal and their colleagues that this was a risky venture and they should expect failure as well as success. But the principal and certain colleagues also assured them that their competence, their worth as teachers, was not "on the line." Even in failure they would be supported. They had a psychological "safety net." Of course, there were also others on the school staff who were less than supportive. The Riversedge teachers who ventured forth with the MAGIC experiment knew well that some would likely pounce on any sign of failure with a not-so-subtle "I told you so." And inevitably, in proceeding to try something new and different, old allegiances are broken and new allegiances are formed. Perhaps few stand to lose more when ventures fail than those in leadership roles. Often a job or even a career is at stake. Given that one's identity is often intertwined with any significant change, it is evident that more than "cold cognition" is involved.

Purposes, goals, and values.

The third category of thoughts involved in change concerns what may be simply termed the "why" questions. Again there are many issues that can be noted in this regard. One might simply argue that innovation is a value that some individuals and organizations, for whatever reason, hold dear. There are conservatives and progressives in any organization; there are conservative as well as venturesome organizations. And, of course, each person may have his own reason for trying or not trying something: "It might be interesting." "We need to be current." "It would look good to central administration." "We need to grow and improve." Building on our earlier expositions on the role of task and ability goals, we suggest that the importance of these two goals within the work context, and of school leadership is likely to be critical. When emphasis on innovation and excellence (an accomplishment goal) characterizes the work world, it is likely that staff members will as a group be more venturesome and be more likely to try the untried. They will be more apt to examine and revise the way they think about and teach school. We would predict also that innovation on the part of some will not be so readily interpreted as an attempt to upstage others. Indeed, we would specifically argue that a work environment emphasizing accomplishment rather than power or social solidarity, while not sufficient to make good things happen, is sufficient to encourage people to be more innovative.

Causes of Cognitive Change

What prompts people as individuals and as participants in groups or organizations to recognize alternatives to what they are currently pursuing and to think about their tasks and their relationship to that task differently? Complete answers to such questions are not easy to come by. However, recent work on cognitive change (cf. Pintrich, Marx, & Boyle, 1993) does provide helpful clues.

A Recognized Need

A primary initiating factor is likely to be some perceived need to change. As conceptual change theorists (for example, Posner, Strike, Hewson, & Gertzog, 1982) point out, scientists shift paradigms and young scholars begin to think differently when their current ways are not working and when they feel some dissatisfaction with accepted theory or practice.

School staff and leadership too must see some reason for change. In particular, it is when recognized practices are not compatible with organizational values that individuals in the organization are likely to see the need for change. As a result, those involved in organizational change and development often focus on the existence of conflict between practices and principles (cf. for example, Schein, 1985). The assumption is that the cognitive need for consistency and the reduction of salient contradictions will serve as a need for action. Clearly, some of the action we took was in the nature of describing policies and practices that were incompatible with stated beliefs of school staff, such as "All children can learn." "This school values children." We then asked them to look at whether certain of their policies and practices were in line with those beliefs.

Of course, when the dissonance is severe it can also lead to defensive reactions. It may "freeze" thought and prevent further consideration of change. One can paralyze as well as energize by creating situations that engender dissonance and conflict. In effecting change, one has to be sensitive to the fact that dissonance creation is a two-edged sword and behave accordingly. Recall that emotional statements were part and parcel of the dialogue that ensued during the change efforts at both Riversedge and Plainview (Chapters 6 and 7). There were occasional bursts of anger, expressions of hurt directed at those who presumably prompted the conflict—the university group. Sometimes the outbursts were not really directed at anyone in particular. A poignant moment occurred when a parent attending the Riversedge discussions portrayed her failure as a parent in pushing for the "competitive advantage." One could not have gone through the process we have described without realizing it was painful for those in the school who were rethinking what they were as well as what they were doing. The university team too sensed and felt some angst as we recognized that yes, indeed, we could be seen as bringing some of this pain. They had a right to express anger and resentment toward us.

In summary, we learned again what others involved in change have also learned; dissonance and a sense of dissatisfaction with what one is currently doing are at the root of change. Our entree to the school district in which we worked was undoubtedly occasioned in large part by a felt need on the part of the school staff involved. Teachers and administrators were aware of the challenges facing them; they were worried about their abilities to come up with the "right" solutions. Had they not recognized a need, we feel reasonably sure they would have found reasons not to consent to work with us. They knew, and we acknowledged at the outset, that what we were proposing demanded much effort and possibly some pain. But our presence also promised hope and opportunity. Although it stretched their conceptions of what schools should be doing, it also reinforced a belief that was a part of their repertory: School should be about learning—for *all* children. This primary belief was tied up with notions of enhancing self-esteem, especially in "at-risk" children, which certainly helped. The school needed a change but was not traumatized by the thought of it—a necessary ingredient for making a change.

A Plausible Alternative

Equally important in recognizing a need to change is that there must be an intelligible and acceptable option. It is not enough to feel negative about what one is doing. It is clear to us now that the inclination of school staff to visit other schools that were pursuing some of the options we were discussing served three important purposes in this regard. First, Riversedge and Plainview staff saw that an alternative to what they were doing did exist. Second, there was a plausible solution to *their* problems. And third, they saw real teachers, much like themselves, actually using new methods. There was a model to emulate; there were adaptable, adoptable routines with which they could identify. What they were considering was intelligible and could be assimilated into their thinking.

It is difficult to overestimate the importance of visits to classes. Simply considering new options in the abstract will not by itself prompt change. Certainly, it is unlikely to effect change in notions of purpose and in basic beliefs about the goals of teaching and learning. But in-depth and focused exposure to concrete examples that embody new possibilities will help. They may well be the *sine qua non* in making the preferred alternative plausible.

A Growth Experience with Change

A plausible alternative attracts one to the possibility of change. It may prompt imagining oneself in the role of a different kind of teacher or picturing what one might try and do. But finally, it is only as one tries something with a sense of growth and movement toward valued ends that the alternative holds the potential of becoming part and parcel of the individual's life. We observed teachers Jeri and Doris initiate their multiage classrooms with a combination of hope and fear. Sure, they had read more than they had ever read before about how to manage such classrooms. They had attended workshops. And they had observed classrooms with teachers like themselves who were managing to move from traditional classrooms to a multiage concept. Jeri and Doris recognized the need; they sensed that the multiage classroom was a plausible route to follow; they experienced the kinds of information input and modeling we have suggested are needed to transform them into thinking and instructing differently. Yet we all learned that there was another important step. They could not actually retain this course of action if they should experience a disaster of sorts. If they were to compare what was happening in their multiage classrooms with the order exhibited in other classrooms, including ones they had previously managed, they would have quickly become quite discouraged. And if they had been forced to think about producing better test scores by the end of the year, their change would have been ephemeral. "Success" needed to be redefined. Certainly, they couldn't be compared to others not attempting this venture. Nor could their own past experiences be too firmly controlling of their orientation. Jeri and Doris had to consider the changes occurring in their classrooms, perhaps at first as "how things were settling down." Later, there were times when they and their students surprised themselves with what they were doing, and they were able to take pleasure in it.

A Task-Focused Work Environment

The quality of culture experienced by staff members in their work environment is important in growing and sustaining the process of change. In the examples just cited, the principal and the rest of the staff not only gave the teachers introducing a comprehensive programmatic change "some slack," they gave them other ingredients needed for a true test of the usefulness of what they were doing: necessary resources, not too many students, and kind words. But of greater importance was that these teachers were given a work context that emulated what they were trying to present to their students: a task-focused work context in which the stress was on the worth of venturing forth to try something new and challenging, where progress in the task was defined as success, where comparisons with others was minimized, and where resources were provided in reasonable amounts.

Of course, it is helpful when the innovation proceeds from a shared understanding of what schools should be. If the school has a clear sense of mission, any venture perceived as compatible is more likely to receive and retain support. We observed that as more members of the Riversedge staff saw the multiage experiment as compatible with a larger vision of school and as a possible way to realize broadly shared goals, they saw the experiment as less of a threat and more of a possibility. Profound shifts in cognitive life seldom come easily, nor do they occur in the exact same way for everyone in the organization. Yet there must be a degree of sharing if the cognitive changes are to be functional in the operation of the school as a whole and if they are capable of sustained support that eventuates in established patterns of productive action.

An Initiating Force

Planned change is occasioned by certain events and actions. Change may be inevitable but working toward a specific kind of change requires focused action. Someone has to introduce the idea. Someone has to call attention to the need for change. Realistic alternatives have to be described and convergence around one and not other things requires such social psychological processes as persuasion, social influence, the exercise of power perhaps, the ability to motivate and inspire. In brief, there is a critical role for leadership. It may or may not be a member of the school staff who provides the initiating force. Someone finally has to "stick out her neck" and say, "Let's do it!" If someone with influence in the school does not identify with the impetus, respond to it, exploit and direct it, the kind of culture change we call for will not result. The school principal is key (Leithwood, Jantzi, Fernandez, 1994; Maehr, Midgley & Urdan, 1992) but cannot do it alone. Staff support and leadership are likewise critical.

Riversedge and Plainview presented somewhat different patterns in this regard. In both cases, staff leadership was key. At Riversedge, for example, the MAGIC program was created and promoted by a certain group of teachers. However, at some point the principal said, "Let's do it" and began promoting it as a major project of the school. The small group of innovators at Plainview had to struggle to be heard. But they persisted and finally, when the project was almost concluded they were "allowed" to experiment with the small house concept. The leadership in this case was actually a bit more than "tolerant." It seemed to be intrigued but hesitant to identify fully with the effort. In both cases, however, what was done could not have been done if those in formal leadership roles had said "no." Some form of agreement was an absolute prerequisite.

Conclusion

Our involvement in two continuing experiments in school change brought a special touch of reality to our overall concerns with the nature of schools and the need for school reform. The vision was not lost in the reality of practice. It was enhanced, specified, and perhaps adjusted a bit but overall served us well in guiding the change efforts. Yes, it was difficult to nudge these two schools toward the pervasive change in culture we envisioned.

But there was rather solid evidence of systematic movement in this direction. School cultures can change. Not without effort, not without commitment, not without leadership, not without some pain—but our experiences at Riversedge and Plainview and the data we gathered bear witness to the possibility of transforming school cultures toward a learning-focused, child-centered vision. Moreover, our experiences and analyses may provide a template for implementing change. We hope some are motivated to try.

Notes

1. We are indebted to Willy Lens for many insights on putting theory into practice. It was he who suggested these two quotes to capture a theme we were endeavoring to express.

2. Several integrative reviews have been published including: Anderman & Maehr, 1994; Collopy & Green, 1995; Maehr & Parker, 1993; Midgley, 1993; Midgley & Wood, 1993; Midgley & Urdan, 1992; Urdan, Midgley, & Wood, 1995.

3. For an expanded description and discussion see Wood & Midgley, 1995.

4. See Appendix for the survey instrument used.

5. The inventory items and further explanatory information are in the Appendix.

6. Described in detail in Midgley, Maehr, Collopy, & Roeser, 1994.

7. For a more complete description of this study see Anderman, Maehr, & Midgley, 1996.

Part Four

Conclusion

9 A Hopeful Word

To turn our public schools around we need to adopt that legendary Noah
principle: no more prizes for predicting rain. Prizes only for building arks.
—Louis V. Gerstner, Jr.[1]

Each year, millions of children begin an important adventure.
They enter school. Prior to that, they have preconceived notions about
what "school" is. Brothers, sisters, parents, TV, and preschool orientation
sessions have made sure of that. But at age five or six, children have much to
learn about the world, about school, and about themselves as learners. They
will become increasingly cognizant of what they know and do not know and
what they can and cannot do—and they may define this as "success" or "failure." They may avoid these categories, at least to a degree, and focus on the
sheer process of using their capacities, exercising their skills, and applying
the knowledge they have learned to learn more. In short, they may simply
become involved in a growth process that is itself engaging and rewarding—and forget about whether what happens is an achievement or an accomplishment. Remarkably, they might—and some often do—become
captivated by nothing more—and nothing less—than the thrill of grasping
an ever-expanding social, physical, aesthetic, and intellectual world. They
may also come to view school as a competitive game.

In the words we have used throughout this volume, children come to
adopt an ability or a task goal orientation toward schooling. This is seldom
an either-or choice, of course. Most will adopt a task orientation in one or
another facet of school, and most will also from time to time adopt an ability orientation. But it is likely that one of these two orientations will dominate in certain classrooms *and* be more prevalent in some schools than others. One or the other may be more evident at certain life stages than at

others. And task and ability goals will probably loom larger in the lives of some children than in the lives of others.

But children will inevitably define school and various parts of school—math, reading, physical education, music, and sports—in terms of purposes, goals, expectations, conventions, knowledge, possibilities, and limitations. Especially important, they will define themselves as learners. How children define themselves is important to their motivation in school and to their continuing investment in learning. It will also influence how they relate to life in general, the kind of people they become, the optimism they exhibit, and the way they cope with life. What children think about school, in short, is more critical than is often recognized and is the first and most important message of this book. It underscores the necessity of continuing to study and take account of these thoughts that children develop and hold in the course of spending countless hours in a place called school.

A second message, one that we hope will be taken seriously by educators, is that children's thoughts about school are influenced by school policies and practices. Teachers and administrators, in their instructional practices and in the way they manage and relate to students, will frame school more in terms of task or ability goals. They will define the purpose of school as learning or performing. That in our view is really the critical facet of what we have come to call "school cultures." As schools establish what is to be done and how, set procedures for evaluation, define patterns of conduct, recognize and reward, and schedule and organize, they not only reflect a set of assumptions but promote the perceptions of why the student is there. And as they do that, they will determine how children will invest in what the school has to offer and in the kind of activities it espouses. In some ways, this should be obvious. Of course schools and school staff affect the kind of learners that students become! Yet, one still hears educators express the inevitability of failure and too quickly blame the student or her family when things go awry. As forcefully as we can, we suggest that principals and teachers ought to give more attention to what they are saying to children about the nature of learning and schooling through the policies and practices they allow and promote.

A third message is even more critical. Not only do educators fail to recognize that they can do something to enhance motivation and learning—even for students at most risk for school failure—they behave incorrectly (Midgley, 1993; Anderman & Maehr, 1994; Eccles et al., 1993). Too often it is assumed that learning is work and, therefore, must be paid for (cf. Lepper and Cordova, 1992). Too often, school is made to be a competitive game in which some become losers and others become winners—but not learners. Too seldom do children experience the intrinsic and inherent joy of learning for its own sake. And, when and as this happens, schools and school staff carry a heavy burden of responsibility. For the root cause is a misdefinition of schooling where demonstrating ability relative to others is the stated or unstated desideratum. Sorting and classifying is the modus operandi. This will not serve the child-student well.

And so, we end as we began. Well, not quite. Schools today face severe and sometimes overwhelming challenges. Many are in a state of crisis. It is easy to blame society, the family, lack of resources. But the bitter pill is that schools too must shoulder part of the blame— especially if they have given up—but also if they rely on the wrong solutions. And the fact of the matter is that many have given up and many more are relying on the wrong solutions. There is something that can be done. There is a cause for hope that does not rely on higher standards, new technology, or increased resources. While these may be welcome, they will do little unless there is a serious and pervasive concern with first principles.

A Return to First Principles

It is by returning to a serious commitment to first principles of what education and schools should be that crisis becomes hope. We stated these first principles at the outset. We restate them now with even greater confidence that they must be at the heart of how school and instruction are designed.

1. The child-student is and must be at the center of school and school-ing. The practice and theory of education is only secondarily about standards, curriculum, pedagogy, teacher education, or the organiza-tion and management of schools. It is about *children* and students.
2. Schools and education must especially be about the enhancement and sustaining of motivation for *learning*—for a lifetime! Among the many good things that students can and must do, the "bottom line" must be learning and the love of learning.
3. By stressing that schools are about learning, a third principle is im-plied. Learning is obviously *not* the province of a few. *Learning is the characteristic of ALL*. Children come to school with different "advan-tages" and "disadvantages." They have experienced different lives prior to school; they live in different worlds outside of school. But they retain one element common to humanity: the capacity to learn. All children can make progress in acquiring skills, knowledge, and

understanding. Effort, progress, and growth must be valued in students. The focus cannot be on who performs best. The practice of education cannot devolve into simply selecting, classifying, and labeling. Yes, the public school has to be "inclusive" but in the sense that learning, an all-inclusive characteristic, is primary.

Schools get into trouble and children and society are not served well when these principles are ignored.

Toward Practice Built on First Principles

And so in conclusion we stress these first principles with which we began. But it is equally important to remember that these principles, like any worthy assumptions, beliefs, guidelines, or values, must be elaborated on and operationalized if they are to find their way into practice. The story of this book is not just of belief in the worth of all children and the importance of learning. That argument has been often made and more forcefully than we have made it here. The prose, the numbers, and the tables that make up these pages sum up to a statement regarding what taking these first principles seriously might mean. We outlined a theory of school based not just on our ruminations regarding the problems of schools or limited by our own unique observations and experiences; rather, the theory is based on current research and open to further testing, validation, and enhancement. It can be put to the severest of empirical and scientific tests. But equally important, it can be used—by practitioners as well as researchers. And so we do not exactly conclude as we began.

Beyond Predicting Rain

The quote at the outset of this chapter should give us all pause. We too began with a recital of the problems of education. And in the immediately preceding paragraphs, we have repeated some of these concerns. That is easy to do. For, as we said, hardly a day goes by without an item in the popular media that provides grist for this mill. And it is in fact hard to deny that here and elsewhere in the world schools confront severe problems. Here and there in the United States and elsewhere, those problems have become crises. It is not just that "schools aren't as good as they used to be" because, as Will Rogers added, "they never were"—it is that they are not what we want them to be to provide some hope for our future. We trust, at a minimum, we have gone beyond predicting rain.

A Somewhat Novel Diagnosis

Yes, we offer a critique of schools. We like to think of it as a diagnosis—and a somewhat novel one at that. Our analysis is not only based on sound and established theory, it has now been grounded in the real world of school. As a diagnosis, it is more than just blaming or criticizing schools; there is an implied solution. There is a prescription for what ails schools. The answer resides within the school's capacity to act. Many of the solutions in recent years have asked more of schools and their staffs than can be produced. We have shown, we believe, that typical schools can follow our path—if they so choose. They can do so with no major change in their budgets, no firing or hiring, no purchase of new programs and technology—simply by reaffirming some basic notions of what a student is and what the business of teaching and learning should be. This is not to imply that organizational focus and changes in thinking and doing are easy to accomplish—but they can happen. Schools, school leadership, and staff can make them happen!

We hope we have done more than simply identify another "school problem." We trust that our diagnosis has put a new gloss on the problems, crises, and failings of which schools are accused. Perhaps now the problem has been redefined so it can·be better understood—and solved.

Putting Theory into Practice

Somewhat incidental to our effort perhaps, we have provided a perspective and insight into process and procedure that can be used in translating theory into practice and in assisting theorists to learn from practitioners.

During the past decade or so, considerable research has been conducted on cognition, motivation, and social processes and has only been applied intermittently to the real world of schools. At the very least, we have shown the relevance of that work and thereby perhaps encouraged a few to follow our path in putting theory into practice. For example, the effects of holding task and ability goals are established in the research literature. In somewhat abstract and general terms we know also how people come to hold these goals. Evaluation, for example, has always been seen as playing an important role in this regard. Forms of reward and recognition have, too. What we did not know, at least as profoundly as we now know, were the ways in which school policies and everyday practices shape these definitions of purpose for schooling. One has to spend time in schools and observe what is happening in order to understand the forms evaluation takes. The important role of the task is often acknowledged and studied in artificial settings remote from the day-to-day teaching of reading, math, social studies, and science. What is the student really asked to do? How is that shaped by time and scheduling? By teacher control? By classroom materials and working in groups? One does not answer these questions by conducting a fifty-minute "experiment" in seven 5th grade science classes. One does not begin to fully appreciate school culture and its effects unless one views the multiple inter-actions that occur in the hallways and at schoolwide assemblies and is aware of general policies on assessment, grading, discipline, and student recognition. Research on student motivation and learning has focused heavily on how students interact with selected materials and sometimes on student-teacher interactions—but seldom if at all on school context in its multiple forms and varied effects. We had not expected that "time," how learning is blocked, scheduled, and placed within designated periods, could be so pro-foundly important. Time likely frames the science (or anything else) that can be taught. It restricts cooperation among teachers and experimentation in the grouping of students. It can make learning tasks unnecessarily artifi-cial. It is a source of conflict among teachers and the instigator of serious political battles. Mess with the schedule and you touch the most sensitive nerves of the school. Avoid tampering with the schedule, and you retain re-straints on the possibility of experimenting, innovating, and relating to stu-dents differently.

We hope we have conveyed that theory and practice are not mutually ex-clusive. Indeed, one separates them only at a price.

Whether and How School Cultures Can Change

This volume stands and falls on whether we have contributed to the under-standing of if and how school cultures can change. In reaching conclusions on that point, consider the following.

We do not claim that our school change effort worked out as perfectly as we would have liked. Yet, at the very least these efforts give cause for opti-mism that school cultures can change. School culture is not just something that the school *has* or *is*; it is about what school leadership and staff can do. The perceived stress on task and ability goals is rooted in everyday policies and practices that teachers and administrators create, employ, and pro-mote. School staff members are largely the creators and almost always are heavily involved in the interpretation of these goals as they reach down to the lives of students. The individual school, principal, and teachers are not helpless to do something about how schooling is defined for children. In this area, they are substantially masters of their own fate.

Of course, change is not easy. Perhaps our portrayal of change can serve as a heuristic if not a set of guidelines for transforming the school of your choice. At the least, we encourage the reader not only to follow but to build on what we have described, taking our mistakes as seriously as our successes.

But Have We Built an Ark?

We are somewhat confident that we have gone a step or so beyond "predicting rain." Only the reader and the experiences of the future can determine whether we have actually "built an ark." Perhaps, at the least, we have provided sketches for the design of that ark.

Notes

1. Chairman and CEO, IBM Corporation. Louis V. Gerstner, Jr., with Roger D. Semerad, Denis Philip Doyle, and William B. Johnston, *Reinventing Education: Entrepreneurship in America's Schools* (New York: Dutton, 1994) p. xiv.

Appendix: Selected Scales from the Patterns of Adaptive Learning Survey (PALS)

Carol Midgley, Martin L. Maehr, Lynley Hicks,
Robert Roeser, Tim Urdan, Eric Anderman,
and Avi Kaplan   *University of Michigan, 1996*

Student Scales*

Personal Goal Orientation

Task orientation

(6 items, alpha=.85)

I like schoolwork that I'll learn from even if I make a lot of mistakes.

An important reason why I do my schoolwork is because I like to learn new things.

I like schoolwork best when it really makes me think.

An important reason why I do my work in school is because I want to get better at it.

An important reason I do my schoolwork is because I enjoy it.

I do my schoolwork because I'm interested in it.

Ability orientation

(6 items, alpha=.86)

I want to do better than other students in my class.

---

*These scales have been developed and improved over time. The scales used to assess the effectiveness of the interventions are similar to, but not identical to, the scales listed here. The items have also been adapted to measure domain specific (math and English) goals and goal structures, with alpha coefficients that are equally high or higher than those reported here. Five-point Likert-type scales are used. For example, the items on the student scales that measure personal goal orientation are on a scale from 1 = not at all true of me; 3 = somewhat true of me; 5 = very true of me. We do not recommend using these scales with children who are in 3rd grade or lower.

I would feel successful if I did better than most of the other students in my class.

I'd like to show my teacher that I'm smarter than the other kids in this class.

Doing better than other students in this class is important to me.

I would feel really good if I were the only one who could answer the teacher's questions in class.

It's important to me that the other students in this class think that I am good at my work.

Perceptions of the Classroom Goal Structure

Task goal structure

(5 items, alpha=.78)

In this class:

Our teacher thinks mistakes are okay as long as we are learning.

Our teacher wants us to understand our work, not just memorize it.

Our teacher really wants us to enjoy learning new things.

Our teacher recognizes us for trying hard.

Our teacher gives us time to really explore and understand new ideas.

Ability goal structure

(6 items, alpha=.73)

In this class:

Our teacher tells us how we compare to other students.

Our teacher makes it obvious when students are not doing well on their work.

Only a few students do really well.

Our teacher points out those students who get good grades as an example to all of us.

Our teacher lets us know which students get the highest scores on tests.

Our teacher calls on smart students more than other students.

Perceptions of the School Goal Structure*

Task goal structure

(6 items, alpha=.81)

---

*The scales measuring students' perceptions of the school goal structure are currently in revision. Please contact the authors for further information relative to their use.

In this school:

Teachers believe all students can learn.

Understanding the work is more important than getting the right answers.

Mistakes are okay as long as we are learning.

Teachers think how much you learn is more important than test scores or grades.

Teachers want students to really understand their work not just memorize it.

Trying hard counts a lot.

Ability goal structure

(5 items, alpha=.80)

In this school, teachers treat kids who get good grades better than other kids.

In this school, only a few kids get praised for their schoolwork.

In this school, teachers only care about the smart kids.

This school has given up on some of its students.

In this school, special privileges are given to students who get the highest grades.

Teacher Scales

Perceptions of the School Goal Structure

Task goal structure for students

(7 items, alpha=.81)

In this school:

A real effort is made to recognize students for effort and improvement.

A real effort is made to show students how the work they do in school is related to their lives outside of school.

The importance of trying hard is really stressed to students.

Students are told that making mistakes is OK as long as they are learning and improving.

The emphasis is on really understanding schoolwork not just memorizing it.

Students are frequently told that learning should be fun.

A lot of the work students do is boring and repetitious. (reversed)

Performance goal structure for students

(8 items, alpha=.70)

In this school:

It's easy to tell which students get the highest grades and which students get the lowest grades.

Students hear a lot about the importance of making the honor roll or being recognized at honor assemblies.

Students are encouraged to compete with each other academically.

Grades and test scores are not talked about a lot. (reversed)

Students hear a lot about the importance of getting high test scores.

Students who get good grades are pointed out as an example to others.

Perceptions of the School Goal Structure for Teachers

Accomplishment

(6 items, alpha=.82)

In this school, teachers have many opportunities to learn new things.

If someone has a good idea or project, the administration in this school listens and supports it.

In this school, the administration is always working to improve teaching.

This school makes teachers want to work hard.

This school supports instructional innovations.

In this school, practical restraints severely limit teachers' ability to implement new ideas. (reversed)

Power

(7 items, alpha=.84)

In this school, some teachers have more influence than other teachers.

In this school, the administration shows favoritism to some teachers.

In this school, some teachers have greater access to resources than others.

In this school, teachers compete with one another.

In this school, teachers try to outdo each other.

Power and influence count a lot around this school.

In this school, the administration actively encourages competition among teachers.

Instructional Strategies

Task-oriented instructional strategies

(4 items, alpha=.75)

In my classroom:

I make a special effort to give my students work that is creative and imaginative.

I stress to students that I want them to understand the work, not just memorize it.

I frequently tell my students I want them to enjoy learning.

I make a special effort to give my students work that has meaning in their everyday lives.

Ability-oriented instructional strategies

(5 items, alpha=.79)

In my classroom:

I display the work of the highest achieving students as an example.

I give special privileges to students who do the best academically.

I help students understand how their performance compares to others.

I point out those children who do well academically as a model for the other students.

I encourage students to compete with each other academically.

References

Amabile, T. M. (1983). Social psychology of creativity: A componential conceptualization. *Journal of Personality and Social Psychology, 45*, 357–376.

Amabile, T. M., & Hennessey, B. A. (1992). The motivation for creativity in children. In A. K. Boggiano & T. S. Pittman (Eds.), *Achievement and motivation: A social-developmental perspective* (pp. 54–74). New York: Cambridge University Press.

Ames, C. (1984). Competitive, cooperative, and individualistic goal structures: A motivational analysis. In R. E. Ames & C. Ames (Eds.), *Research on motivation in education: Vol. 1* (pp. 177–207). New York: Academic Press.

Ames, C. A. (1990). Motivation: What teachers need to know. *Teachers College Record, 91*, 409–421.

Ames, C. (1992). Classrooms: Goals, structures, and student motivation. *Journal of Educational Psychology, 84*, 261–271.

Ames, C., & Ames, R. (Eds.), (1989). *Research on motivation in education: Goals and cognitions.* New York: Academic Press.

Ames, R., & Ames, C. (1993). Creating a mastery-oriented school-wide culture: A team leadership perspective. In M. Sashkin & H. J. Walberg (Eds.), *Educational leadership and school culture* (pp. 124–145). Berkeley, CA: McCutchan.

Ames, C., & Archer, J. (1987). Mothers' beliefs about the role of ability and effort in school learning. *Journal of Educational Psychology, 79*, 409–414.

Ames, C., & Archer, J. (1988). Achievement goals in the classroom: Students' learning strategies and motivation processes. *Journal of Educational Psychology, 80*, 260–267.

Anderman, E. (1992, March). *The effects of personal and school-wide goals on deep processing strategies of at risk, not at risk, and special education students.* Paper presented at the annual meeting of the Society for Research on Adolescence, Washington, DC.

Anderman, E., & Maehr, M. L. (1994). Motivation and schooling in the middle grades. *Review of Educational Research, 64*, 287–309.

Anderman, E., & Midgley, C. (1995). *Changes in personal achievement goals and perceived classroom goal structures across the transition to middle level schools.* Manuscript submitted for publication.

Anderman, E., Maehr, M. L., & Midgley, C. (1996). *Is it inevitable for motivation to decline in the middle grades? Promising results of a school intervention.* Manuscript in preparation.

227

Anderman, E. M., & Young, A. J. (1994). Motivation and strategy use in science: Individual differences and classroom effects. *Journal of Research in Science Teaching, 31*, 811–831.

Anderson, J. (1980). *Cognitive psychology and its implications.* San Francisco: Freeman.

Arbreton, A. (1993). *When getting help is helpful: Developmental, cognitive, and motivational influences on students' academic help-seeking.* Unpublished doctoral dissertation, University of Michigan, Ann Arbor.

Archer, J. (1990). *Motivation and creativity: The relationship between achievement goals and creativity in writing short stories and poems.* Unpublished doctoral dissertation, University of Illinois, Urbana-Champaign.

Bandura, A. (1993). Perceived self-efficacy in cognitive development and functioning. *Educational Psychologist, 28(2)*, 117–148.

Bass, B. M. (1985). *Leadership and performance beyond expectations.* New York: Free Press.

Beck, J. S., Urdan, T., & Midgley, C. (1992, April). *Moving toward a task-focus in middle level schools.* Paper presented at the Annual Meeting of the American Educational Research Association, San Francisco.

Bloom, B. S., Engelhart, M. D., Furst, E. J., Hill, W. H., & Krathwohl, D. R. (1956). *Taxonomy of educational objectives. The classification of educational goals: Handbook 1. Cognitive domain.* New York: Longmans, Green.

Bloom, B. S., Krathwohl, D. R., & Masia, B. B. (1964). *Taxonomy of educational objectives. Book 2: Affective domain.* London: Longman.

Blumenfeld, P. C., & Meece, J. (1988). Task factors, teacher behavior and students' involvement and use of learning strategies in science. *Elementary School Journal, 88*, 235–250.

Blumenfeld, P. C., Soloway, E., Marx, R. W., Krajcik, J. S., Guzdial, M., & Palincsar, A. (1991). Motivating project-based learning: Sustaining the doing, supporting the learning. *Educational Psychologist, 26*, 369–398.

Bock, R. D., & Wiley, D. E. (1967). Quasi-experimentation in educational settings: Comment. *School Review, 75*, 353–366.

Bolman, L. G., & Deal, T. E. (1991). *Reforming organizations.* San Francisco: Jossey-Bass.

Braskamp, L. A., & Maehr, M. L. (1985). *SPECTRUM: An organizational development tool.* Champaign, IL: MetriTech.

Brookover, W., Beady, C., Flood, P., Schweitzer, J., & Wisenbaker, J. (1979). *School social systems and student achievement: Schools can make a difference.* New York: J. R. Bergin.

Brookover, W., Beamer, L., Efthim, H., Hathaway, D., Lezotte, L., Miller, S., Passalacque, J., & Tornatzky, L. (1982). *Creating effective schools: An inservice program for enhancing school learning climate and achievement.* Holmes Beach, FL: Learning Publications.

Brophy, J. (1987). Socializing students' motivation to learn. In M. L. Maehr & D. A. Kleiber (Eds.), *Advances in motivation and achievement:Vol. 5, Enhancing motivation* (pp. 181–210). Greenwich, CT: JAI Press.

Brown, A., Bransford, J., Ferrara, R., & Campione, J. (1983). Learning, remembering and understanding. In P. H. Mossen (Ed.), *Handbook of child psychology,Vol. 3* (pp. 77–166). NewYork: Wiley.

Brown, A. L., & Palincsar, A. S. (1989). Guided cooperative learning and individual knowledge acquisition. In L. B. Resnick (Ed.), *Knowing and learning. Issues for a cognitive psychology of learning. Essays in honor of Robert Glaser* (pp. 393–451). Hillsdale, NJ: Lawrence Erlbaum.

Bryk, A. S., & Raudenbush, S. W. (1992). *Hierarchical linear models: Applications and data analysis methods.* Newbury Park, CA: Sage.

Buck, R. M., & Schweingruber, H. A. (1992, August). *Effects of parents' and teachers' educational goals on students' learning.* Poster presented at the annual meeting of the American Psychological Association, Washington, DC.

Carnegie Corporation (1992). Adolescent health: A generation at risk. *Carnegie Quarterly, 37.*

Carnegie Council on Adolescent Development (1989). *Turning points: Preparing American youth for the 21st century.* Report of the Task Force on Education of Young Adolescents. NewYork: Author.

Cartwright, D. (1978). Theory and practice. *Journal of Social Issue, 34*, 168–180.

Chira, S. (1991, May 15). Schools to help with life as well as learning. *New York Times*, pp. A1, B7.

Cialdini, R. B. (1995). Principles and techniques of social influence. In A. Tesser (Ed.), *Advanced Social Psychology* (pp. 257–281). NewYork: McGraw-Hill.

Clifford, M. M. (1988). Failure tolerance and academic risk-taking in ten- to twelve-year-old students. *British Journal of Educational Psychology, 58*, 15–27.

Cohen, E. G. (1994). Restructuring the classroom: Conditions for productive small groups. *Review of Educational Research, 64*, 1–35.

Coleman, J. S., et al. (1966). *Equality of educational opportunity.* U.S. Department of Health, Education, and Welfare. Washington, DC: U.S. Government Printing Office.

Collopy, R. B., & Green, T. (1995). Using motivational theory with at-risk children. *Educational Leadership, 53*, 37–40.

Covington, M. V. (1992). *Making the grade: A self-worth perspective on motivation and school reform.* Cambridge, MA: Cambridge University Press.

Cross, C. T. (1990). National goals: Four priorities for educational researchers. *Educational Researcher: Research News and Comment, 19*, 21–24.

Csikszentmihalyi, M., & Nakamura, J. (1989). The dynamics of intrinsic motivation: A study of adolescents. In C. Ames & R. Ames (Eds.), *Research on motivation and education: Vol. 3* (pp. 45–71). NewYork: Academic Press.

Csikszentmihalyi, M., Rathunde, K., & Whalen, S. (1993). *Talented teenagers.* New York: Cambridge University Press.

Cuban, L. (1990). Reforming again, again, and again. *Educational Researcher, 19,* 3–13.

Davis, K. S. (1972). *FDR: The beckoning of destiny 1882–1928.* New York: Random House.

Deci, E. L., & Ryan, R. M. (1985). *Intrinsic motivation and self-determination in human behavior.* New York: Plenum.

Deci, E. L., & Ryan, R. M. (1992). The initiation and registration of intrinsically motivated learning and achievement. In A. K. Boggiano and T. Pittman (Eds.), *Achievement and motivation: A social-developmental perspective* (pp. 9–36). New York: Cambridge University Press.

Deal, T. E., & Kennedy, A. A. (1982). *Corporate culture: The rites and rituals of corporate life.* Reading, MA: Addison-Wesley.

Deal, T. E., & Peterson, K. D. (1990). *The principal's role in shaping school culture.* Washington, DC: U.S. Department of Education, Office of Educational Research and Improvement.

Denison, D. R. (1984). Bringing corporate culture to the bottom line. *Organizational Dynamics, 13,* 5–22.

Denison, D. R. (1985). *Corporate culture and organizational effectiveness: A behavioral approach to financial performance.* New York: Wiley.

Duda, J. L., & Nicholls, J. G. (1992). Dimensions of achievement motivation in schoolwork and sport. *Journal of Educational Psychology, 84,* 290–299.

Dweck, C. (1991). Self-theories and goals: Their role in motivation, personality, and development. In R. A. Dieastbier (Ed.), *Nebraska Symposium on Motivation, 1990* (pp. 199–235). Lincoln: University of Nebraska Press.

Dyer, H. S., Linn, R. L., & Patton, M. J. (1969). A comparison of four methods of obtaining observed and predicted school system means on achievement tests. *American Educational Research Journal, 6,* 591–605.

Eccles, J. S., & Midgley, C. (1989). Stage/environment fit: Developmentally appropriate classrooms for early adolescents. In R. E. Ames & C. Ames (Eds.), *Research on motivation in education: Vol. 3* (pp. 139–186). New York: Academic Press.

Eccles, J. S., Midgley, C., Wigfield, A., Miller-Buchanan, C., Reuman, D., Flanagan, C., & MacIver, D. (1993). Development during adolescence: The impact of stage-environment fit on young adolescents' experiences in schools and families. *American Psychologist, 48,* 90–101.

Edmonds, R. R., & Frederiksen, J. R. (1979). *Search for effective schools: The identification and analysis of city schools that are instructionally effective for poor children.* East Lansing: Michigan State University, Institute for Research on Teaching.

Elliot, A. J., & Harackiewicz, J. M. (1994). Goal setting, achievement orientation, and intrinsic motivation: A mediational analysis. *Journal of Personality & Social Psychology 66,* 968–980.

Entwistle, N. J., & Ramsden, P. (1983). *Understanding student learning.* London: Croom Helm.

Epstein, J. (1989). Family structures and student motivation: A developmental perspective. In C. Ames & R. Ames (Eds.), *Research on motivation in education:Vol. 3* (pp. 259–295). New York: Academic Press.

Epstein, J L. (1983). Longitudinal effects of family-school-person interactions on student outcomes. *Research in Sociology of Education and Socialization:Vol. 4* (pp. 101–127). Greenwich, CT: JAI Press.

Farmer, H. S., Vispoel, W., & Maehr, M. L. (1991). Achievement contexts: Effect on achievement values and causal attributions. *Journal of Educational Research, 85*, 26–38.

Fink, C., Boggiamo, A. K., & Barrett, M. (1990). Controlling teaching strategies. Undermining children's self-determination and performance. *Journal of Personality and Social Psychology, 59,* 916–924.

Fraser, B. J., & Walberg, H. J. (Eds.) (1991). *Educational environments: Evaluation, antecedents and consequences.* New York: Pergamon Press.

Garcia, T., & Pintrich, P. R. (1994). Regulating motivation and cognition in the classroom: The role of self-schemas and self-regulating strategies. In D. H. Schunk & B. J. Zimmerman (Eds.), *Self-regulation of learning and performance: Issues and educational applications* (pp. 127–153). Hillsdale, NJ: Lawrence Erlbaum.

Glenn, B. C., & McLean, T. (1981). *What works? An examination of effective schools for poor black children.* Cambridge, MA: Harvard University, Center for Law and Education.

Good, T. L., & Weinstein, R. S. (1986). Schools make a difference: Evidence, criticisms, and new directions. *American Psychologist, 41*, 1090–1097.

Goodlad, J. (1984). *A place called school: Prospects for the future.* New York: McGraw Hill.

Gutierrez, R., & Slavin, R. E. (1992). Achievement effects of the nongraded elementary school: A best evidence synthesis. *Review of Educational Research, 62*, 333–376.

Hackman, J. R. (1986). The psychology of self-management in organization. In M. S. Pallak, & R. O. Perloff (Eds.), *Psychology and work: Productivity, change, and employment* (pp. 85–136). Washington, DC: American Psychological Association.

Hackman, J. R., & Oldham, G. F. (1980). *Work redesign.* Reading, MA: Addison-Wesley.

Harackiewicz, J. M., & Elliot, A. J. (1993). Achievement goals and intrinsic motivation. *Journal of Personality & Social Psychology, 65*, 904–915.

Harter, S. (1992). The relationship betwen perceived competence, effect, and motivational orientation within the classroom: Processes and patterns of change. In A. K. Boggiano and T. Pittman (Eds.), *Achievement and motivation:A social-developmental perspective* (pp. 77–114). New York: Cambridge University Press.

Harter, S., Whitesell, N. R., & Kowalski, P. (1992). Individual differences in the effects of educational transitions on young adolescents' perceptions of competence and motivational orientation. *American Educational Research Journal, 29*, 777–808.

Havighurst, R. J. (1952). *Developmental tasks and education* (2nd ed.). New York: David McKay.

Hill, K. T. (1977). The relation of evaluative practices to test anxiety and achievement motivation. *UCLA Educator, 19*, 15–21.

Hill, K. T. (1980). Motivation, evaluation, and educational test policy. In L. J. Fyans (Ed.), *Achievement motivation: Recent trends in theory and research*. New York: Plenum Press.

Hill, K. T. (1984). Debilitating motivation and testing: A major educational problem—possible solutions and policy application. In R. E. Ames & C. Ames (Eds.), *Research on motivation in education: Student Motivation: Vol. 1*. New York: Academic Press.

Hill, K. T., & Wigfield, A. (1984). Test anxiety: A major educational problem and what can be done about it. *Elementary School Journal, 85*, 105–126.

Hoffman, L. M. (1992). *Continuing motivation in elementary school children: A naturalistic case study*. Unpublished doctoral dissertation, Ohio State University, Columbus.

Hofstede, G. (1991). *Culture and organizations*. New York: McGraw-Hill.

Hopfenberg, W. S., Levin, H., & Associates. (1993). *The accelerated schools*. San Francisco: Jossey-Bass.

Howe, K. R. (1994). Standards, assessment, and equality of educational opportunity. *Educational Researcher, 23*, 27–33.

Howell, J. M., & Avolio, B. J. (1993). Transformational leadership, transactional leadership, locus of control, and support for innovation: Key predictors of consolidated-business-unit performance. *Journal of Applied Psychology, 78*, 891–902.

Hoy, W. K., & Miskel, C. G. (1995). *Educational Administration: Theory, research, and practice* (4th ed.). New York: McGraw-Hill.

Hughes, B., Sullivan, H. J., & Mosley, M. L. (1985). External evaluation, task difficulty, and continuing motivation. *Journal of Educational Research, 78*, 210–215.

Hunt, J. G. (1991). *Leadership: A new synthesis*. Newbury Park, CA: Sage.

Jencks, C. (1972). *Inequality: A reassessment of the effect of family and schooling in America*. New York: Basic Books.

Johnson, P. (1988). *Intellectuals*. New York: Harper and Row.

Kanter, R. M. (1983). *The change masters: Innovation and entrepreneurship in the American corporation*. New York: Simon & Schuster.

Kanter, R. M. (1989). *When giants learn to dance: Mastering the challenges of strategy, management, and careers in the 1990's*. New York: Simon & Schuster.

Kaplan, A., & Maehr, M. (in press). School cultures: A critical variable in student motivation and learning. In Walberg, H. J., & Haertel, G. D. (Eds.), *Educational psychology: effective practices and policies*. NSSE's Series on Contemporary Issues. Berkeley, CA: McCutchan.

Kilmann, R. H., Saxton, M. J., Serpa, R., and associates (Eds.). (1985). *Gaining control of the corporate culture*. San Francisco: Jossey-Bass.

Kluckhohn, F. (1961). Dominant and variant value orientations. In C. Kluckhohn & H. Murray (Eds.), *Personality in nature, culture and society*. New York: Alfred A. Knopf.

Kohn, A. (1990). *The brighter side of human nature*. New York: Basic Books.

Kohn, A. (1993). *Punished by rewards: The trouble with gold stars, incentive plans, A's, praise, and other bribes*. Boston: Houghton-Mifflin.

Kohn, A. (1994). The truth about self-esteem. *Phi Delta Kappan*, 272–283.

Krug, S. (1989). Leadership and learning: A measurement-based approach for analyzing school effectiveness and developing effective leaders. In M. L. Maehr & C. Ames (Eds.), *Advances in motivation and achievement: Vol. 6. Motivation enhancing environments* (pp. 249–277). Greenwich, CT: JAI Press.

Krug, S. E. (1991, April). *A large-scale comparison of perceived school cultures in the United States and Australia*. Paper presented at the Annual Meeting of the American Educational Research Association, Chicago.

Leithwood, K. (1994). Leadership for school restructuring. *Educational Administration Quarterly, 30*, 498–518.

Leithwood, K., Jantzi, D., & Fernandez, A. (1994). In J. Murphy & K. Seashore-Levis (Eds.), *Reshaping the principalship: Insights from transformational reform efforts* (pp. 77–98). Thousand Oaks, CA: Corwin Press, Inc.

Lepper, M. R., & Cordova, D. I. (1992). A desire to be taught: Instructional consequences of intrinsic motivation. *Motivation and Emotion, 16*, 187–208.

Lepper, M. R., & Greene, D. (Eds.). (1978). *The hidden costs of work*. Hillsdale, NJ: Lawrence Erlbaum.

Lepper, M. R., & Hodell, M. (1989). Intrinsic motivation in the classroom. In C. Ames, & R. Ames (Eds.), *Research on motivation and education: Goals and cognitions: Vol. 3* (pp. 73–105). New York: Academic Press.

Lepper, M. R., Keavney, M., & Drake, M. (in press). Intrinsic motivation and extrinsic rewards: A commentary on Cameron and Pierce's meta-analysis. *Review of Educational Research*.

Lewin, K. (1952). *Field theory in social science: Selected papers by Kurt Lewin*. Edited by D. Cartwright. London: Tavistock Publications.

Lieberman, A., & Miller, L. (1990). Restructuring schools: What matters and what works. *Phi Delta Kappan, 71*, 759–764.

Lightfoot, S. L. (1983). *The good high school: Portraits of character and culture*. New York: Basic Books.

Linn, R. L. (1983, April). *Measuring school effectiveness: How achievement data can and cannot be used*. Paper presented at the annual meeting of the American Educational Research Association, Montreal, Quebec.

Maehr, M. L. (1974a). Toward a framework for the cross-cultural study of achievement motivation: McClelland considered and redirected. In M. G. Wade & R. M. Martens (Eds.), *Psychology of motor behavior and sport* (pp. 146–163). Proceed-ings of the Annual Conference of the North American Society for the Psychology of Sport and Physical Activity, Urbana, IL: Human Kinetics Publishers.

Maehr, M. L. (1974b). *Sociocultural origins of achievement*. Monterey, CA: Brooks/Cole.

Maehr, M. L. (1976). Continuing motivation: An analysis of a seldom considered educational outcome. *Review of Educational Research, 46*, 443–462.

Maehr, M. L. (1983). On doing well in science: Why Johnny no longer excels—why Sarah never did. In S. Paris (Ed.), *Learning and motivation in the classroom*. Hillsdale, NJ: Lawrence Erlbaum.

Maehr, M. L. (1989). Thoughts about motivation. In C. Ames, & R. Ames (Eds.), *Research on motivation in education,Vol. 3: Goals and cognitions*. New York: Academic Press.

Maehr, M. L. (1991). The "psychological environment" of the school: A focus for school leadership. In P. Thurston and P. Zodhiatas (Eds.), *Advances in educational administration:Vol. 2*. Greenwich, CT: JAI Press.

Maehr, M. L., Ames, R., & Braskamp, L. A. (1988). *Instructional leadership evaluation and development program (I LEAD)*. Champaign, IL: MetriTech, Inc.

Maehr, M. L., & Braskamp, L. A. (1986). *The motivation factor: A theory of personal investment*. Lexington, MA: Heath & Co.

Maehr, M. L., & Buck, R. (1993). Transforming school culture. In H. Walberg and M. Sashkin (Eds.), *Educational leadership and school culture: Current research and practice* (pp. 40–57). Berkeley, CA: McCutchan.

Maehr, M. L., & Fyans, L. J., Jr. (1989). School culture, motivation, and achievement. In M. L. Maehr & C. Ames (Eds.), *Advances in motivation and achievement: Vol. 6, Motivation enhancing environments*. Greenwich, CT: JAI Press.

Maehr, M. L., & Midgley, C. (1991). Enhancing student motivation: A school-wide approach. *Educational Psychologist, 26,* 399–427.

Maehr, M. L., Midgley, C., & Urdan, T. (1992). School leader as motivator. *Educational Administration Quarterly, 18*, 412–431.

Maehr, M. L., & Parker, S. (1993). A tale of two schools—and the primary task of leadership. *Phi Delta Kappan, 75,* 233–239.

Maehr, M. L., & Pintrich, P. R. (1991). *Advances in motivation and achievement: Goals and self-regulation:Vol. 7*. Greenwich, CT: JAI Press.

McCaslin, M., & Good, T. L. (1992). Compliant cognition: The misalliance of management and instructional goals in current school reform. *Educational Researcher, 21*, 4–16.

McCaslin, M. M., & Murdock, T. B. (1991). The emergent interaction of home and school in the development of students' adaptive learning. In M. L. Maehr & P. R. Pintrich (Eds.), *Advances in motivation and achievement,Vol. 7* (pp. 213–259). Greenwich, CT: JAI Press.

McClelland, D. C. (1961). *The achieving society*. Princeton, NJ: Van Nostrand.

McClelland, D. C., Koestner, R., & Weinberger, J. (1989). How do self-attributed and implicit motives differ? *Psychological Review, 96*, 690–702.

Meece, J. L. (1991). The classroom context and students' motivational goals. In P. Pintrich & M. L. Maehr, (Eds.), *Advances in motivation and achievement ,Vol 7; Goals and self-regulatory processes.* Greenwich, CT: JAI Press.

Meece, J. L., Blumenfeld, P. C., & Hoyle, R. H. (1988). Students' goal orientation and cognitive engagement in classroom activities. *Journal of Educational Psychology, 80,* 514–523.

Midgley, C. (1993). Motivation and middle level schools. In P. Pintrich. & M. L. Maehr, (Eds.), *Advances in motivation and achievement,Vol. 8: Motivation in the adolescent years* (pp. 219–276). Greenwich, CT: JAI Press.

Midgley, C., Anderman, E., & Hicks, L. (1995). Differences between elementary and middle school teachers and students: A goal theory approach. *Journal of Early Adolescence, 15,* 90–113.

Midgley, C., Arunkumar, R., & Urdan, T. (in press). If I don't do well tomorrow there's a reason: Predictors of adolescents' use of academic self-handicapping strategies. *Journal of Educational Psychology.*

Midgley, C., Feldlaufer, H., & Eccles, J. S. (1989a). Change in teacher efficacy and student self- and task-related beliefs during the transition to junior high school. *Journal of Educational Psychology, 81,* 247–258.

Midgley, C., Feldlaufer, H., & Eccles, J. S. (1989b). Student/teacher relations and attitudes toward mathematics before and after the transition to junior high school. *Child Development, 60,* 375–395.

Midgley, C., Maehr, M. L., Collopy, R., & Roeser, R. (1994). *Enhancing the motivation and learning of underachieving students: A school-wide approach.* Final report to the U.S. Department of Education, Grant No. R215A00430.

Midgley, C., Maehr, M. L., Hicks, L., Roeser, R., Urdan, T., Anderman, E., & Kaplan, A. (1996). *Manual: Patterns of Adaptive Learning Survey (PALS).* Leadership and Learning Laboratory, University of Michigan, Ann Arbor.

Midgley, C., & Urdan, T. (1992). The transition to middle level schools: Making it a good experience for all students. *Middle School Journal, 24,* 5–14.

Midgley, C., & Urdan, T. (1995). Predictors of middle school students' use of self-handicapping strategies. *Journal of Early Adolescence, 15,* 90–113.

Midgley, C., & Wood, S. (1993). Beyond site-based management: Empowering teachers to reform schools. *Phi Delta Kappan, 75,* 245–252.

Moss, P. A., Beck, J. S., Ebbs, C., Matson, B., Muchmore, J., Steele, D., Taylor, C., & Herter, R. (1992). Portfolios, accountability, and an interpretive approach to validity. *Educational Measurement: Issues and Practice, 3 (11),* 12–21.

Murphy, J. (1991). *Restructuring schools: Capturing and assessing the phenomena.* New York: Teachers College Press.

Murphy, J., & Seashore-Louis, K. (Eds.). (1994). *Reshaping the principalship: Insights from transformational reform efforts.* Thousand Oaks, CA: Corwin Press, Inc.

Newmann, F. M. (1993). Beyond common sense in educational restructuring: The issues of content and linkage. *Educational Researcher, 22,* 4–13, 22.

Nicholls, J. G. (1972). Creativity in the person who will never produce anything original and useful: The concept of creativity and normally distributed trait. *American Psychologist, 27*, 717–727.

Nicholls, J. G. (1984). Achievement motivation: Conceptions of ability, subjective experience, task choice, and performance. *Psychological Review, 91*, 328–346.

Nicholls, J. G. (1989). *The competitive ethos and democratic education.* Cambridge, MA: Harvard University Press.

Nicholls, J. G., & Hazzard, S. P. (1993). *Education as adventure: Lessons from the second grade.* New York: Teachers College Press.

Nicholls, J. G., Patashnick, M., & Nolen, S. B. (1985). Adolescents' theories of education. *Journal of Educational Psychology, 77*, 683–692.

Nisbett, R. E. (1993). Violence and U.S. regional culture. *American Psychologist, 48*, 441–449.

Oakes, J. (1992). Can tracking research inform practice? Technical, normative, and political considerations. *Educational Researcher, 21*, 12–21.

Ouchi, W. (1986). *Theory Z: How American business can meet the Japanese challenge.* Reading, MA: Addison-Wesley.

Palincsar, A. S., & Klenk, L. (1992). Fostering literacy learning in supportive contexts. *Journal of Learning Disabilities, 25*, 211–225, 229.

Paris, S. G., Lawton, T. A., Turner, J. C., & Roth, J. L. (1991). A developmental perspective on standardized achievement testing. *Educational Researcher, 20*, 12–20.

Pascarella, E. T., Walberg, H. J., Junker, L. K., & Haertel, G. D. (1981). Continuing motivation in science for early and late adolescents. *American Educational Research Journal, 18*, 439–452.

Perkins, D. (1992). *Smart schools.* New York: Free Press.

Peshkin, A. (1986). *God's choice: The total world of a fundamentalist Christian school.* Chicago: The University of Chicago Press.

Peters, T. J., & Austin, N. (1985). *A passion for excellence: The leadership difference.* New York: Random House.

Peters, T. J., & Waterman, R. H., Jr. (1982). *In search of excellence: Lessons from America's best-run companies.* New York: Harper.

Pintrich, P. R., Cross, D. R., Kozma, R. B., & McKeachie, W. J. (1986). Instructional psychology. *Annual Review of Psychology, 37*, 611–651.

Pintrich, P. R. & De Groot, E. (1990a). Motivational and self-regulated learning components of classroom academic performance. *Journal of Educational Psychology, 82*, 66–78.

Pintrich, P. R., & De Groot, E. (1990b, April). *Quantitative and qualitative perspectives on student motivational beliefs and self-regulated learning.* Paper presented at the annual meeting of the American Educational Research Association, Boston.

Pintrich, P. R., & Garcia, T. (1991). Student goal orientation and self-regulation in the college classroom. In M. Maehr and P. R. Pintrich (Eds.), *Advances in motivation and achievement: Vol. 7. Goals and self-regulatory processes.* Greenwich, CT: JAI Press.

Pintrich, P. R., & Garcia, T. (1994). Self-regulated learning in college students: Knowledge, strategies, and motivation. In P. R. Pintrich, D. Brown & C. E. Weinstein (Eds.), *Student motivation, cognition, and learning: Essays in honor of Wilbert J. McKeachie* (pp. 113–133). Hillsdale, NJ: Lawrence Erlbaum.

Pintrich, P. R., Marx, R., & Boyle, R. (1993). Beyond "cold" conceptual change: The role of motivational beliefs and classroom contextual factors in the process of conceptual change. *Review of Educational Research, 63,* 167–199.

Pintrich, P. R., & Schrauben, B. (1992). Students' motivational beliefs and their cognitive engagement in academic tasks. In D. Schunk and J. Meece (Eds.), *Student perceptions in the classroom: Causes and consequences* (pp. 149–183). Hillsdale, NJ: Lawrence Erlbaum.

Pintrich, P. R., & Schunk, D. (in press). *Motivation in education: Theory, research, and applications.* Columbus, OH: Prentice-Hall/Merrill College.

Posner, G., Strike, K., Hewson, P., & Gertzog, W. (1982). Accommodation of a scientific conception: Toward a theory of conceptual change. *Science Education, 66,* 211–227.

Purkey, S. C., & Smith, M. S. (1982). Too soon to cheer? Synthesis of research on effective schools. *Educational Leadership, 40,* 64–69.

Qin, Z., Johnson, D. W., & Johnson, R. T. (1995). Cooperative versus competitive efforts and problem solving. *Review of Educational Research, 65,* 129–143.

Roeser, R., Midgley, C., & Urdan, T. (in press). Perceptions of the school psychological climate and early adolescents' self-appraisals and academic engagement. *Journal of Educational Psychology.*

Rogers, C. R. (1969). *Freedom to learn.* Columbus, OH: Charles E. Merrill.

Rosenholtz, S. J. (1985). Effective schools: Interpreting the evidence. *American Journal of Education, 93,* 352–387.

Rutter, M., Maughan, B., Mortimer, P., & Ouston, J. (1979). *Fifteen thousand hours: Secondary schools and their effects on children.* Cambridge, MA: Harvard University Press.

Sarason, S. B. (1982). *The culture of the school and the problem of change* (2nd ed.). Boston: Allyn & Bacon.

Sarason, S. B. (1990). *The predictable failure of educational reform.* San Francisco: Jossey-Bass.

Sashkin, M. (1988). The visionary leader. In J. A. Conger & R. M. Kamingo (Eds.), *Charismatic leadership* (pp. 122–160). San Francisco: Jossey-Bass.

Sashkin, M., & Walberg, H. J. (1993). *Educational leadership and school culture.* Berkeley, CA: McCutchan.

Schein, E. H. (1984). Coming to a new awareness of organizational culture. *Sloan Management Review, 25,* 3–16.

Schein, E. H. (1985). *Organizational culture and leadership.* San Francisco: Jossey-Bass.

Schein, E. H. (1990). Organizational culture. *American Psychologist, 45,* 109–119.

Sergiovanni, T. J. & Corbally, J. E. (Eds.). (1984). *Leadership and organizational culture*. Urbana: University of Illinois Press.

Seidman, E., Allen, L., Aber, J. L., Mitchell, C., & Feinman, J. (1994). The impact of school transition in early adolescence on the self-esteem and perceived social context of poor urban youth. *Child Development, 65,* 507–522.

Simmons, R. G., & Blyth, D. A. (1987). *Moving into adolescence: The impact of pubertal change and school context*. Hawthorne, NY: Aldine de Gruyler.

Sizer, T. R. (1992). *Horace's school: Redesigning the American high school*. Boston: Houghton-Mifflin.

Smylie, M. A. (1994). Redesigning teachers' work: Connections to the classroom. In A. Hart, & A. Lieberman. (Eds.), *Review of Research in Education, 20,* 129–175.

Steinkamp, M., & Maehr, M. L. (1984). *Advances in motivation and achievement. Vol. 2: Women in science*. Greenwich, CT: JAI Press.

Stevenson, H. W., & Stigler, J. W. (1992). *The learning gap: Why our schools are failing and what we can learn from Japanese and Chinese education*. New York: Summit Books/Simon & Schuster.

Thurow, L. (1992). *Head to head: The coming economic battle among Japan, Europe, and America*. New York: Morrow.

Timar, T. (1989). The politics of school restructuring. *Phi Delta Kappan, 71,* 265–275.

Triandis, H. C. (1972). *The analysis of subjective culture*. New York: Wiley.

Triandis, H. C. (1994). *Culture and social behavior*. New York: McGraw-Hill.

Triandis, H. C. (1995). Motivation and achievement in collectivist and individualist cultures. In M. L. Maehr & P. R. Pintrich (Eds.), *Culture, motivation and achievement: Vol. 9. Advances in motivation and achievement*. Greenwich, CT: JAI Press.

Urdan, T. C., Hicks, L., & Anderman, E. M. (1994, April). *Perceptions of school culture: Differences by gender, ethnicity, and ability*. Paper presented at the annual meeting of the American Educational Research Association, New Orleans.

Urdan, T. C., & Maehr, M. L. (1995). Beyond a two-goal theory of motivation and achievement: A case for social goals. *Review of Educational Research, 65,* 213–243.

Urdan, T., Midgley, C., & Wood, S. (1995). Special issues in reforming middle level schools. *Journal of Early Adolescence, 15,* 9–37.

U. S. Department of Education, National Center for Education Statistics (1993). *America's teachers: Profile of a profession*. Washington, DC.

VanderStoep, S. W., Anderman, D. M., & Midgley, C. (1994). The relationship among principal "venturesomeness," a stress on excellence, and the personal engagement of teachers and students. *School Effectiveness and School Improvement, 5,* 254–271.

Weber, G. (1971). *Inner-city children can be taught to read: Four successful schools*. Washington, DC: Council for Basic Education.

Wentzel, K. (1991). Social and academic goals at school: Motivation and achievement in context. In P. Pintrich & M. L. Maehr, (Eds.), *Advances in motivation and achievement:Vol 7. Goals and self-regulatory processes*. Greenwich, CT: JAI Press.

Westbury, I. (1992). Comparing American and Japanese achievement: Is the United States really a low achiever? *Educational Researcher, 21,* 18–24.

Wigfield, A., Eccles, J. S., Mac Iver, D., Reuman, D. A., & Midgley, C. (1991). Transitions during early adolescence: Changes in children's domain-specific self-perceptions and general self-esteem across the transition to junior high school. *Developmental Psychology, 27,* 552–565.

Wood, S., & Midgley, C. (1995). *Collaborating to change school goals: Effects on teachers.* Manuscript submitted for publication.

Wood, S., Roeser, R., & Linnenbrink, L. (1996, April). *Toward a further understanding of school goal structure: Objective and subjective measures.* Paper presented at the annual meeting of the American Educational Research Association, New York.

Wynne, E. A. (1980). *Looking at schools: Good, bad and indifferent.* Lexington, MA: Lexington Books.

Young, A., Arbreton, A., & Midgley, C. (1992, April). *All content areas may not be created equal: An investigation of motivational orientation and cognitive strategy use in four academic domains.* Paper presented at the annual meeting of the American Educational Research Association, San Francisco.

Yukl, G. (1989). *Leadership in organizations.* Englewood Cliffs, NJ: Prentice Hall.

About the Book and Authors

This book outlines a vision of school that can be used for school reform. At the heart of this vision is a culture that focuses students' attention on learning and on its intrinsic worth and value for all, while minimizing the stress on competing within a social hierarchy. The fruits of this vision are clear in the level and quality of engagement exhibited by students. Its practicality is demonstrated in extensive case studies of two schools in the process of realizing this vision.

In response to the crises and challenges confronted by schools, the book proposes an avenue to school reform based on current research on motivation and learning. First, school reform demands that we change school cultures—emphasizing learning for all students. Many schools—to their detriment and certainly to the harm of their students- —recognize, reward, and promote school as a competitive game in which some win and others lose. Going beyond making a case against school as a venue for academic competition, the authors next lay out what can be done to move schools toward a focus on learning and growth for all students. In addition to numerous examples from the real world of school, two extensive case studies show schools in the process of enhancing their emphasis on learning and minimizing the stress on demonstrating ability. Along with a *course* of change, special attention is given to the *processes* of change.

The work presented is based on cutting-edge efforts in the area of motivation, learning, and cognition as related to teaching and learning. An accessible volume, it should appeal to upper-level undergraduates and graduate students in educational psychology. Those in leadership and policy roles, such as school administrators, school staff, teachers, and principals, as well as those in governmental agencies should find the book useful. Even though the book is based on current theory and research, the narrative is framed in terms of the day-to-day tasks of schools.

Martin L. Maehr is professor of education and psychology, University of Michigan at Ann Arbor, coauthor of *The Motivation Factor: A Theory of Personal Investment,* and author of *Sociological Origins of Achievement,* among other titles. **Carol Midgley** is an associate research scientist in the Combined Program in education and psychology at the same institution.

Index